# Errancies of Desire

*Television and Popular Culture*
Robert J. Thompson, *Series Editor*

**Select Titles in Television and Popular Culture**

For a full list of titles in this series,
visit https://press.syr.edu/supressbook-series
/television-and-popular-culture/.

# Errancies
## of Desire

Monstrous Masculinities
across the Atlantic

Vartan P. Messier

SYU

Syracuse University Press

∞ The paper used in this publication meets the minimum requirements
of the American National Standard for Information Sciences—Permanence
of Paper for Printed Library Materials, ANSI Z39.48-1992.

For a listing of books published and distributed by Syracuse University Press,
visit https://press.syr.edu.

ISBN: 978-0-8156-3778-3 (hardcover)
        978-0-8156-3787-5 (paperback)
        978-0-8156-5571-8 (e-book)

**Library of Congress Cataloging-in-Publication Data**

Names: Messier, Vartan P., author.
Title: Errancies of desire : monstrous masculinities across the Atlantic / Vartan P. Messier.
Description: First edition. | Syracuse, New York : Syracuse University Press, 2023. |
    Series: Television and popular culture | Includes bibliographical references and index.
Identifiers: LCCN 2022026382 (print) | LCCN 2022026383 (ebook) |
    ISBN 9780815637783 (hardcover ; alk. paper) | ISBN 9780815637875 (paperback ; alk. paper) |
    ISBN 9780815655718 (ebook)
Subjects: LCSH: Fiction—20th century—History and criticism. | Masculinity in literature. |
    Men in literature | Misogyny in literature. | Sex crimes in literature. | Desire in literature. |
    LCGFT: Literary criticism.
Classification: LCC PN3403 .M47 2023 (print) | LCC PN3403 (ebook) | DDC 809.3/935211—
    dc23/eng/20220926
LC record available at https://lccn.loc.gov/2022026382
LC ebook record available at https://lccn.loc.gov/2022026383

*Manufactured in the United States of America*

# Contents

# Acknowledgments

Special thanks to the late Margie Waller for her unparalleled support and guidance in the writing of the doctoral dissertation that inspired the present book, as well as to Sabine Doran and the late Marcel Hénaff for their enormous generosity during that process. I am also grateful to Jennifer Doyle who provided valuable feedback to the original manuscript and suggested the idea of a focus on masculinity for the book project.

Friends and colleagues at the City University of New York (CUNY) have also contributed significantly. I specifically appreciate the commentary and suggestions of Agnieszka Tuszynska and Matthew Lau on different chapters of the manuscript.

A number of grants and awards from the Professional Staff Congress (PSC), the union that represents CUNY faculty, enabled me to dedicate time to writing and revising, and to present sections of the book as works-in-progress at international conferences. A fellowship leave from Queensborough Community College (QCC) allowed me to attend the Graduate Center (CUNY), Center for Place, Culture and Politics (CPCP) seminar for a year, where I presented and discussed this project. The consideration Peter Hitchcock devoted to an early draft of the introductory chapter was noteworthy.

I also thank the journals that have allowed me to reprint materials herein. Earlier drafts of chapter three appeared in *Revista Atenea* and *Interdisciplinary Literary Studies*, and a section of the conclusion appeared in *The Journal of Adaptation in Film and Performance*.

Finally, I am as ever grateful to my wife, Nicole, for her unparalleled support and for the blessing that is our firstborn, Luca Byron, to whom this book is dedicated.

# Errancies of Desire

# Introduction

Between appetite and desire there is no difference, except that desire
is generally related to men insofar as they are conscious of their appetite. So desire can be defined as appetite together with consciousness
of the appetite.
    —Spinoza, *Ethics*

Self-consciousness is Desire in general.
    —Hegel, *Phenomenology of Spirit*

The cover of the September 27, 2010, edition of *Newsweek* depicts the mus-
cular back of a man holding a young boy over his shoulder. The child's
gaze is fixed directly at the camera in a wanting expression. The title called
upon the (assumed male reader) to "Man Up!" claiming "The Traditional
Male Is an Endangered Species" and "It's Time to Rethink Masculinity."
Both the cover and the title had gathered significant media attention at the
time. Inspired by the growing media prognostic that the "End of Men" had
arrived,[1] the corresponding article by Andrew Romano and Tony Dokoupil
endeavored to uncover why men, at least in the United States, were at a
point of crisis, and what could be done to rescue them.

Despite the seemingly provocative stance of the magazine cover, the
fact is the Great Recession did not spur the first occurrence of such a crisis in
the United States or elsewhere.[2] Nevertheless, the renewed attention to the
predicament of men points to a series of misgivings about what it means to
be a man at any critical point in history. The traditional "macho" or "strong,
silent" archetypes of masculinity[3] that have long defined the modern man
are ill-fitted to operate in the postindustrial, information age of the new era of
globalization, especially as they have been linked to widespread concerns of

1

angst and depression and, more importantly, to the endemic issues of sexual violence and aggression. Correspondingly, I probe these two pervasive matters in *Errancies of Desire* since they continuously plague traditional constructions of masculinity across the world.[4] As detailed below, this book draws from a diverse corpus of contemporary literary works from Africa, Europe, and the United States to provide a cross-cultural analysis of discourses on subjectivity and masculine identity connected to patterns of oppressive, sexist behavior, especially when men feel marginalized or disenfranchised by the changing socioeconomic complexities that affect their lives.

**The Crisis of Masculinity—Redux**

The contention that the third millennium presents itself as a challenge for men has been long in the making. As women's presence in the workforce steadily increased since the mid-twentieth century following the shift from a male-dominated manufacturing economy to a service economy, their image and what is expected of them also changed. This has not been the case for most men, who are seemingly caught in conservative expectations of their own making. Romano and Dokoupil argue that rather than recoiling into reactionary forms of masculine machismo, men's attitudes and anxieties regarding gender roles and identity as well as our collective understanding thereof should be expanded so that societies prosper for everyone's benefit: men, women, and children.

As the Great Recession reportedly impacted men's livelihood more drastically than women's, the *Newsweek* article set a precedent for other US media channels to more openly discuss masculinity as a means to help diffuse the perceived crisis, and gathered a wide range of comments and responses on the internet in its wake.[5] Since then, there has been increased attention from different corners of the globe to the question of whether masculinity is in crisis.[6] While mainstream media reporters and authors tried to persuade their audiences that rethinking conceptions of gender norms and roles may eventually lead to a more equitable, harmonious, and prosperous society, it appears it did not garner much traction during the ensuing US electoral cycle of 2016, where essentialist notions about sex and gender attributes and abilities seem to have not only largely prevailed[7] but have also galvanized the Republican party into becoming an enduring bastion of traditional masculinity.[8]

Seldom before have issues pertaining to gender and sexuality occupied the national public sphere as they did during the 2016 US elections. For the first time in the nation's history, a woman was elected as the primary candidate of one of the two dominating parties. And, according to most pundits and experts, she was prognosticated to defeat a man widely decried as misogynistic and labeled to embody a "toxic masculinity."[9] But history is not without a sense of irony, as the events that unfolded proved how wrong those predictions were.

One dominating narrative is that Donald Trump's rise to the presidency was fueled by an electoral majority of angry white men who felt the effects of the aforementioned crisis more than any other demographic;[10] in other words, men who felt that Trump's brand of masculinity—however debatable[11]—would restore America to its former glory (as his notorious campaign slogan suggested) or men who believed the livelihood and privileges they had traditionally enjoyed have eroded as a result of liberal progressivism and the global multiculturalist agenda of the Obama era.

**Men Behaving Badly**

As a symptom of the Great Recession, economic anxiety was the oft-cited reason why so many white men voted for Trump. A reboot of the "Angry White Male" of the 1990s, the angry white man of the new millennium feels disenfranchised by the direction of national politics and globalization and blames everyone else: immigrants, ethnic minorities, and women. While this narrative may not be consistent with the realities of the electorate,[12] it has garnered a mythic quality that bestows on it a sense of permanency in the media cycle, extending itself through the very end of the Trump presidency and beyond.[13] Like all myths, it contains a kernel of truth, in particular for an eager public willing to engage with it as a means to explain and understand current events since it relates to the aggressive attitudes and violent behavior of men.

Perhaps not so coincidentally, the cultural zeitgeist surrounding the Trump presidency has been swamped by reports of sexual misbehavior from men in positions of power. While the extramarital affairs of Trump were allegedly consensual and transactional, the sexual assault allegations against Supreme Court Justice Brett Kavanaugh revitalized a fierce debate surrounding questions of white male privilege and its related abuses. It is out of the same sense of paternalistic entitlement to economic resources that men felt it was their right to assault and harass women (and sometimes other men). However, whereas much attention is focused on white phallocentrism in a country beset with racial tension and oppression in light of the #BlackLivesMatter movement, it seems important to note that white men have not been the only ones behaving badly.

On the one hand, Christine Blasey Ford's testimony in front of the Senate Judiciary Committee brought back some people's memories of Anita Hill's 1991 testimony detailing allegations of sexual harassment against Justice Clarence Thomas. On the other hand, in the wake of the #MeToo movement[14] spurred by the sexual harassment accusations against Hollywood mogul Harvey Weinstein, a number of prominent men of color were also accused of misconduct, including musician R. Kelly, actor Morgan Freeman, and most notably comedian Bill Cosby. Furthermore, such cases are not strictly endemic to the United States. As a global movement with varying rates of success,[15] #MeToo has also claimed the resignation of prominent men abroad; a number of British, South Korean, Japanese, Israeli, and Indian politicians were compelled to resign.[16] Regardless of the location or context, whether in the majority or in the minority, these cases reveal that on a global stage, the so-called "crisis" of masculinity cannot be reductively attributed to economic anxiety or racist attitudes, but to issues that pertain more specifically to heteronormative configurations of gender relations and sexual expression that cross national borders.

**Between Fact and Fiction**

This constellation of reports focusing on the (mis)behavior of men from major news outlets in the United States and abroad seems to emphasize the contemporaneous nature of the conundrum and the need to examine it more closely.[17] One could argue that the study of men's lives has always formed an intrinsic part of the study of human behavior. Perhaps the focus on men has even been too exclusive and excessive, one could easily point out, since feminism's rise in prominence in both academia and the public sphere in the second half of the twentieth century was spurred from the necessity to shift the focus away from men and toward women as well as other underrepresented groups.[18] Yet as Anne-Marie Slaughter claims in her 2015 book, *Unfinished Business,* "The next phase of the Women's Movement is a Men's Movement."[19] It is safe to say Slaughter was not making a reference to the conservative Men's Rights Movement (MRM), but rather to the idea that at this juncture any improvements to the lives of women are unlikely without addressing the lives of men as well. Even if the concept of gender fluidity were to supplant the more traditional binary formations that inform gender differences, any genuine progress with regard to women's lives requires renewed attention to men's lives as long as we continue to engage with problems concerning gender and sexuality in a world where men and women's interests collide as much as they coexist. The abusive comportment of some men, whether it be in politics, sports, the entertainment industry, or at home, seems prevalent enough to continue or reinitiate discussions about how men express their sexuality in an era when traditional masculinity and its associated sexist ideology of dominance and aggression is increasingly criticized[20] at the same time it appears to persist.[21]

This provides an adequate backdrop for this book wherein I examine the propensity for aggression and sexual violence embedded in cultural configurations of masculine identity in works of contemporary fiction: namely, J. M. Coetzee's *Disgrace* (1999),[22] Michel Houellebecq's *The Elementary Particles* (1998),[23] Bret Easton Ellis's *American Psycho* (1991),[24] and Alain Mabanckou's *African Psycho* (2003).[25] Spanning four subcontinents, these novels published at the dawn of the twenty-first century were remarkably prescient of the present cultural moment, as they all address different masculinities in crisis, both in and out of their specific contexts. In conjunction, these texts notably underline the idea that sexual violence and oppression are not only persistent signs of male behavior but are also consistent in various expressions of masculine identity across the globe.

One could easily argue that the simultaneous attention to a crisis in masculinity and male sexual misconduct is not coincidental. In fact, the premise of this study is based on the idea that insofar as masculinity is an identity that one assumes and performs, it remains intrinsically connected with problematic issues of desire and subjectivity; with the ways in which men see themselves, envision their lives, and understand their relationships with others and the institutions they inhabit in a world in constant flux.

In contemporary film and literature this predicament has often been specifically portrayed as a problem of desire, and particularly, of heterosexual desire. Male libido, it appears, is unpredictable and misguided, predatory, and potentially destructive. Yet the geneses of these problematic constructions of masculinity are not consistently diagnosed. While some texts may situate it in the unbridled expression of human sexuality and its associated discourses, others contend it is the perverse result of popular constructions of sex and gender.

Like the variety of responses provided in the aforementioned reports, works of fiction may not provide definite answers, but as living agents of culture, voices of a national consciousness or the collective unconscious, as well as carriers of language and ideology, they may offer unique insights on the topic at hand through the ways they lend themselves to meanings and interpretations. Even if Plato is famously wary of poets' propensity to lie, and Guy de Maupassant claims that novelists merely capture the "illusion" of reality,[26] thereby casting doubt on the uses of fiction to reflect or comment on current events, in a more mediated perspective, Ato Quayson explains that literary texts are not merely mimetic of reality, but that they are *"restructurations* of various cultural subtexts." Like any other "text"—conceptually speaking, any type of human discourse—with which the public engages, literary and filmic texts are firmly involved in an intricate matrix of interrelationships between the realities they create and the ones that create them. Joseph Campbell convincingly points to the ways in which the study of myth is "the experience of meaning," not only because their fictions may carry with them truths that transcend their immediate context, but also because they directly relate to our simultaneous experiences of being and becoming, of understanding who we are as human beings since we are bound to language to make "sense" of our experiences at any given time and place.

If one merely were to consider the controversies and discussions surrounding the publication of *American Psycho*, *Disgrace*, and *Elementary Particles* as well as their persistent popularity, it seems a given that novels provide a commentary as much as they are open to it, and it is this dialogic quality that makes them particularly apt for this study on the desires that shape male subjectivities and their identities. With that purpose in mind, the aim of this book is to examine the ways in which masculine identities are informed by mediated processes of subject formation that reinforce traditional sex and gender configurations and the pathos of phallocratic violence and oppression, systems that are as coercive as they are damaging, not only to women as the obvious victims, but to men as well.

## The Desiring Subject and the Object of Fantasy

In Spike Jonze's 2002 film *Adaptation*, the main character Charlie (Nicolas Cage)—based on real-life screenwriter Charlie Kaufmann—finds himself at an impasse because he has thus far failed to adapt Susan Orlean's non-fiction bestseller *The Orchid Thief* for the screen. Since "the book has no story" per se, as it contains long digressions and no clear narrative unity, he initially intended the screenplay to "exist" rather than be "artificially" plot or character driven. However, because his multiple attempts at creating a truly experimental work do not produce anything viable, he follows his (fictitious) twin brother Donald's advice and decides to attend a screenwriting seminar taught by Robert McKee (Brian Cox), author of *Story*, an immensely popular screenwriting guide. There, McKee explains that desire is the major driving force that lies at the heart of every story; answering one of the audience's questions he yells, "You can't have a protagonist without desire. It doesn't make sense! Any fucking sense!" In thus emphasizing the integral role of desire as the essential motivating factor for productive and meaningful experiences of subject formation, the McKee character echoes Spinoza's claim and epigraph above that desire is "the very essence of man"[27] and touches upon the foundational concept of poststructuralist or postmodern theories of the subject as constituted on desire.[28]

However, while modern thinkers sought to rescue desire from the deterministic hold of reason by recasting it as a liberating and productive force,[29] the Western intellectual tradition from Plato to Freud has warned us against the ways in which desire may also present itself as destructive. This paradox is best exemplified in the myth of Orpheus and Eurydice, which recounts how the poet ventures into the Underworld to reclaim his wife. Seduced by the music of Orpheus, Hades agrees to release Eurydice on condition that the poet does not look back at her throughout their journey to the world of the living. This, however, proves to be unbearable for Orpheus, whose anxious gaze causes his wife to disappear, sending her back to Hades for eternity. Forever mourning his loss, Orpheus is eventually killed. His body is torn to shreds by the Maenads at the behest of a jealous Dionysus, but his head keeps singing the sorrows of lost love as it floats down to Lesbos.

In "The Gaze of Orpheus," Maurice Blanchot argues the myth serves as a parable for the artistic process, which relies on the constitutive powers of desire as the inspiration that guides the writer in his creative journey before eventually offering his work as sacrifice.[30] However, Orpheus's desire to hold and behold Eurydice is also marked by the two notable transgressions that punctuate his journey to the Underworld and back: on the one hand, he wanders into the forbidden space of the Underworld and on the other, he errs in looking back at Eurydice. Yet desire is also constitutive of the myth itself, because without desire, there would be no love, transgression, myth, or any proper experience thereof; in fact, desire is both myth *and* the experience of myth. While Blanchot emphasizes the productive and inspirational qualities of desire in his interpretation, the myth also reveals the sacrificial potential of the desiring gaze as well as the anxieties it may exert on the beholder because of its devastating consequences. To that effect, Jacques Lacan considers Orpheus's desire to recover Eurydice's body a male fetishistic fantasy, and his failure marks the inevitable consequence of attempting to turn fantasy into reality.[31]

Blanchot and Lacan's interpretations and the implications outlined above provide the title and theoretical impetus of *Errancies of Desire*. Interrelating desire with error and *"errance"* (the French for "to wander"), I use the term "errancies" to signify both to err and to wander. The guiding hypothesis is that processes of subject formation are channeled by the sometimes erroneous and itinerant impulses of intersubjective desire—as both motivational inspiration and more conventionally as a "lack" or void—while remaining intricately linked to the historical and cultural complexities of gender roles and identity. Poststructuralist theorists such as Rosi Braidotti (following Deleuze) posit that the fluidity of desire produces heterogeneous and nomadic subjects that undermine essentialist notions of cultural difference and specificity.[32] My main argument is that although the desiring subject may be deterritorialized, the subjectivities of the male protagonists depicted in the works I analyze are insidiously confined within hegemonic and dominant forms of mediated desire that promote phallocratic structures of oppression. In other words, these characters reinforce essentialist concepts of male subjectivities even as they reveal the fluidity and permeability of cultural identities within shifting local and global contexts.

**Masculinity, Mediation, and the Transnational**

As a seemingly incredulous 2015 *New York Times* article entitled "A Master's Degree in . . . Masculinity?"[33] testifies, specialized courses of study on masculinities remain mostly invisible to the public at large. But for social scientists and other scholars in the humanities, the study of men and masculinity is certainly not a new phenomenon. Since the 1980s, the field of study has focused on dismantling traditional, stereotypical, and monolithic ideas about men; who they are, what they should be, how they behave or ought to handle themselves.

In *Bodies That Matter* and *Gender Trouble*, Judith Butler argues that identity in general and gender identities in particular are not only constructed but are also performative. In that sense, not only are they assumed, repetitively situated, and potentially alter over time,[34] they are not inherently bound to one's being. In other words, there is nothing in the male DNA that tells a man he must be strong, seemingly unemotional, and dress the part. Rather, these characteristics inform a sense of masculine identity in accordance with other contiguous or previous performances coded as such. This point is particularly important when considering the overwhelming emphasis on heteronormativity or compulsory heterosexuality attached to such configurations of masculinity, and how any deviation from the norm may threaten the very identity of the male subject. Part of my argument, however, is that ironically, it is these same heteronormative performances that imperil the psyche of the subject, not systematically as a repressive mechanism, but as a mediated one, a singular optic I will elucidate below.

Following the pioneering work of Michael Kimmel and R. W. Connell, among others, ideas surrounding "hegemonic masculinity" have given way to the understanding that men exist in their plurality; there are multiple masculinities because the construction of masculinity is defined temporally across various cultural, political, historical, and psychological domains. Moreover, as there has remained a bias and tendency to study men within sociocultural and geographical boundaries, Connell went on to advocate in the introduction to the second edition of *Masculinities* (2005) that, in this era of rapid globalization, men should not only be studied in their plurality but also through the more comparative lens of the transnational, which represents a "crucial frontier of research." In fact, he argues that apart from his own work on "transnational business masculinities,"[35] few studies have considered how processes of globalization affect masculinities from a transnational perspective.[36] Recently, the American Men's Studies Association chose "Transnational Masculinities and Relationalities" as the theme of their 2016 International Conference in Izmir, Turkey, pointing out that as transnational processes have affected the construction of identities they also "draw legitimacy from the previously established gender relations."[37]

While many scholars in the social sciences have responded to the call by producing a number of excellent anthologies,[38] there has been almost no book-length comparative study of masculinity or transnational masculinities in the field of literary studies, a void the present work aims to fill. Two recent works, Sabrina Qiong Yu's *Jet Li: Chinese Masculinity and Transnational Film Stardom* (2012)[39] and *John Wayne's World: Transnational Masculinity in the Fifties* (2013)[40] by Russell Meeuf purport to look beyond their theaters of national production and circulation. Clearly inscribed within the disciplines of film and screen studies, both books examine the ways in which the two iconic stars' most typified masculinities, the martial artist and the cowboy, successfully crossed geographical boundaries to resonate with global audiences. On the one hand, the transnational appeal of Jet Li resides mostly in the simultaneous nationalization and orientalization of the kung fu hero (somewhat following in Bruce Lee's footsteps). On the other, Meeuf posits that Wayne's popular films not only showcased the American masculine ideals of "toughness, patriotism, militarism"[41] abroad but also "a set of styles and values at the core of an American-style capitalist modernity."[42] Even if my focus is not on star studies, Qiong Yu's perspective is not dissimilar to that which I propose here, as she "reveals the ways in which star image is constructed and transformed within transcultural contexts in relation to the discourses of gender, sexuality, genre, nation and cultural identity."[43] The notable difference is that in my study, I argue that mediated constructions of masculinity are powerful homogenizing forces as they undergo minimal transformation across cultural contexts.

The interrelated issues of male subjectivity and masculine identity I investigate in this book address many of the concerns regarding forms of patriarchal and imperial exploitation shared by scholars in postcolonial and gender studies as they intersect with the transnational turn. In *Minor Transnationalism*,[44] Françoise Lionnet and Shu-mei Shih claim that a transnational approach tends to respect the heterogeneity and multiplicity of subjective differences while resisting the homogenizing and dominant model proposed by capitalist globalization. In this book I engage with processes of globalization and transnationalism to effectively map out experiences of deterritorialization. In turn, I ask whether the world has been restructured in such a way that experiential differences are increasingly diminished as they grow more interconnected. The perspective I adopt herein argues that the very processes of mediation that inform paternalistic projections of identity are capable of undermining the locality of cultural differences.

My distinct line of inquiry focuses on identifying and delineating the role mediation plays in shaping male subjectivity and desire, and correspondingly, how pervasively it informs gendered identity and associated norms of performativity, especially as they can lead to expressions of phallocratic violence and oppression. In a fundamental sense, we, humans, are *mediated* beings; we understand the world around us and our experiences foremost through the medium of language. However, because language is a culturally specific social construct, wherein the relationships between the words and the concepts they signify are arbitrary,[45] it does not provide a necessarily faithful translation of our sensible perceptions. Nietzsche considered that because of the human drive to translate the world into meaningful language through the use of metaphors, it is quite impossible to know the world as it truly is, as the use of language merely aims to reinforce and/or validate certain systems of beliefs for the sake of social cohesion.[46]

Since discursive practices in all mediums aim to establish social norms, my analysis considers how discourses about sex, gender, and sexuality mediate perception, consciousness, *and* desire. My contention, therefore, is that one's desires are not necessary expressions of oneself, but of a mediated self, a social construction or "simulation," to use a term made popular by Jean Baudrillard,[47] which corresponds to accepted and/or popular models of identity and behavior. This is especially pervasive in the media-saturated information age, infamously dubbed "The Society of the Spectacle" by Guy Debord, who reminds us, "The spectacle is not a collection of images, but a social relation among people, mediated by images."[48] In *Mediated: How the Media Shapes Your World and the Way You Live in It*,[49] Thomas de Zengotita considers that the wide-ranging, all-encompassing phenomenon of mediation of the current era is increasingly narcissistic. Echoing Baudrillard, he points out that the celebrated heroes of yesteryear "were not known as people at all. They *were* their works and deeds, they *were* their myths. Nelson and Byron and Lincoln were basically fictional constructs, even in their own lifetimes. They were the inventions of the people who idolized them, on the basis of a few stories and images."[50] As media-generated discourses, these popular models of masculine identity and the virtues they glorify potentially set norms for generations, even if they are firmly at odds with past and present realities of constantly shifting political, economic, and sociocultural landscapes. If anything, the "Time's Up" and #MeToo movements have revealed how such performative benchmarks of male behavior, regardless of their immediate or relative contexts, only exacerbate societal tensions with damaging repercussions for all subject positions and relations.

Addressing the crux of the issues outlined at the beginning of this introduction, chapter one explores the ways in which J. M. Coetzee's *Disgrace* unravels the crisis of white masculinity as a problem of heterosexual desire in post-apartheid South Africa. In my exegesis, I analyze how the narrative's opening lines present sex as a "problem" for David Lurie, the white middle-aged English professor and main protagonist. This perspective is altogether informed by his aging predicament and the growing irrelevance of the Western ideals of Romanticism by which he abides. My analysis reveals that sex is problematic because in Lurie's case its expression is linked with power and related abuses in general, and with forms of phallocratic violence directed toward gendered and/or racial others in particular. Dismissed for having sex with one of his "coloured" (a term used to specifically describe mixed race individuals in South Africa) students, he stubbornly refuses to recognize the abhorrent nature of his ravenous libido and the ways in which it perpetuates a history of exploitation in a nation in transition. The nexus of power and privilege is further complicated in the story when the romantic idealization of the natural law of desire by which Lurie abides backfires when Lucy, his lesbian daughter, is raped by three young black males at her farm while he is unconscious. *Disgrace* provides a telling reflection on the complex relations between sexuality and masculine identity as, alongside Lurie, we are compelled to witness and contend with the destructive potential of male libidinal energy when it is unfettered and misguided. Weighing in the dynamic between sex, race, and privilege in contemporary South Africa, my contention is that Lurie's actions and attitudes are representative of a male heterosexual subjectivity entrapped within a paradigm of Western thought that perpetuates hegemonic structures of masculine identity and violent forms of gendered oppression and repercussions.

Similarly addressing the modern predicament of the aging white male body, the next chapter discusses Michel Houellebecq's 1998 award-winning novel *The Elementary Particles*, which draws a sharp critique of modern consumer society's economies of desire. The text suggests that the sexual revolution of the 1960s has merely displaced the mechanisms of oppression without undermining them. In doing so, Houellebecq's novel also articulates a vigorous critique of poststructuralist thought that runs parallel to the *nouveaux philosophes'* refutation of the previous generation's more radical ideas. I argue that this critique relies on a reactionary form of traditional historicism and inscribes male heterosexual desire within a model of a restricted economy following the Lacanian conception of desire as "lack," which is similar to the ways in which Lurie experiences desire in *Disgrace*. Conversely, I demonstrate through a poststructuralist reading that, far from being the inherited condition of the postwar generation's advocacy for self-expression, the social alienation felt by the male protagonists is in fact the perverse production of a "society of control" operating under a postmodern variation of Guy Debord's spectacular model for late-twentieth-century culture industries.

Under this perspective, *Elementary Particles* comes within sight of the subject work of chapter three: Bret Easton Ellis's *American Psycho*, his infamous novel about a Wall Street serial killer. Although both novels address some of the main theses of Debord's *Society of the Spectacle*, I examine how they do so through different agents: Houellebecq's novel attempts to shape a critique of the economies of sexual desire by drawing precise individuated pathologies whereas Ellis's text provides an ideological critique of consumer capitalism and media culture by voiding the psychological background of its main character Patrick Bateman. By thus contrasting narrative strategies, I demonstrate how in *American Psycho* the distance between reader and narrator is narrowed through a forced process of narrativized identification, thus producing a visceral critique of consumerism and media violence by relegating the responsibility of Bateman's actions to the reader. Similar to how *Disgrace* individuates the problem of desire, *Elementary Particles* draws a precise portrait of its protagonist as a discernable "other" by emphasizing the castrated (in)ability for Bruno, one of the main protagonists, to fulfill his libidinal wishes as a result of his personal failure to resolve the pre-oedipal and oedipal stages of sexual maturity. In contrast, *American Psycho* provides a subjectivizing "I/eye" whose mediated experiences are relived and reproduced by the reader, thus positing phallocratic violence as a collective phenomenon of a society in crisis, rather than an individual one.

This discussion of *American Psycho* is then juxtaposed in the fourth chapter to an examination of Alain Mabanckou's *African Psycho*, a lesser-known francophone novel whose paratextual reference to Ellis's text establishes an unavoidable dialogic relationship between the two. In this sense, *African Psycho* engages both the "America-ness" and the "psycho-ness" of Ellis's text by transposing them to sub-Saharan Africa, a postcolonial context whose political, economic, and social histories have been largely affected by capitalist excess. Concentrating on the transformation of the violent psychopathology of modern consumer culture when it crosses the Atlantic, I interrogate whether this reconfiguration relies on assumptions of cultural difference between Africa and America. In turn, I trace the impact of this dyadic relationship to the discursive formation of African cultural identity and subjectivity. Since the media-induced psychoses of Bateman and Grégoire are reflections of each other, my argument here is that the psychotic expression of male desire in *African Psycho* undermines seemingly fixed and antithetical notions of continental identity. Carla Freccero[51] notes that the figure of the psycho is a "consoling fantasy," a product of the collective imaginary that condenses the institutional violence of American historicity; my demonstration shows the fantasy function of the psycho is not confined within these national borders.

As *African Psycho* effectively triangulates the discussion of the errancies of desire across three continents and their related political and cultural histories, my comparative analysis reveals that the syndrome that defines male heterosexual subjectivity transcends cultural and national boundaries. What is more troublesome, however, are the ways in which the mediated desires that inform Lurie, Bruno, Bateman, and Grégoire's subject positions are bound to anxieties and neuroses that produce abhorrent, oppressive, and sometimes psychotic behavior toward others. Consequently, the boundary-crossing and wide-ranging institutionalization of such violent and misogynistic potentialities misconstrues benchmarks of masculine performativity, therefore revealing the potential to turn all men into monsters.

# 1

## Predatory Desire

*Sex, Race, and Privilege in J. M. Coetzee's* Disgrace

> Tis an old lesson; time approves it true, And those who know it best,
> deplore it most; When all is won that all desire to woo, The paltry
> prize is hardly worth the cost.
> —Lord Byron, "Childe Harold's Pilgrimage"

> This is no country for old men
> —Yeats, "Sailing to Byzantium"

In the margins of the publicized controversy surrounding inappropriate sexual behavior by privileged men in positions of power outlined in the introduction, J. M. Coetzee's 1999 award-winning novel *Disgrace* illuminates certain concerns regarding the abusive behavior of men in general, and, considering the more specific post-apartheid South African context of the text, toward gendered and racial others in particular. Highlighting the intersections of the private and the public in consideration of the waves of recent political and historical changes operating in South Africa, Pamela Cooper insightfully points out, "throughout the novel the demise of white advantage, both sexual and racial, shows itself in continuous re-drawing—and inflaming—of the line between personal conduct and public implication."[1]

Coetzee had already garnered an international reputation with *Waiting for the Barbarians* (1980), and *Life and Times of Michael K.* (1983) by the time he won his second Booker Prize with *Disgrace*, which first aroused controversy in the author's native South Africa for the novel's perceived pessimistic outlook of the future of interracial relations and negative representation of native characters.[2] Part of the outcry was triggered by the

16

ways in which the novel reinforces the "worst nightmares and clichés about South Africa as a violent society."[3] At the heart of the discussion is the rape of a white settler by a gang of black youths, reminiscent of what has been identified as a "black peril" narrative of the colonial mindset that pits the vulnerable white female against unbridled black male sexuality. Echoing the perspective of many other South African critics, Ian Glenn argues that "the book was surely intended as a commentary, from a white point of view, on 'life in the liberated zone,' as a pessimistic view of the nation and the future of South Africans in it."[4] While the novel may appear to perpetuate what Glenn categorizes as "liberal Afro-pessimism,"[5] it is my contention that, given the extremely individuated point of view of its protagonist, it is more revealing of the ways in which individual actions are informed by the spheres of influence that shape one's consciousness as a form of mediated desire than as cultural commentary on the future of race relations in a nation in transition. With that objective in mind, this chapter focuses on the intersections between phallocratic violence and masculine identity across racial and generational divides in post-apartheid South Africa.

The novel initially locates the crisis of masculinity in David Lurie, the main protagonist, and his relationship with gendered and racial others. As a white, aging professor who finds himself dismissed for having sex with one of his "coloured"[6] students, he stubbornly refuses to recognize the abhorrent nature of his ravenous libido how it perpetuates a history of exploitation. It is only after three young black men rape his daughter Lucy at her farm while he is unconscious that he is forced to confront the predatory nature and devastating effects of his own acts. Weighing in the dynamic between sex, race, and privilege in contemporary South Africa, my argument is that Lurie is representative of male heterosexual subjectivity entrapped within an economy of desire that perpetuates misguided configurations of masculine identity and gendered oppression. I begin with an analysis of the ways in which Lurie's sexuality is predicated on a Eurocentric model of Byronic virility. While the actualization of his lustful desires on his student revives the specter of imperial exploitation, the attack on his daughter invokes a reciprocity that further perpetuates forms of male violence and patriarchal dominance, even as it crosses historically determined racial and cultural boundaries.

### "Mad, Bad, and Dangerous to Know":
### A Lur(i)e to the Lascivious and Licentious

Lord Byron is certainly not the only literary ghost that haunts the text of *Disgrace*, yet his mediated presence in the projections of the protagonist marks his influence as mystical as it is mythical, especially in light of de Zengotita's remarks cited in the introduction. In a first telling reference, Lurie fancies working on a piece of music inspired by Byron's time in Italy as, quite tellingly, "a mediation on love between the sexes in the form of a chamber opera" (4). Lurie may not be a Byronic Hero, but there is little doubt that the mythicized image of the infamous poet as a promiscuous philanderer impresses itself heavily onto Lurie's consciousness. In fact, his subjectivity is significantly mediated by his admiration for the Romantic poets: Byron, most predominantly, but Wordsworth as well, and to a lesser extent, Blake and Yeats.[7] On the one hand, and this is a point which will be elaborated throughout this section, as a Romanticist by trade and temperament, Lurie configures Byron as an ideal of masculine virility with which he aligns himself.[8] His daughter even appoints the famous description of Byron by Lady Caroline Lamb to her father when he declares his dogged determination to remain unrepentant for his perceived sexual misbehavior. On the other, as perhaps justifying the former, their life trajectory and in particular their fall from grace can be easily compared.

As the story goes, Byron was not only a celebrated London literary figure at the beginning of the nineteenth century, but also a noted Lothario with reputed good looks. Eventually, rumors surrounding his scandalous liaison with his half-sister led him to his permanent exile and self-destruction. Lurie's exile to the Eastern Cape is similarly driven by a scandalous affair. More essentially, however, not unlike Byron whose father deserted him while he was very young, Lurie was brought up by women, which consequently turned him into a womanizer (7). Apparently free from Oedipal anxieties, Lurie was destined to an existence shaped by sexual conquests, and it should not be surprising his views on women, sex, love, and desire are solipsistic and narcissistic to a fault. First, Lurie's views on women are traditionally sexist and objectifying. He scorns the women of the Eastern Cape, his own daughter included, who are either unattractive or do not make an effort to keep up appearances. Conversely, his student Melanie has "plenty of beauty" (78), which "she has a duty to share" (18), thus clearly positioning female-embodied beauty to be an object for male consumption. Secondly, although he has a strong sexual temperament (2) his needs are preferably met outside of the constraints of marriage, an enterprise he failed twice. Thirdly, however contained his emotions may seem, Lurie is continuously subjected to the stirrings of desire, surrendering to what he considers to be the natural order of things as instilled by lofty Romanticist ideals.

Lurie's egotistical views are perhaps best illustrated when Lucy asks him to explain his affair with his student. However inappropriate one's desires, he nonetheless believes it is against one's nature to resist them, and quoting Blake, he proclaims "Sooner murder an infant in its cradle than nurse unacted desires" (69). Hence, desire presents itself as a categorical imperative for Lurie, even if it often subverts dominant societal codes of sexual conduct. To that end, Lurie seems to be particularly taken by desire as a form of transgression—"lured" in, purportedly, by the forbidden, the taboo. In a revelatory passage that focuses on a class lecture on Byron's "Lara," Lurie is implicitly compared to Lucifer: a "thing," or "monster" with a "mad heart" that demands not to be judged but sympathized with, even if he acts impetuously as he pleases (33–34). Lurie has an affair with his student who presents child-like qualities, and he fantasizes about having a threesome with her even younger sister. Quite conveniently, this licentious penchant can also be attributed to Byron's own incestuous inclinations.

In contrast to Byron's own trajectory of self-destruction post-exile, Lurie's decline partly originated before the scandal-driven departure. However, it should not come as a surprise that during his exile in the Eastern Cape, Lurie reflects on his predicament through the prism of Byron's declining years in Italy. Alluding to the march of time, the text intimates the problem arose incrementally, before his powers of seduction vanished altogether (7). This apparent loss of a privileged position in the libidinal economy has triggered an unbearable anxiety, which he seeks to suppress through a series of promiscuous encounters with married women, tourists, and, eventually, prostitutes. This feeling of relative invisibility and his diminished capacity to attract the opposite sex is echoed in the growing insignificance of his profession as stated in the first pages of the text. Lurie views the current, "rationalized" educational landscape, where the more traditional department of Classics and Modern Languages has been absorbed into the more pragmatic Communications, to be "an emasculated institution" in which he doesn't fit (4).

Within this context, Lurie considers himself a scholar and not a teacher because he only teaches to earn a living in order to write books about the romantics of yore (162). This opposition between the dead and the living, and Lurie's preference for keeping company with the dead, white males of his area of specialization, highlights his growing disconnect with his students in this particular place and time. Accordingly, they are unaffected by his class on the Romantic poets. For example, his discussion of Wordsworth fails to captivate their attention, and consequently he imagines his students doubt whether he can possibly know anything about love (23). This misunderstanding is notably echoed in Melanie's disdain for the Romantics and her more pointed interest in feminist authors. More importantly, this gap is not only representative of their age differences, but is also endemic of the rift between him as a representative of white masculinity based on ideals of Romantic humanism and the young, gendered, mixed-race generations of Cape Town and the material realities of the new South Africa.

While the comparison between Lurie and Byron is maintained through Lurie's artistic project, Lurie's Byronic ideal is increasingly revealed to be an inadequate mediator for his life-altering experiences in the country. The decline is first noted when Lurie compares the Eastern Cape to Italy, and himself to an aging, fat Byron. However, it is only after the attack on him and Lucy and the consequences thereof that Lurie realizes that he was consumed by a fantasy. Once Lucy opens up to him about what happened to her, he contemplates Byron's own dalliances, realizing there must have been numerous instances that would have been considered rape, thus making him seem out of touch (160). This realization marks a significant turning point for Lurie; as Graham points out, "Discarding a Romantic tradition that has legitimised his mistreatment of Melanie, Lurie moves away from an emphasis on Byron, and scripts the voices of Byron's abandoned daughter, and of Teresa."[9]

His opera project, originally conceived as "a chamber-play about love and death, with a passionate young woman and a once passionate but now less than passionate old man" (180), was rather ambitious but he felt it had potential. But in the no-man's-land of the Eastern Cape, his Byron undertaking is going nowhere, very much like himself. If artworks always contain a biographic element, then it should not come as a surprise that as a fantasy, the initial concept does not adequately mediate his present reality.

Emblematic of his own disconnect with women, Lurie admits that although he is able to pinpoint the Byron character, he is at loss with the historical Teresa: "young, greedy, willful, petulant" (181). Therefore, he decides to imagine Teresa as a middle-aged woman who is nostalgic about her affair with Byron, as it represents the pinnacle of her existence (182) and her sole claim to immortality. His thinly veiled sexism notwithstanding, he nonetheless asks himself whether he can find love for such an unremarkable woman (182). It is not a stretch to see Bev Shaw, the unattractive middle-aged veterinarian with whom he has an affair in the Eastern Cape, in this version of Teresa. So, the question Lurie asks is whether, he, as Byron, could ever love someone like Bev? With the slight progression marked by this shift in emphasis rooted in an acceptance of the present, the music comes slowly; as the opera is toned down, it becomes less grandiose and more honest. Notably, Lurie seems to let go of the categorical imperative; like Bev, Teresa is everywoman, and by accepting women at face value, and not some sort of object of fantasy, he is adapting to his newfound reality.[10] Progressively, as events outside of his control unfold around him, he accepts Teresa as his guide because in the humility of his service to the dead and dying dogs, he has little dignity, like her (209). Finally, Lurie learns to hear others speak through Teresa, the scorned, abandoned lover of the mythical Byron, now only a pale shadow of his former virile self.

This "reparative reading," to use a term coined by Eve Sedgwick,[11] of Lurie's position is popular with critics who have more closely focused on the interspecies discourse contained in *Disgrace*.[12] Contrary to the more negative appraisal of the novel's overall grim forecast regarding the future of race relations, this interpretation paints the narrative with a type of redemptive aura, even if the reader remains suspicious of such a closure given the ambiguously complex ethics of the text and Lurie's relationships with gendered others.

## White Privilege and a Heart of Darkness

Since the weight of the Byronic fantasy of virility informs Lurie's consciousness to such great extent, the opening sentence of the novel appropriately frontloads issues pertaining to masculinity and sexuality: "For a man of his age, fifty-two, divorced, he has, to his mind, solved the problem of sex rather well" (1). The argument here is rather unequivocal: "sex" is qualified as a "problem" and therefore needs to be "solved" in some manner or form. Further examination of the sentence yields that sex is a problem "For a man of his age," that is, a middle-aged man, a threshold that invariably connotes an unavoidable decline, a dimension explored later in the chapter. Additionally, the qualifier "divorced" points to a history of failed commitments. In other words, sex *is* a problem for men with commitment issues past their physical prime. However, this perspective is entirely *his* as the phrase "to his mind" clearly posits. Thereby it appears the problematic nature of sex—and its solution—is more of a psychological quandary than a physiological or physical one. This distinction is noteworthy since it evokes a mind/body dualism that fits within the traditional, if not antiquated, western epistemological framework that Lurie favors. As a prism of social relations in post-apartheid South Africa, Lurie's quandary is located, somewhat ironically, in a social type of masculinity that has traditionally been dominant. As Pamela Cooper accurately points out, "at fifty-two, Lurie is broadly representative of an older social order: the officially defunct South Africa of Afrikaner dominance, statutory racial oppression, and the uneasy pleasures of white privilege."[13]

However, far from being the pitiful victim of an unfair market of libidinal exchange that idolizes the young, Lurie still manages his transactions from a place of privilege. In South Africa, unlike Lurie's seductive powers, privilege languishes, even when one considers the fact that he often has to pay to get the woman he wants (7). Like most coveted things, sex can be considered a commodity; it is a transaction subjected to market rules of supply and demand. For someone still privileged enough to enjoy a comfortable standard of living, when attraction fails, money prevails.

His anxiety is cured by the regularity of his encounters with "Soraya," whose compliant and discreet temperament is "satisfactory" and very much to his liking (6), and so they meet every Thursday to "make love" (1). *Satisfaction* seems like an understatement but these weekly encounters are a source of happiness; "a moderated bliss" (6), he tells himself. Bliss, yes, but in *moderation*: a form of civilized restraint, a regulated release of libidinal energy that keeps the instincts in check. Lurie's rationalization of his predicament and the solution he enacts is rooted in the belief so firmly anchored in Western thought that one can (and ought to) control and regulate one's bodily impulses. Here, Wordsworth's definition of poetry from the *Preface to Lyrical Ballads* could be easily transposed to Lurie's sexual regimen. However, Lurie is quick to find ways to elude reason altogether and preach Byronic ideals that privilege the unabated pursuit of one's sensual appetites.

The story Lurie tells himself is certainly convenient, yet it is revealed to be self-defeating. And while the regulated encounters with Soraya may allow for the safe and ordained expression of sexual desire, this system and its rationale contain traces of the mechanism of repression. This becomes evident when he spots Soraya in town with her two children and follows her before he eventually gets caught. His ordained and seemingly detached approach to the needs of the flesh is put to the test because the tacit agreement with Soraya does not take into account the unpredictable stirrings of desire, as he seemingly confuses her professional affections for personal intimacies. Consequently, his affection for her increases (6), as if knowing her personal life grants him privileged access surpassing the anonymous confines allotted by their contractual transaction, until she puts a stop to their encounters.

Since the next "Soraya" the escort agency provides does not live up to her name, he goes back to pursuing married women—perhaps as sublimation—but when one encounter with his department's new secretary proves to be entirely dissatisfactory since she does not exhibit Soraya's docility and pliancy, he feels weary and contemplates giving up the hunt (9). As experience dictates, however, the stirrings of desire are not so easily quelled, and he cannot get rid of the *idea* of Soraya as the antidote to his predicament, even if he acknowledges he should (9). Like a predator, he stalks her and calls her at her home, making advances that she abruptly and expectedly rejects. This episode both frames and forecasts the ways in which desire in general and male desire in particular is borne by unruly fluctuations that operate independently of reason and cannot be harnessed within a framework that attempts to regulate it accordingly. More specifically, however, *Disgrace* situates this problematic within the white male body, a body which has traditionally been privileged as the locus of imperial power, but whose aging predicament, like colonization itself, has stripped it of its historically determined superiority, as it no longer possesses privileged access to the colonized female body.[14]

Beyond its inherent association with white privilege, Lurie's desire is predatory and his sexual behavior exploitative, as he uses women for his own gratification. Hence, there is a condemning correlation to "the problem of sex" alluded to initially: sex is problematic because it is linked with power and its related abuses. More specifically, it is interconnected with forms of violence directed toward gendered and racial others. While this is undoubtedly the case with Lurie, the attack on Lucy later reveals that acts of sexual violence are not solely carried out by privileged white men. Even if the reader is not privy to the psychological dispositions of Lucy's rapists to the extent of Lurie's, the parallelisms between the two acts lead us to draw certain deductions regarding both hegemonic and non-hegemonic forms of predatory desire as it intersects with histories of race relations.

Following the debacle with Soraya, his illicit affair with his student Melanie rapidly turns into abuse, rape, and Lurie's eventual fall and disgrace in the span of three weeks and a handful of encounters. Like Soraya, Melanie is "coloured," a feature Lurie further exoticizes by calling her "Meláni: the dark one" (18). This is not a coincidence, as he readily admits he is not interested in another student, Amanda, a slender blonde (29). This fascination and fetishization of the native woman as exotic can be traced back to Joseph Conrad, at the very least, and has a long, sustained history in Western colonial literature.[15] In this case, however, Melanie is also excessively young since Lurie compares her body to that of a pubescent girl (19), which tints their relationship with the incestuous hues of paternal colonialism. Whereas his initial courtship already violates codes of ethical conduct, his quasi-obsession with her—looking up her student file, assisting at her play rehearsal, storming into her flat unannounced—not only leads to the misguided consummation of their relationship (19), but eventually to rape. To fully evaluate Lurie's actions, nonetheless, the free indirect speech mode of narration that shapes the novel's voice presents the reader with a challenge.

In "Rape and the Violence of Representation in J. M. Coetzee's *Disgrace*," Carine M. Mardorossian makes the somewhat reaching argument that the focalizing of the narrative through the free indirect discourse of Lurie's consciousness—which is certainly pedantic and self-interested, but also critically self-aware—prompts the reader to trust him and to be "thus brought into an uncomfortable proximity to and complicity with the white masculinist subject's way of thinking."[16] While I agree the reader comes into close contact with Lurie's thoughts, the properties of free indirect discourse provide a frame of reference from which the reader can distance oneself, a point I elaborate further in chapters two and three, wherein I explain that such distancing is more strenuous when confronted with a first person narrative characterized by the absence of an individuated consciousness. In other words, I would argue the reader can clearly identify Lurie's distinct voice and is consequently more at ease in choosing to adopt or reject Lurie's account. To that effect, there is genuine tension between the narrator and Lurie's own thoughts, which sends the reader pondering whether Lurie is aware of the impropriety of his acts and the consequences therein, or whether the narrator is judging the protagonist.

There is perhaps no irony in the fact that Melanie is a student in his course on the Romantic poets since Lurie periodically falls for his students; he admits he is infatuated with her (11) and believes she is probably aware of his "desiring gaze" (12). At the very least, she is curious since she accepts his invitation for a drink at his apartment. There, Lurie's infatuation grows, even if he senses a profound disconnect between them, as she appears indifferent to his discourse on how poetic discourse is similar to love at first sight (13). In a foreshadowing of events to unfold, she frowns at his query regarding her literary interests and declares she prefers the more politically engaged work of women writers Adrienne Rich, Toni Morrison, and Alice Walker (13–14). Consequently, his first attempt to seduce her with a brief expose on Byron, on a woman's duty to share her beauty, and a quote from Shakespeare's "From fairest creatures we desire increase" fails due to its overtly pedantic tone (17).

However, as with Soraya, Lurie perseveres, even if the narrator (or is it Lurie?) declares "he ought to end it" (18). As a sexual predator in selfish disregard of private boundaries, he stalks her and calls her at home. Unlike Soraya, however, Melanie is too inexperienced to elude Lurie's inappropriate advances. Although he is seemingly aware he should not pursue her, he is under the impervious tyranny of desire that does not allow itself to be allayed with commonsense (18). He reassures her the affair will not "go too far"; all the while the narrator is aware of the inevitable incongruity between two minds: "Too far. What is far, what is too far, in a matter like this? Is her too far the same as his too far?" (19). Defying all reason, they go back to his apartment where

> he makes love to her. Her body is clear, simple, in its way perfect; though she is passive throughout, he finds the act pleasurable, so pleasurable that from its climax he tumbles into blank oblivion. (19)

This first of three sexual encounters is one-sided and confirms earlier observations about Lurie's exploitative ways and objectifying gaze. He may very well "make love to her" (in the same way he "made love" to Soraya) but there is no mutual reciprocity: while it may be "pleasurable" from his perspective, she is not only "passive" but apparently completely silent, if not seemingly lifeless, and her quiet, almost shameful, exit from the scene confirms her discomposure (19). But her well-being does not seem to concern him since the text informs us he awakes the next day feeling particularly content about the entire episode (19).

From there on, things escalate quickly. Two days after their first tryst, he finds her on campus and gives her a car ride to her flat. Although he notices she is *"No more than a child!"* (emphasis in text, 20) and briefly questions his behavior, he still very much desires her (20). Lurie is well aware of this overbearing paradox, but yet he welcomingly submits to his lustful desire. Whereas Melanie has enough sense to reject his proposal to come in to her flat in that instance, her presence in class the next day agitates him enough that he chooses to assist at the rehearsal of a play she is in the next day. As was the case in his pursuit of Soraya, conscious he is luridly spying on her in the darkness, he is aware he should not be there (24). But seeing her perform has quite the adverse effect since he shows up at her flat unannounced shortly thereafter:

> He has given her no warning; she is too surprised to resist the intruder who thrusts himself upon her. When he takes her in his arms, her limbs crumple like a marionette's. Words heavy as clubs thud into the delicate whorl of her ear. "No, not now!" she says, struggling. "My cousin will be back!"
>
> But nothing will stop him. [ . . . ]
>
> She does not resist. All she does is avert herself—avert her lips, avert her eyes. She lets him lay her out on the bed and undress her: she even helps him, raising her arms and then her hips. Little shivers of cold run through her; as soon as she is bare, she slips under the quilted counterpane like a mole burrowing, and turns her back on him.
>
> Not rape, not quite that, but undesired nevertheless, undesired to the core. As though she had decided to go slack, die within herself for the duration, like a rabbit when the jaws of the fox close on its neck. So that everything done to her might be done, as it were, far away. (24–25)

Even if Lurie believes his forceful actions were "undesired" but do not "quite" constitute "rape," it is clear they do. First, the diction is unequivocal: he is an "intruder" who "thrusts" himself upon her using the element of "surprise." The implicit violence of his behavior is rendered through his "words" which, unsuccessful at seducing her previously, are now as "heavy as clubs." Secondly, even if "she does not resist" and "helps him" get her undressed, there is no expressed or implied consent on her part. Finally, her bodily reactions shed any remaining possible doubt: after a brief struggle, she freezes, gives in, and phases out, as it were, to the force to which she is subjected. The predator has consumed its prey; in this instance, desire is reduced to an appetite, an animal hunger that only serves the self and neglects as well as negates the other.

During and in the immediate aftermath, however, as if actualizing some fantasy from stage to reality, Lurie claims to be possessed by the goddess of beauty—a mythological incantation he will resort to again in an attempt to explain himself; first, during the academic hearing that investigates his actions and later, when he thinks about how to answer Lucy's questions. The mythical and the phantasmagorical belong to the realm of the unconscious; actualizing one's desire shatters all safeguards as the consequences are all too real. Lurie realizes, too late, that he has gone too far as he admits to himself his actions were "a mistake, a huge mistake" and imagines Melanie "trying to cleanse herself of it, of him" (25). Within an implicit code of acceptable behavior, Lurie knows he behaved badly, that, as a professor, an adult, a father, and in an extended sense a white man in a country bereft with racial inequalities, he abused his position of power, even if he fails to recognize it as such at first.

The juxtaposition of the aforementioned masculine roles comes into full effect when the errancy of Lurie's desire backfires. The reckoning unfurls first through Melanie herself, then in a series of confrontations with her boyfriend, her father, and finally the administration. When Melanie shows up at Lurie's doorstep a week later asking for shelter, he takes her in and lets her sleep in his daughter's bedroom. In the moment, he feels like comforting her as a father would, even if he cannot ignore that he still desires her (26). Lurie understands the precariousness of his predicament, and believes Melanie may be capable of manipulating him. However, he is quickly reminded that even if she is using him, his actions have been far worse, especially given he has exclusively been in the driver's seat (28). Memory, it seems, is as fleeting as reason or wisdom because soon thereafter "he makes love to her one more time, on the bed in his daughter's bedroom" (29). Whereas the glaring incestuous implication will be addressed later in the chapter, there is little to indicate that this third episode is not again one-sided. The phrase "he makes love" is a catchall that redirects to Lurie's exclusive pleasure, and he rationalizes her lack of eagerness to her age and want of experience. Singling out an intimate gesture that hints at her willingness, "he feels a surge of joy and desire. Who knows, he thinks: there might, despite all, be a future" (29). Lurie's delusions about their future are perhaps as palpable as they are unnerving, but his state of blissful oblivion recedes as soon as the scandalous nature of the affair becomes a public matter.

The first sign of his demise is brought about by Melanie's boyfriend, a "bravo" (31), who warns him to keep to himself by showing up at his office and his lectures on Byron. Seemingly ashamed, Melanie remains silent, keeps her distance, and eludes Lurie's request to comply with the course requirements in order to avoid further problems (34). As much as he would like to reenter into a more traditional teacher-student relationship, she tells him *"I am no longer your student"* (emphasis in the text) in a tone that is more deferential than defiant (35). Next, her father intervenes and implores Lurie to speak to her to change her mind about quitting school, as he is unaware of their affair at first. When he eventually finds out, he coerces Melanie to file an administrative complaint against Lurie. While Lurie may entertain the idea that "she is too innocent . . . too ignorant of her power" to have brought the charges on her own (39) because she never speaks out against him, his view also undermines her capacity for independent action. This is reminiscent of the ways in which the subaltern is denied a voice and agency;[17] not only by Lurie, but also by her father and the academy (ostensibly) since her personal concerns are never divulged to the reader.

In a misguided display of vanity, Lurie acts as if the administrative hearing is beneath him and makes a mockery of it. He attempts to end the inquiry immediately by abiding strictly to the language of the rule of law; a language that precisely delineates acceptable conduct from disorderly behavior. However, the law is an ethical minimum, a language devoid of emotion. But without emotion, there is no narrative that provides meaningful resolution: a catharsis Lurie is set to deny to the committee out of spite for their seemingly conservative views about sex. When brought to explain his motivations, he paints himself as a victim of desire, a "servant of Eros," all the while acknowledging his lustful impulse could have been reined in (52). Whereas he readily admits the error of his ways (48–49) he is unrepentant because, on the one hand, under the romanticist worldview that informs his logos, he should not repent (58), and on the other, he believes his "inappropriate desires" are not a deviancy that ought to be cured (43).

However cognizant of his actions, Lurie fails to see how his relationship with Melanie constitutes an abuse of his privileged position of authority. Solipsistically, he considers the inquiry to be based on puritan and ageist principles (52), which Farodia Rassool, the chair of the Committee on Discrimination, vehemently decries. "As teachers we occupy positions of power," Rassool explains, "but when we try to get to specificity, all of a sudden it is not abuse of a young woman he is confessing to, just an impulse he could not resist, with no mention of the pain he has caused, no mention of the long history of exploitation of which this is part" (53). Lurie snickers at her outburst because he finds ridiculous the idea that he is a male predator in the pursuit of innocent young girls (53). However, contemplating Melanie's appearance in front of the committee, he admits they are not equal. Whereas he may recognize the uneven power dynamics between teacher and student, Lurie remains colorblind to the "long history of exploitation" of race relationships in South Africa.[18]

Amid the repeated pleas to genuinely acknowledge the nature of his actions, he merely "pleads guilty" to the Byronic imperative that governs his actions and validates desire as a natural right in an irritating display of arrogant vanity. The university wants to resolve what it considers to be a public matter that affects the community as a whole. In contrast, Lurie considers this mostly a private affair, and he is only willing to admit that he behaved illegally, not shamefully, and hence, he dismisses the idea that sacrificing his dignity in a repentant statement will ease the tensions ignited in the larger context of the university community. What he does not understand is the larger issue at stake here; he abused his authority but dismissed the idea that what he did constitutes an abuse of human rights. As Graham argues, "Lurie's relationship with Melanie in *Disgrace* is depicted as a betrayal of ethical responsibility, as he violates and will not take responsibility for her as an embodied human being,"[19] thus further perpetuating the objectification of women of color as his own private entitlement.

### Desire Degree Zero?

It is only after Lucy is raped at her farm that Lurie is forced to reconsider his position since the natural logic that he holds up as justification for his behavior falters when the line between victimhood and perpetrator is blurred. But prior to that, the series of conversations he entertains with Lucy on his affair reveal the complicit ways in which they both participate in structural models of racial inequality and fail to acknowledge their own privilege.

Discussing the consequences of the hearing, Lurie tells Lucy the administration wanted him to admit his character faults and denounces the puritanical atmosphere of the proceeding (66). Silently telling himself "they wanted me castrated" (66), he tries to explain his position by citing the example of a dog that was punished for getting excited over a bitch in heat, effectively leading it to despise itself (90). Scoffing at his solipsism, Lucy asks whether men should give free rein to their lustful instincts, to which he answers, "Sometimes I have felt just the opposite. That desire is a burden we could well do without" (90). While this may mark a surprising reversal on Lurie's part as a result of his resignation, interestingly enough this perspective is precisely connected to the discussion in chapter two, on the eschatology of desire in Houellebecq's *Elementary Particles*.

Lucy does not absolve Lurie of his deeds, yet she cajoles him when he presumes it was Melanie's father and/or boyfriend who pressured Melanie to denounce him, hinting that she may eventually forgive him (69). There is a palpable sense of dramatic irony in Lucy's statement considering the events that will unfold and the pressure Lurie will exert on her to seek justice. Yet it also seems rather preposterous for Lucy to think she can speak of Melanie's experience. Like her father, she too will eventually have to reckon with the erosion of the historical privilege of her racial identity; with the added dimension, however, that she will also need come to grips with her own relatively underprivileged gender position.

Facing his daughter's witticisms, Lurie's misogynistic views remain paramount. Rooted in his own narcissism, his marked obtuseness in matters of female sexuality is a revelatory blind spot; one could argue that his marked disdain for "Sapphic Love" as a reason for gaining weight (86), for example, is rooted in the possibility that it threatens the heteronormative imperative of the patriarchy and the conditioning of male desire to lust over youthful female bodies.

This is the reason he deflects Lucy's hint that as an older man, he should not be pursuing young women (69), claiming that "unacted desires . . . can turn ugly in the old as in the young" (69–70). As Lucy appears incredulous, he doubles down by saying, "Every woman I have been close to has . . . made me a better person," to which Lucy jokingly responds whether he thinks the women feel the same way (70). The reality underlying Lucy's "joke" has a chilling effect on Lurie, as he later tells Bev that living there is a form of penance away from temptation (148). There is perhaps no irony that his work for Bev, a woman who specializes in euthanizing and sterilizing animals as if she were part of a mechanism of repression (91) foreshadows his own fate since he finds himself rejected and undesirable, very much like the dogs for which he eventually learns to care. Even the affair Bev initiates appears to be some type of duty he performs somewhat willfully (149–50). Like the undesirable dogs, Lurie the unwanted caters to the unattractive Bev who "has no breasts to speak of. Sturdy, almost waistless, like a squat little tub" (149); a sharp contrast "to the sweet young flesh" of Melanie (150). Nonetheless, he seems to have accepted his lot; when they have sex, they may not be "making love" as he did with Melanie or Soraya—the phrase seems exclusively reserved for interracial intercourse that threads on the exploitative—but there are clear signs of affection from Bev. On the cold floor of the sanitized clinic, their encounters are sobering, and stand in sharp contrast to sex with Melanie where pleasure is tainted with traces of violence, conquest, and exploitation.[20]

While Bev may not arouse any particular lustful feelings in Lurie, there are a number of instances wherein desire manifests itself insidiously in the Eastern Cape, once again revealing its ubiquitous and tyrannical presence. As he contemplates life in the country soon after his arrival, he still feels the pang of desire when he suddenly thinks of his former student as he envisions her youthful body (65). Shortly thereafter, gazing upon a trio of geese, he fantasizes about having a threesome with Melanie and Soraya (88). Lurie's later visit to the Isaacs' household to recount his version of the events further confirms the inevitable allure of the young for someone in Lurie's predicament. When Melanie's younger sister opens the door dressed in her school uniform, he can immediately recognize the similar physical traits to the sole, yet important, distinction that she is even more attractive than her older sister (163). He realizes that coming to the Isaacs' home may have been an error of judgment as he may succumb to temptation; not only do memories of his affair with Melanie resurface, he also experiences desire for the apt-named Desirée and imagines having a threesome with the both of them (164).

Even if his desire for young bodies of racial others is persistent, Lurie readdresses some of his previously held beliefs on sex in the aftermath of the attack. Because Lucy is not open about her experience at first, he feels like an outcast and contemplates whether women would lead better lives on their own since lesbian women get on well without men (104), perhaps a veiled allusion to Adrienne Rich's essay, "Compulsory Heterosexuality and Lesbian Existence." He further ponders whether for a lesbian, rape is the worst violation possible (104). His intuition is confirmed when Lucy eventually discloses her feelings about her rape, as she is prone to consider hatred as an integral part of male heterosexual desire:

> . . . When it comes to men and sex, David, nothing surprises me any more. Maybe, for men, hating the woman makes sex more exciting. You are a man, you ought to know. When you have sex with someone strange—when you trap her, hold her down, get her under you, put all your weight on her—isn't it a bit like killing? Pushing the knife in; exiting afterwards, leaving the body behind covered in blood—doesn't it feel like murder, like getting away with murder? (158)

For Lucy, penetrative sex is as violent as rape, and Lurie is initially taken aback because of the implication of his own complicity. But even as he tries to imagine Lucy's horror, he still fails to make the connection with his own behavior, especially toward Melanie.

His inability to understand the meaning and implication of sexual violence is first brought up by Lucy and Bev Shaw who insist he cannot comprehend what happened to his daughter. Rebuked by their assertion, he acts outraged by their claim that he has no understanding of what rape is, in part because he is a man (140–41). Not only is his outrage misguided; while Lurie may very well believe he understands what happened to Lucy, or even Melanie for that matter, his consideration is limited to his own male perspective. After Lucy's disclosure, he recollects searching the term in the dictionary as a child and seeing representations of *The Rape of the Sabine Women*, which led him to conclude that, in close similitude to Lucy's perspective, rape seems to equate itself to sex (160). What he eventually grasps, in fact, is that whereas he could visualize himself as a male perpetrator, he doubts he could ever incorporate the point of view of a female victim (160).

Lurie's incapacity to truly empathize with the pain of these young women is situated in his inability to experience the degree zero of desire, as it continuously reappears at the most incongruous moments. For instance, upon briefly returning to Cape Town to put his affairs in order, his ex-wife Rosalind calls to check in on him, and he soon remembers his first tryst with her (187). This brief memory flash only leads Lurie further into the errancy of desire when Rosalind tells Lurie she saw Melanie perform, which stirs up his blood and awakens his fantasy; he believes that chapter has not come to an end because he believes she has "the smell of a mate" (190). Calling in the animality of desire, Lurie cannot cast off her "smell" so he is curious to know whether the affair is truly over (190). At the theater, he notices Melanie has flourished in his absence; not only does he see her talent as a performer, but sees also that she may have very well found herself. Yet he still lusts after her. He thinks of their last night together in Lucy's room (as it retains its incestuous nature), takes pride in the success of her comic delivery, and is inflated with the desire to call her "*Mine!* . . . as if she were his daughter" (191). But soon enough, he is woken from his reverie by Melanie's boyfriend, who spots him in the audience and reminds him to "stay with your own kind" (193). One is entitled to ask, as Lurie certainly does, who is his "kind": middle-aged white women like Bev as the older Teresa to his aging Byron?

## The Sins of the Father

Being a middle-aged man is a double-edged sword for Lurie; he is called to be a responsible father to his daughter, especially in times of crisis, but as a man subjected to the tyranny of desire he is stereotypically ensnared into lusting for girls that are considerably younger and more vulnerable than his daughter. The archetypical perspective that considers a man's life as evolving from boyhood to adulthood through defining stages toward maturity and responsibility[21] appears to falter in the face of exceptional events and the realities they engender. Therefore, there is a parallel of causality between Lurie's behavior with Melanie and the actions of Lucy's attackers.

The foreshadowing of the event is enacted not only through the rape of Melanie, but also in the ways in which the text develops a tension between Lurie's desire for his young student and the parental gestures of care and affection he expresses toward her. While this tension is already evident in the company of Soraya, with Melanie, the impression arises soon after their first coitus, when upon giving her a ride home, he realizes she is *"No more than a child!"* (emphasis in the text) and addresses her with the voice of a reassuring father, all the while feeling desirous for her (20). However, it is when a distraught Melanie seeks refuge in his apartment shortly after he rapes her that the tension climaxes. Looking after her as he would his own child by providing his daughter's bed, he comforts her to the point of almost saying "Tell Daddy what is wrong" (26–27). This predicament should have alerted Lurie to the errancy of his ways, and especially to the abusive associations of the incestuous overtones of their relationship, but it is there, in his daughter's bedroom, that he has sex with Melanie one last time, a pleasurable experience he delusionally believes is mutual. While this fantasy is ultimately derailed, the overlap between Lurie's desiring gaze and his fatherly feelings carries over to a number of interactions with his daughter, before eventually giving way to something more ordinary, which will render him vulnerable enough to prove his undoing and ultimate disgrace.

Perhaps because of Byron's spectral influence, the shadow of incest appears on a number of occasions, including when the thought of Melanie is conjured by Lurie's gazing at his daughter; though he considers her to be overweight (59, 65) she remains attractive, and he even has a brief flash of envisioning her with Melanie (88). However, he realizes such projected male standards of beauty do not apply to his lesbian daughter (76). Simultaneously, considering he may no longer be the lothario of his youth, Lurie acknowledges his debt to her and pities children in general, and daughters in particular, having to care for their fathers as they grow older. In these instances, Lurie accepts his position as an aging parent, which strongly contrasts with his identification of a younger, virile Byronic lover.

One would perhaps be inclined to view Lurie more kindly in this light. However, one must acknowledge that his consideration to spare his daughter the intimate, unsightly workings of the elderly is not the same concern he displayed toward Melanie, and how she may have looked at him as an older man; a father like her own father, a protective, providing figure rather than a predatory one. In the interplay between these two identity positions, Lurie fails to recognize that he should have taken on the responsibility of the former as his prerogative given his position of authority as both parent and professor.

In Lucy's company, desire sporadically gives way to more homely feelings given the measure of self-awareness required of all parents, even if Lurie confesses, "being a father is a rather abstract business" (63). Despite staking a claim in the rather amorphous role fathers play in their children's lives, he admits that he has always generously and unconditionally loved his daughter from the very beginning (76). At first, he expresses how proud he feels about Lucy's accomplishments when he looks at her settlement and realizes she is no longer a child but has become a "solid countrywoman, a *boervrou*" (60). Contemplating the question of his legacy, he ponders whether history played a larger part in shaping his daughter's character (61). On the one hand, Lurie's observation lends credence to the truism that nature plays a greater share into shaping individuals than nurture does, and therefore deceivingly validates his (misguided) belief regarding the "abstract business" of fatherhood. On another more interestingly prophetic level, the idea of history introduced herein hints at the larger discourse of colonization. One could argue therefore that, as a settler herself, Lucy is somewhat complicit in that scheme, however liberal she appears. In turn, this will eventually support Lurie's view that the attack was a result of the forces of history coming full circle. However cynical the idea, there is a way in which, despite Lucy's attempt to elude the patriarchal values of heteronormativity and other systems of paternal oppression, she falls back into the fold through the tautology of a history written in blood. And while Lurie initially refuses to acknowledge how his own actions toward Melanie have contributed to "a long history of exploitation," the plight and suffering of his daughter should serve as a violent reminder of the inevitable consequences thereof.

Lurie's fatherly love and his role as provider and protector are directly put to the test during the attack. Knocked unconscious and locked in the lavatory, he wonders if he will be able to pass this trial (94). When one of the men douses him with methylated spirits and sets him on fire, he realizes they may not be spared, and notwithstanding his own plight he thinks foremost of his daughter (96). Downplaying his own injuries after the attackers leave, Lurie displays genuine concern for Lucy's well-being. However, he is unable to comfort her; in shock, her mind drifts far away from her father and this place since she does not respond to his consoling embrace (99). This failed attempt marks the moment at which the relationship between Lurie and Lucy, as father and daughter, breaks down; not only because of the traumatic yet separate injuries they have suffered in the hands of their attackers, but because of the uniqueness of the perspective through which the events are presented.

It is of considerable note that, like most significant events in the novel, the entire episode is exclusively related through Lurie's limited point of view. Even though they are both victims of the same perpetrators, their experiences are dramatically distinct, one which Lucy will emphasize repeatedly, mostly because she considers it her own private issue (112). Apart from revealing the difficulty she feels about speaking of her own trauma, Lucy's decree points to the fact that one simply cannot speak for the other, a concept which Lurie does not comprehend because of his marked tendency to project his own thoughts and desires onto others, as was the case with Melanie wherein he appeared oblivious to her own singular feelings.

Since she does not confide in Lurie until some time afterward, like him, the reader can only suspect what happened. On the one hand, as the affair between Melanie and Lurie and its consequences foreshadow later events, one can infer that Lucy's reluctance in sharing stems from the extreme difficulty with which victims speak of their experience of sexual assault because it makes them relive the trauma, a concept first hinted at by the reference to Adrienne Rich whose poem "Rape" specifically addresses that conundrum. On the other, Lucy's silence is more expressly situated in the ways she regards heterosexual intercourse as inherently violent, an act which directly implicates her father as guilty perpetrator.

In Lurie's mind, however, Lucy's decision not to share her experience reflects back onto his own insecurities. In the immediate aftermath of the incident, Lucy's silence makes it seem to Lurie that she is holding it together while he feels incredibly feeble (103). Lurie's physical scars bear witness to his shortcomings as a father and guide, something he had already alluded to before the incident. One night, he has an elaborate dream wherein Lucy vividly cries out for his help with her arms stretched out (103). When he goes to see her immediately thereafter, she rebukes him patronizingly (104). Lucy's response indicates he is incapable of acting as his daughter's protector, as his dream unearths his own unconscious fears.

From his border of exclusion, he tries to act as a responsible parent. On the one hand, he asks Lucy whether she and her doctor have addressed all undesirable consequences, and on the other, he manifests his opposition to returning to the farm in order to stay out of harm's way, which she dismisses on the grounds that safety is relative (105). While the former concern will unravel its own set of consequences, the latter issue is Lurie's main preoccupation. Despite his repeated attempts to reason with Lucy regarding her perilous situation, her determination to stay on amid the precariousness of her position makes Lurie realize she is no longer "her father's little girl" (105), a reality Lucy later confirms (161). Lucy may not mean to reject her father for who he is, but she nonetheless seems to indicate that being a father is not an identity one assumes freely, independently of contextual circumstances. Whereas he may be genuinely concerned for her safety, as any responsible parent would be, it is debatable whether he is in the rightful position to offer any counsel, most notably because of his own tenuous relationship with the concept of fatherhood. In discussing Lucy's safety with Bev, when she suggests he needs to let her go, he responds that he already has, adding, "I have been the least protective of parents" (140). Lurie's statement is not without a sense of incriminatory irony: his hands-off approach to parenting would have indeed foreshadowed how he effectively failed to protect his daughter. In fact, his past absenteeism reverberates into the events of the day, as during the same conversation Bev reminds Lurie that, contrary to his claim that he was present during the ordeal, he was locked in the bathroom and not actually "there" (140). Not only did Lurie not witness what happened to Lucy that day, one can also infer he also was not "there" as a father, to *protect* her from harm. His absence and failure to live up to the expectations of fatherhood reveal a fissure in the traditional model of white colonial patriarchy Lurie embodies.[22] This literal and inferred absence renders his present attempts to act as a responsible parent all the more questionable. This is especially true if one extends this unfortunate irony to the ways in which, as a parent, he should have also considered Melanie's vulnerability, especially when her father, Mr. Isaacs, voiced similar concerns about the well-being of his own daughter to Lurie; "abstract business" indeed.

Lurie's paradoxical positionality of protector and predator can arguably lead one to conclude there may be more than his identity as father at play. Regardless of how well-intentioned he is regarding the health and safety of his daughter, Lucy's repeated rejections may be rooted not only in their diverging views regarding her future, but in the fundamental difference of their individual experiences as well as his own complicity in the power dynamics that shape them.

Her silence, like that of Melanie earlier, is testimony enough of the paralyzing and debilitating force of the trauma caused by sexual assault. Yet it is amplified through Lurie's limited perspective precisely because of who he is, not only as a father but also as a man whose very actions have been associated with the victimization of others, thereby participating in a system that imposes such silences.[23] Lurie's constant queries about what happened, as well as Lucy's feelings and intentions (155), prompt her to tell him she "cannot talk anymore . . . because of who you are and who I am" (155).

Whereas Lucy clearly indicates her aversion to talking, what is the more precise nature of her implication regarding their particular subject positions? Lurie's first reaction is linked to his perceived failure as a father and his inability to effectively comfort his daughter. Lucy wants to decide for herself what to do next, because even if he is well-intentioned, she tells him he cannot possibly comprehend her particular experience (157). Given their opposite sex and distinct sexuality, she claims he cannot guide her (161) in this particular matter because the attack only further emphasized the violent inequalities of the codes of conduct to which he has adhered for the majority of his life.

Lurie's gestures are inadequate and misguided because they do not take into account the experiential differences between the sexes. He cannot "possibly comprehend," not only because he was not "there," but also because he has participated in forms of phallocratic oppression through his own complicity in a long history of acts of violence perpetrated against female others, thereby revealing that "his story"—and his disgrace—forms an intrinsic part of it. What is disgraceful, therefore, is what one individual inflicts upon other, and ultimately, oneself, when perpetuating the structures of a dreadful legacy of violence forever imprinted not only on people's minds and bodies, but also in the deafening silences that inhabit the vast physical and psychological territories they inhabit.

Lurie's father status and his capacity to be a guide for Lucy reaches a boiling point when he learns she is pregnant as a consequence of her rape, and that the father may very well be Pollux, a seemingly deranged young man that Petrus, Lucy's neighbor and soon-to-be landlord, is harboring due to their family ties. This news, and Lucy's determination to keep the child and get into some type of protective arrangement with Petrus, ruptures their already tense relationship.

Soon after Pollux was spotted at Petrus's party, Lurie tries to recruit Petrus's help to bring the boy to justice. At first, Petrus responds that the boy is too young to be tried and dismisses Lurie's request. In pleading Lucy's case, Lurie tells Petrus she wants to be "a good citizen and a good neighbor," but that he is foremost worried about her safety (138). To Lurie's incredulity, Petrus responds confidently that she will be safe because he is a capable guardian (139)—in contrast to Lurie. Accordingly, Lucy points out that her decision to enter into a protective agreement with Petrus is partly due to Lurie being rather unfit for successfully resolving the issues at hand (204). Not only is Lurie unable to effectively protect Lucy but he is being overshadowed by Petrus's rise to prominence. The latter's graduation from "dog-man" to landowner, all the while asserting his own right to self-determination, has displaced Lurie in whatever parental role he may have previously occupied, marking a symbolic shift in the terms of the patriarchy, a topic which will be investigated in detail in the next section.

With regard to Lucy's pregnancy, Lurie is surprised she did not take any precautions and is even more shocked that she will keep the child. Inquiring why she did not tell him earlier, she answers she wanted to avoid his tantrums:

> Because I couldn't face one of your eruptions. David, I can't run my life according to whether or not you like what I do. Not any more. You behave as if everything I do is part of the story of your life. You are the main character, I am a minor character who doesn't make an appearance until halfway through. Well, contrary to what you think, people are not divided

into major and minor. I am not minor. I have a life of my own, just as important to me as yours is to you, and in my life I am the one who makes the decisions. (198)

Lucy's response not only reaffirms her independence through her right to make her own decisions, but also illuminates the limited—sexist and pater-nal—perspective of the text's main point of view; the irony being, of course, that within the novel's diegesis, Lurie *is* the main character. Yet, Lucy's plea fails to make him aware of his paternalistic narrowmindedness. In light of the shifting dynamics alluded to earlier, it appears this last-ditch effort is fueled more by his own degraded sense of self-worth than hers, as he comes to grips with his displacement, not only as a man, but also as a father.

Given these new circumstances, Lucy and Lurie are at each other's throats mostly because Lurie remains blind to her legitimate attempts at writing her own story. The tension between them reaches another climax when he beats Pollux because he catches him spying on her while she is bathing. Lurie may believe he acted righteously, but Lucy clearly hints at the idea that her father's presence and actions are a menace to Lucy's wishes to try to foster peace between the concerned parties (208). Despite her pre-dicament, she reveals herself as a motherly, self-sacrificing figure, and her desire for peace contrasts strongly with Lurie's raging, paternalistic figure. In fact, she had hinted at this earlier when he asked her why she is keeping the child: "I am a woman, David [ . . . ] Should I choose against the child because of who its father is?" (198). In this thinly veiled attack, Lucy voices the burden that women must bear and the wrongs they have to right as the law of succession makes them inherit the sins of their fathers.

It would not be farfetched to argue that Lurie acted out of his own instinct of self-preservation. Realizing that his impassioned actions (209) do not suit him, Lurie appears consequently to reject the virile figure of Byron and turns to Teresa's exemplary passivity as a better guide given the circumstances. In other words, he is aware his actions were not necessarily guided by his concern for Lucy's safety but, rather, by the misguided anger and frustrations of a failed man and father.

Lurie confesses his vexations to Bev, who reassures him as she had done previously when he first voiced his concerns: under Petrus's eye, Lucy will be safe, and that perhaps it is time he steps back and lets Lucy live her life on her own terms because she can adapt to her circumstances (210) and is more grounded than either of them, which concurs with Petrus's views of Lucy as "forward-looking" (136). Lurie is hesitant to do so because he wonders whether he will survive if another disaster strikes (210). Bev puts him on the spot and asks him if therein lies his real concern, therefore underlining Lurie's (unconscious) obsession with "his-story" more than Lucy's, a sign of his persistent narcissism.

Humbled by these experiences, he seems to abandon his delusions by relinquishing his idealization of the Romantics, as his project of an opera based on Byron's affair with Teresa in Italy is at an impasse. As a reflection of his change of perspective, he considers writing about Teresa instead. Lurie imagines her singing, asking the *solitudine immensa* (the immense solitude), "*che sono?*"—what am I? To some extent, one wonders if Lurie is projecting his own thoughts onto Teresa, as she is "embracing the darkness" and what will come of it (213). No longer inspired by Byron's ravenous exploits, but putting himself in Teresa's shoes, Lurie appears to have embarked on a journey of psychological transformation as he awaits what the future will bring.

Observing Lucy working on the flower beds from a distance, Lurie realizes she is "becoming a peasant" (217), a much humbler description than the earlier "*boervrou.*" For some reason, this realization has sent him into a calm, contemplative mood about life and lineages; realizing he will soon be a grandfather, he asks himself whether he will be a better grandfather than he ever was a father given he can find new virtues in life, in which case "Victor Hugo, poet of grandfatherhood" may have things to teach him (217–28). There may be a shift in Lurie's consciousness, an acceptance of the inevitable march of history, but also of the passing of time, as one travels from one stage of life to another. In the case for Lurie, the switch from Byron to Hugo by way of Teresa seems fitting, as he also appears to understand the shift by coming to terms with his own vanishing libido (217). Ultimately, as Lucy invites him in for tea, the first visit since he left and took a room in town, he concludes this could be the sign for new beginnings (218).

Therein surfaces another reparative reading under the guise of a narrative of redemption or salvation and new beginnings: the disgraced father crosses the threshold, leaves the past behind, and accepts the future promises of becoming a grandfather. Interestingly, this is the interpretation Steve Jacobs chose in his mostly faithful film adaptation, *Disgrace* (2009). One can arguably see how the final sequence, where he parks his truck on a country road some distance from the farm and decides to walk to meet Lucy in the garden, encapsulates Lurie's journey: his rocky descent to the bottom, his slow winding walk up the dirt path as a sign of hardship and sterility, his arrival at the garden of (new) life, symbolized by the water, the earth, and the new growth, all embodied in the image of his pregnant daughter. He appears from behind a bush, seemingly humbled by the journey, and calls out her name timidly. On his second attempt, the dog (a sprightly Labrador, as opposed to the old bulldog Katy of the novel) runs to greet him as a friend. Lucy finally sees him, inspects his seeming penance, and invites him back into her life. A new chapter begins as he hops the small bench that separates the garden from the brush, the symbolic threshold that separates the destitute from the living. The final shot positions Lucy's dwelling at the center of the story, atop the hill, dominating Petrus's smaller house at the bottom of the shot. This image stands in sharp opposition to the ending of the novel, wherein the shift in the relation of power between Lucy, the white settler/colonizer, and Petrus, the black worker/colonized, is concretized visually through Lurie's thought that Petrus's newly built house overshadows Lucy's old farmhouse (197). To that effect, Theo Tait claims "there's a loss of nerve at the end,"[24] as the film concludes on a more hopeful note than the novel, wherein Lurie puts to sleep a partially disabled dog for which he has taken a liking, itself a symbol of Lurie's disgraced and reduced ego. Jacobs and his screenwriter/wife Anna Maria Monticelli may have chosen to purposely "trump"[25] Coetzee's novel for that desired effect. In light of the sharp critiques of the novel as a paranoid fantasy of black peril/white flight, the film aims to provide a more conciliatory ending, even if in turn it can be accused of maintaining the status of white privilege.

**No Country for Old (White) Men (and White Women?)**

While the film's ending may symbolically envision that white settlers remain at the top of the mountain so to speak, present realities in fact and fiction both point to the white minority's irreversible decline and gradual dispossession; in many ways, Lurie, and by extension, Lucy, are its figurative metaphors. As the first president in the fully representative democracy of post-apartheid South Africa, Nelson Mandela believed the country could only prosper if it included the white minority and strived to address their fears and hopes in shaping the future policies of the country. Recognizing that whites still controlled and dominated large sectors of the economy, Mandela endeavored for racial reconciliation and interracial cooperation on many fronts (with various rates of success).[26] Since then, however, relationships between the black majority heralded by an African National Congress (ANC) in internal crisis and the white minority have tensed up. As a result, the latter have been wary and suspicious of what the future holds for them, especially regarding the thorny issue of land ownership, a majority of which remains in their hands as a result of apartheid's 1913 Natives Land Act that prevented Africans from acquiring agricultural land.[27] Consequently, one could arguably consider Coetzee's novel in the context of that rising uncertainty, as Mandela's famous vision of a "rainbow nation" failed to materialize.[28]

As addressed previously, the gradual irrelevance of the white male settler is first announced through the ways in which Lurie pays for sex with Soraya. No longer able to attract or conquer the other as an entitlement, he resorts to using his economic privilege as an alternative. However, as a byproduct of both the colonial and apartheid eras, the white population's financial superiority acts as a stark reminder of the implications of capital regarding class and racial inequality, and its transactional nature is merely a stop-gap measure that veils the uncertainty surrounding the future of their political power and social relevance.

As a cypher for white economic and political privilege, Lurie's loss of seductive prowess and his inconsequential post at the university is indicative of the gradual erosion of such privilege. On the one hand, he finds himself to be less attractive and desirable since he now has to pay for his sexual needs in the stricter market rules of a libidinal economy that favors the young—in contrast to the entitlement of colonial superiority that marked the apartheid era of his youth. On the other hand, his demotion to the position of adjunct professor of communications also points to the loss of prominence of the Eurocentric ideologies of liberal humanism he represents. The

Romantic poets course he teaches is merely a vestige of a bygone epoch, a historical curiosity that fails to capture the interest of his students, symptomatic of the institutional shift that marks the post-apartheid era.[29]

The effacement of these physical and intellectual privileges underlines the ways in which a process of liberation concerns not only subjugated bodies but also the various methods of imperialist acculturation, in which language, education, and literature all play a conspicuous role.[30] One can read Lurie's subsequent pursuit and rape of Melanie as a symbolic last-ditch attempt on the part of the Western epistemologies to reclaim their lost prominence and reassert their power over the recently liberated other. Andrew van der Vlies suggests that Lurie's stake in the Romantic poets serves as a justification for his pursuit of Melanie,[31] and hence the "histories of exploitation" Lurie is accused of perpetuating encompass the complicity of the European intellectual tradition with the ideologies of imperialism. In the same way nineteenth-century European literature rationalized the colonial enterprise by Orientalizing the other,[32] Lurie uses the Romantic poets to justify his actions toward Melanie. In the previous section, I highlighted how Lurie denies his complicity at first because he remains entrenched in a rather abstract understanding of his actions following his own self-interested reading of European Romanticism. It is only much later, once he returns to Cape Town after his first sojourn in the Eastern Cape, that he eventually contemplates the ways in which most of literature is about "young women struggling to escape from under the weight of old men" to ensure the survival of the species (190). While he may not consciously acknowledge the direct implications of his own actions, he realizes the consequences therein as he refers to the lines of Yeats' "Sailing to Byzantium" cited in the epigraph of this chapter.

However caught in the abstract ideas of a past and distant land, this aging and unfit body of thought is indeed inadequate to face the realities of the present. Such failure is most apparent during the attack, where Lurie realizes how his skills, his education, and his knowledge of languages will not assist him. Against the brutality of the moment, his mind recalls the worst stereotypes propagated by European empires as they embarked on the pretext of a religious mission to "civilize" the continent only to realize the utter failure of their supposed campaign of enlightenment (95). There is undoubtedly a bitter irony in his invocation of the supposed work of missionaries to spread the word of God, considering biblical texts were often used to justify the violence associated with colonial expansion.[33] The aftermath also forces Lurie to come to grips with his own position as an aging white man, who feels increasingly out of place and out of touch and despairs about his prospects for a future in what increasingly feels like another country (197).

As the violence comes full circle, Lurie projects how Lucy perceives the attack within a historical perspective of retribution for past crimes. From his viewpoint, the assault was not personal; considering the ubiquity of violence in South Africa, he realizes they are lucky to be alive because "to own anything" (98) in a country plagued by incredible poverty is to make oneself vulnerable. While Lurie may be attempting to rationalize the event by depersonalizing the incident, he does not grasp that, as was the case for Melanie, rape is a private and personal matter for the victim regardless of the motivations of the perpetrator or the wider political context. Nonetheless, Lurie's overtly intellectual disposition impels him to dramatize the extent to which the incident is symptomatic of a state of affairs that imperils the life of his daughter. Bill Shaw seems to concur with Lurie by alluding to the "Black Peril" narratives that haunt the lives of white farmers, even if such instances have been greatly exaggerated to legitimize racial oppression.[34]

Whereas Lurie, as a white heterosexual male of European taste and culture,[35] may be a vestige of the past, Lucy is presented as a citizen of the rainbow nation, a new paradigm of transnational liberal views. But her complicity in the history of colonization cannot simply be brushed aside, however sympathetic the reader may feel toward her and her plight. From the onset, she is presented as a milder version of the colonial settler, as Lurie nostalgically comes to call her a *"boervrou"* (60). Further prompted by their first day at the market together where Lurie feels proud of his daughter and notices how the mix of people, Africans, Brits, and Afrikaners, is an agreeable representation of modern South Africa (even if the Afrikaners do not do as well as the others) (71–72), Lurie romanticizes the pastoral lifestyle of his daughter and goes so far as to think that her sharing the land with Petrus is a sign that "perhaps history has learned a lesson" (62).

One can easily see how Lurie's perspective is largely mediated by a lyrical temperament, a quixotic reverie that suffers a rude awakening by the material realities of country life through the actualization of its inherent dangers. Lurie believes that Lucy has a romantic attachment to the old, "*ländliche* way of life" (113). However, his thoughts are an abstract idealization she expressly rebuts when she tells him she does operate according to abstract ideas (112) and that besides the lack of safety, living on the farm is "not an idea, good or bad" (105). Contemplating Lucy's prospects, he believes that regardless of her own stubbornness to live according to her choices, there is no future for her here; that the land, this country, "Africa" is a place where whites like her and Ettinger, a neighboring German farmer and true vestige of the "old" days, do not belong (134).

Furthermore, against Lurie's repeated allusions that Lucy's victimization and refusal to seek justice are attempts to redress the wrongs of history (133), she reminds him that what happened to her is exclusively her concern and she reserves the right to do as she pleases (134). When she finally opens up, she tells him her attackers are foremost rapists, not thieves (158). Consequently, she is fearful they will come back since they have "marked" her as theirs (158). As Lurie insists she must leave, she replies,

> But isn't there another way of looking at it, David? What if . . . what if *that* is the price one has to pay for staying on? Perhaps that is how they look at it; perhaps that is how I should look at it too. They see me as owing something. They see themselves as debt collectors, tax collectors. Why should I be allowed to live here without paying? (158)

Here, Lucy appears to align herself with Lurie's historical rationalization and his perception that by not seeking justice, she is attempting to atone for past crimes. As a descendant of the colonialists and inheritor of their resources, she feels complicit in the enterprise, and as a farmer, a *boervrou*, she owns land that was taken away from the native inhabitants.

The association of women with the land and nation building is an ancient colonial trope of discovery and conquest, but in this particular instance it can be focalized through Lurie's invocation of *The Rape of the Sabine Women* as he reflects on his encounter with the word "rape" as a child (159–60). However, far from his thoughts are the ways in which sex with Melanie and to some extension the rape of Lucy can be associated with the

Roman myth. The story goes that in order to populate Rome, the mostly male inhabitants had asked the neighboring Sabines to take their women in marriage. As the Sabines refused, fearing the Romans would become their rivals, the latter abducted the Sabine women during a festival used as a pretext to lure them to the city and coerce them into marriage. This episode explains how the body of women is closely associated with nation building, as their capacity to bear children is the key to posterity. In *Disgrace*, the idea is tainted with the treatment of native women in histories of colonialism, as not only was their fertility seen as a threat to imperial dominance, but settlers often quenched their desires by coercing women into sexual relations. As a "coloured" woman, Melanie is a direct product of that practice, and her rape, its reification. Melanie's victimization is a result of what Kirsten Holst Petersen and Anna Rutherford have dubbed "double colonization" in referring to the ways in which women are simultaneously oppressed by the powers of both the empire and the patriarchy.[36] In contrast, Lucy's rape is a symbolic act of reclaiming the land by native populations. Through Frantz Fanon, Charles Sarvan reminds us that "decolonization is a difficult, violent, and ugly process,"[37] yet one is entitled to ask whether Lucy—or any other woman—deserves such treatment since it merely perpetuates structures of patriarchal colonization and phallocratic violence while the male perpetrators remain scot-free.

Regardless of what Lurie and Lucy may think of their attackers, the fact is the reader does not have access to their thoughts or motivations. While the discussion of *African Psycho* in chapter four may provide some psychological insight to a hypothetical characterization of psychotic African masculinities and their predispositions for rape and violence, in *Disgrace*, the perpetrators do not speak, which not only gives way to all sorts of projections and imaginations, but also allows for the worst stereotypes, thereby conferring a negative judgment of their character following an indictment of their monstrous actions. This perspective is further exacerbated by the presence of Pollux, who is categorized as a deranged and troubled young man, a consideration only reinforced by his voyeurism and the expression of his vengeful anger when Lurie catches him. However, while little insight can be gained from this character, some perspective may be provided through a closer look at his guardian, Petrus, who (perhaps quite deliberatively on the part of Coetzee) is the only African given a voice in the text with the exception of Mr. Isaacs, which only further complicates the stakes regarding historical violence, race relations, and land ownership.

Lucy initially describes Petrus as her assistant, but also recently titled coproprietor; according to her, he is reliable (77). Lurie's—and the reader's—first brief encounter with Petrus is in fact quite telling. Lurie's leading query is whether he takes care of the dogs, to which he responds, "I am the gardener and the dog-man" (64), repeating the last phrase almost sarcastically, as an ironic foreshadowing of his eventual change of status. Perhaps even more significant is that when Lurie mentions he is concerned with his daughter's safety Petrus tells him, somewhat reassuringly (and smilingly) that she will be fine here (64). Even before the attack, Lurie feels uneasy about Petrus's presence. For example, when Lucy suggests Lurie help Petrus by working on his land, he finds the idea that Petrus could pay him has "historical piquancy" (77). Brushing off his snide remark, Lucy insists that by relative standards he is quite wealthy as he owns land, cattle, and has two wives, and in many ways he is "his own master" (114).

At times, Lurie seems to accept the fact that these are no longer the days of old and that Petrus is a bona fide neighbor (116) who accepts help for a wage. In fact, part of him even admires Petrus, given what he must have gone through as a "man of his generation" realizing that "his story" cannot be reduced to English, a language Petrus often misuses as it is "an unfit medium for the truth of South Africa" (117). Here, it appears that not only does Lurie display a sensitivity that is rather unusual given his egotism, but also he acknowledges the cultural bias of language and the protean nature of truth as a result. Yet, the possibility of a parallax view is dismissed as Lurie develops a more unilateral and negative viewpoint on Petrus and his relative position of power after the attack.

Suspicious of Petrus's whereabouts during the event, Lurie appears to ascribe to Ettinger's viewpoint that you cannot trust the Africans (109). Petrus may have orchestrated the attack to drive Lucy off the farm because on the one hand, he appears unaffected by the events in a way that enrages Lurie, and on the other, he refuses to bring Pollux to justice in part because of their kinship. He expected Petrus to manifest some anger, but all he gets is a lukewarm response at best. This is in part where Lurie's single-mindedness is evident; what can he realistically expect from a man who, according to his own admittance, must have endured his own share of injustices during his lifetime? In a sense, one could argue that for Petrus's generation, such outrages were not only commonplace, but institutionalized as well. Lurie wants justice to be served (119), but what of the legions of guilty officials who were granted amnesty by the Truth and Reconciliation Commission? Can Petrus be blamed for his willingness to protect his own people? At the same time, one would be pressed to argue the attack is just retribution for what previous generations of Africans suffered in the hands of the apartheid regime. Whereas the case can certainly be made for reparations and restitutions, it seems highly doubtful that an ethical argument can be made for such violence.

Equally as relevant are the ways in which Lurie seems isolated in his quest for justice, since Lucy chooses to remain silent and avoid confrontation at all costs. Defending herself against her father's relentless pressure, Lucy reattempts to affirm her agency, even if she *chooses not to act.* Of course, Lurie's perspective—and incidentally that of the reader's—may be different. One could argue she has a responsibility to identify the perpetrators so that justice can be done. But perhaps the idea of justice to which Lurie appeals does not correspond to this particular place and time, this country, this particular concept of "Africa" that does not operate according to principles based on western ideas and ideals. Lurie believes that justice could provide some type of catharsis, that existing tensions will be resolved. Although that may be true from his point of view, Lucy tells him she cannot afford to make an enemy of Petrus since he is her neighbor and coproprietor, not a hired hand who can be terminated as one pleases. In fact, given her nonconfrontational disposition and desire to maintain the peace for the sake of the future, she is "forward-looking, not backward-looking" as Petrus tells Lurie (136), perhaps as a reminder of how his generation did not pursue justice for past offenses. On another level, lost to Lurie is a sense of perspective he may still unconsciously deny. In some way, it is not too farfetched to think that his own disgrace was triggered by the actions of another daughter, Melanie, yielding to the pleas of her own father to denounce and seek justice for the one who attacked her and likewise shamed and disgraced her.

Concerned about his daughter's safety and unable to gain any traction with Lucy or Petrus, Lurie is prompted to contemplate their future and that of their property. In the shift of power that is unraveling, Lurie has traded places with Petrus since he has now become "the dog-man," as Petrus called himself when they first met. Being a "dog-man" was merely a step for Petrus, a rite of passage, before he was able to affirm his ownership, not only of the land, but of his destiny as well. At his party, Petrus calls Lucy his "benefactor," a word Lurie finds "distasteful" no doubt given its historical connotation in a place where it was widely misused to justify colonial and missionary atrocities (129). Bev hints that Lurie's view of Petrus is misguided because he helped Lucy with the farm and the market in considerable ways to the extent that she may be indebted to him (140). Lurie concedes Petrus's working ability is "All very swift and businesslike; all very unlike Africa," a force Lurie contrasts to that of his own daughter, whom he considers on the verge of collapse (151). In addition to marking a patriarchal shift, the rise of Petrus also coincides with the fall of his daughter, which is only confirmed when Lucy eventually accepts Petrus's offer to marry her and take her under his wing, signifying both a reversal of the racial dynamic and a restoration of traditional gender hierarchies.

Petrus's proposal comes on the heels of Lurie's final attempt to ask Lucy to leave given she is pregnant with Pollux's child, a situation he considers absurd and disturbing (200). Regardless of how dejected she may feel, she is not "giving up"; a position that is rather dumbfounding given she confesses no actual attachment to the farm (200). It is on the very theme of belonging that Petrus tells Lurie that in the same way he wants to take care of his daughter, Petrus must look after Pollux, because he "is a child. He is my family, my people" (201), thereby clearly situating the issue in terms of conflicting interests according to racial divides, a point that is not lost on Lurie. Nonetheless, Petrus admits that what happened to Lucy was lamentable but insists it is now over (201). In other words, the past should be the past, even if Lurie disagrees since the "past" will live on because of Lucy's pregnancy. Petrus's response is that Pollux ought to marry Lucy, but that because the boy is too young, he, Petrus, will. Obviously, this throws Lurie for a loop, and he tells Petrus, "This is not how we [Westerners] do things" (202), thus reinforcing racial and cultural boundaries.

Lurie's further objection stems from the fact that as a lesbian, Lucy does not want to marry a man; reiterating Lucy's own plea for independence, Lurie tells Petrus she wants to remain single (202). However aware of Lucy's preference, Petrus claims that she must have a husband because it is dangerous for a woman to live alone in these parts (202), a reality that firmly reinstates traditional patriarchal rule in post-apartheid South Africa as a stark rejection of the more Western liberal views embodied by Lucy's sexuality.[38] Nonetheless, cognizant of her precarious situation as a single woman, Lucy understands the proposition as a means for Petrus to obtain her farmland as a form of dowry (203). While Lucy is therein confirming Lurie's initial suspicions about Petrus, she also recognizes that she would gain Petrus's protection. Because Lurie's paranoid position is indicative of his entrenchment to his own Western worldview, he may not perceive that regardless of Petrus's ambition to own Lucy's land, his proposal is a solution to the quandary, a way to resolve the conflict: he is accepting a duty to both "peoples"—black and white—by taking on the responsibility of marrying a woman who is a distinct other and, as Lurie points out earlier, marked by her "disgrace" (115).

In a way, Petrus is brokering a legitimate alliance that absolves the disputed issue of land rights and ownership while providing Lucy with the opportunity to continue to live here as she pleases, albeit in a rather powerless position. To that effect, she agrees with her father that

> "It is humiliating. But perhaps that is a good point to start from again. Perhaps that is what I must learn to accept. To start at ground level. With nothing. Not with nothing but. With nothing. No cards, no weapons, no property, no rights, no dignity."
>     "Like a dog."
>     "Yes, like a dog." (205)

On the one hand, Lucy's assertion echoes the ending of the novel wherein Lurie decides to put to death "Driepoot," the disabled dog he grew fond of by "giving him up," which can be read positively as a renunciation of his old self,[39] the castrated, wounded other he has become, toward the new beginning offered by grandfatherhood—a path that appears hopeful for their future relationship amid their destituteness. On the other hand, the reference also markedly points to the ways in which the devalued lives of nonhuman animals in general, and dogs in particular, whether real or symbolic, are presented discursively throughout the novel as interconnected and interrelated to the lives of their human counterparts.[40] In Lucy's objectification, she has effectively become someone else's subject, to live in fear, forever marked as their territory in her subjugation to a new order. By denaturing the white female body, stripping it of its agency into nothingness, the body-without-organs is reclaimed as an animal to be used in its primal utility, similar to the ways in which Africans were oft compared to animals to justify their mistreatment and exploitation. But more importantly, in the perspective that the female body is associated with nation building, in this new South Africa, the white "mother of the nation" is stripped from her historic privilege as land owner and must start from nothing.

In light of Petrus's proposal, Lucy's change of status from an independent, single woman to a married and kept wife directly correlates with her shift from landowner to tenant, or bywoner as Lucy and Lurie point out, a term that at one time may have been used to designate Petrus or any other poor farmer laboring on another's land. This may not present itself as a just outcome. But perhaps therein lies the irony; rather than symbolizing a truly emancipated "rainbow nation," Lucy and her child, the land and her future offspring, are indicative of troubled times that face the nation, wherein the materiality of history and its violent realities cannot be easily swept away.

As some critics have decried, *Disgrace* plays into the (exaggerated) fears of the white landowning minority. However, Lucy's fate deserves further consideration, not only as a victim of retributive violence, but also as a "modern young woman" who was put back "in her place" (115) and must forego her independence and reintegrate the patriarchy.[41] While Petrus may not be the evil Lurie believes he is, he is nonetheless complicit in perpetuating hierarchical structures of male dominance and oppression. Petrus's dominant personality is quite apparent in the way he conducts himself, and his misogyny is rather outspoken. He not only thinks that women cannot live on their own, but also that they should be submissive to men. When Lurie asks him why he hopes his firstborn will be a boy, he explains "it is best [so that] he can show his sisters . . . how to behave" (130). On another level, one cannot entirely dismiss Lucy's voice regarding her own *personal* suffering. Therefore, Petrus's complicity is situated in his choice to harbor one of the perpetrators and his refusal to denounce and condemn the attack outright. As Glenn posits, Lurie's perspective may be that Petrus "becomes a rather sinister embodiment of black claims for the restitution of farmland and even of Black Economic Empowerment (BEE) logic."[42] However, one could argue that he is merely protecting his own, and that Lurie's insistence for justice is misplaced as it does not adequately put into perspective the historical injustices suffered by Africans at the hands of white settlers and colonizers. However ambiguous the novel is on the issue of rape given its dominant yet limited male perspective, justifying the act on the basis of land dispute and redistribution of wealth represents an ethical quandary.

Although Melanie's own fate is discursively distant and more uncertain, even if seemingly more encouraging considering Lurie's own observations, she also remains subjected to dominating male figures. Not only does her boyfriend fit the type rather perfectly, but in the particularities of his own petit-bourgeois context, Melanie's father also perpetuates Judeo-Christian patriarchal traditions. Africans may have justly reclaimed their land, but they have only done so in maintaining forms of paternalistic colonization, which, as Lucy points out, condemns women to "Not Slavery. [but] Subjection. Subjugation" (159).

# 2

# The Eschatology of Desire in Michel Houellebecq's *The Elementary Particles*

> "You like doing this? I don't mean simply me; I mean the thing in itself?"
>
> "I adore it."
>
> That was above all what he wanted to hear. Not merely the love of one person, but the animal instinct, the simple undifferentiated desire: that was the force that would tear the party to pieces.
>
> —George Orwell, *1984*

Alongside Aldous Huxley's *Brave New World*, George Orwell's *1984* is arguably one of the most famous projections of a negative utopia.[1] The totalitarian regime depicted in Orwell's novel presents the pinnacle of Michel Foucault's concept of a "disciplinary society," which classifies, surveys, and disciplines all levels of existence through the relationship of power to its subjects.[2] In Orwell's vision, "Big Brother" is the panoptic apparatus that ensures all citizens observe coercive rules of conduct. In order to eradicate any form of individual freedom that could eventually lead to nonconformist and revolutionary impulses, a series of disciplinary mechanisms guarantee that the population conforms with the ruling ideology.

In his later work, Foucault coined the term "biopolitic" to delineate the ways in which technologies of power in disciplinary societies are centered on sexuality and the body.[3] The totalitarian regime depicted in *1984* provides an uncompromising depiction of the biopolitics of power, wherein sexual reproduction as well as the fulfillment of libidinal desires are strictly regulated for they are perceived to be both potentially disruptive and possibly subversive to the good functioning of society.

In the above epigraph, *1984*'s main protagonist, Winston, voices the belief that the instinctual gratification of unrestrained sexual desire is a politically subversive act. This idea has most pervasively circulated in the history of Western thought by the Marquis de Sade, who wrote *La Philosophie dans le boudoir* two centuries prior to the setting of Orwell's novel in the aftermath of the French revolution. Therein he inserted the brief political pamphlet entitled "Français, encore un effort si vous voulez être Republicains," an ironical response to Robespierre's postrevolutionary discourses in which he precisely argues for a concept of absolute freedom inspired by the natural right of individuals over the potentially despotic sovereignty of the state.[4] Accordingly, popular interpretations of Sade's work have attempted to show that his philosophy of sexual freedom can be read as a revolutionary manifesto against the constraints and hypocrisies of the ruling class as well as the legal and moral constraints of institutionalized dogma.[5]

The idea that the liberalization of sexual politics plays an integral role in equilibrating the balance of power in democratic societies is congruent with the views of various social movements of the 1960s that helped trigger the sexual revolution. Yet, it is precisely the sociopolitical legacy of this generation that is duly criticized in Michel Houellebecq's 1998 award-winning and provocative[6] novel *The Elementary Particles*. In drawing a sharp critique of the economies of desire in modern consumer society through the lives of its various protagonists, the novel suggests that a society that allows for the free expression of human sexuality—the direct heritage of the revolutionary ideals promoted in the work of the Marquis de Sade and its various interpretations—does not permit individuals to achieve a greater state of generalized emancipation because it merely *displaces* the mechanisms of oppression. In fact, such a society not only perversely conflates the public and the private sphere, but also substitutes the power structure of the disciplinary state with the equally unbalanced power relations of a liberal, pleasure-driven society, wherein individuals compete against each other for the fulfillment of their desires.[7]

From a retrospective set in an imaginary, post-human 2079, the frame narrative recounts in a series of fragmentary encounters the rather sordid existence of Bruno Clément and Michel Djerzinski, two half brothers who lived in France at the dawn of the third millennium. The text makes it clear that their failures to adjust to the psycho-realities of modern life can be traced to having been abandoned at an early age by their freethinking and free-loving mother, Janine (later referred to as "Jane"). Her first husband Serge is a plastic surgeon who shares her libertine ideals. Since raising a child is incompatible with their lifestyle, they send Bruno off to live with his maternal grandparents in Algeria before divorcing amicably. Bruno's upbringing is tragic because he is continuously abused and humiliated sexually in boarding school. Later, as a high school literature teacher trapped in a loveless marriage, Bruno becomes an insatiable sex addict and consumer. One day, he sexually propositions one of his students and, consequently, he is sent to a mental institute for evaluation. His marriage ends soon thereafter, but he finds in Christiane, whom he meets at a singles retreat, a supportive woman eager to satisfy him sexually. However, their sexcapades to swinging Paris come to a screeching halt when she dies shortly after an illness paralyzes her from the waist down. This is the final blow for Bruno who checks himself into a mental clinic and lives the rest of his days heavily sedated.

Born in 1958, two years after his older brother, Michel is an introverted molecular biologist who is raised by his paternal grandmother: a hard-working and morally righteous individual—the very antithesis of his freethinking mother. Son of Marc Djerzinski, a documentary filmmaker Janine befriends soon after her divorce, Michel only falls in love once as a teenager with a girl named Annabelle. She eventually leaves him for David di Meola, the son of one of Janine's lovers, who becomes a Satanist cult leader as well as a rapist and murderer. Subsequently, Michel soon grows totally impervious to human emotions. Even when Michel and Annabelle become intimate again when their paths cross years later, he remains cold and impassive, incapable of love. As the epilogue that frames the narrative explains, his depreciative views on love and sex eventually lead him to discover a scientific formula that eliminates desire and affection as variables in the equation for sexual reproduction. In 2029, his research makes human cloning possible, which eventually leads to the extinction of the human race in its present configuration.[8]

## Reactionary Historicism and a Contested *History of Sexuality*

To formulate a critique of contemporary society's model of sexual freedom, Houellebecq's novel draws from the various disciplinary discourses that have shaped Western thought (the social sciences of philosophy, literature, theology, and history, as well as the "hard" sciences of biology, chemistry, and of course, physics) and makes a considerable number of references to prominent intellectual figures (Aldous Huxley, Auguste Comte, Friedrich Nietzsche, etc.), which are interweaved into a wide-ranging argumentative stratagem. This comprehensive heteroglossia endeavors to bestow the narrative an authoritative agency, which in turn aims to validate the veracity of the novel's manifest critique. By laying bare the problematics of desire in contemporary consumer society through the dialogical pattern of this multidisciplinary discourse, the rhetoric of *Elementary Particles* conscientiously outdoes an allegorical reading of the Jamesonian "political unconscious."[9] The Determinism that guides the multiple discursive fronts of the narrative is considerably overt about its ideological function and the sociohistorical context it addresses.

My contention is that it is specifically in this hermeneutic logic of determinism that one finds the weakness of the narrative's ideological critique of the politics of sexual freedom. Likewise, I further argue that the novel's implied criticism of the philosophical movements of the 1960s—the school of poststructuralist thought that specifically endeavored to undermine the absolutism of the Age of Reason and nineteenth-century positivism—also falls short due to a reactionary argument reductively misguided by a traditional form of historicism. Ironically so, I will also demonstrate that it is inevitably through a deconstructive reading that *Elementary Particles* provides for a noteworthy illustration of how the problematics of sexual desire, far from being the inherited condition of the postwar generation's advocacy for self-expression and free will, is actually the perverse product of a society of control operating under the economic model of spectacular consumption.

The interpretative logic of the text's naturalism points to the demise of the determinist project. Similar to Emile Zola's own investment in the experimental novel's potentialities for the determination of the human psyche, Houellebecq's text gets entangled into the tropes of characterization drawn by the dialectics and poetics of the specific genre. Yet, in a self-conscious effort to go beyond Zola's mere characterization of social conditions, the novel's voice expressively draws specific genealogies as well as detailed narrative reconstitutions of the psychological portraits of the main characters. This is further problematized by the structure of the novel, which, instead of attempting to objectively outline a revelatory cartography of male heteronormative dysfunction, displays the ambition by the narrative to clearly prognosticate, through the reconstruction of the post-human narrator, the eschatology of all desire.[10]

Jerry Andrews Varsava aptly argues by way of Karl Popper and Hayden White that the historical perspective presented in *Elementary Particles* and in Houellebecq's other novels is guided by a very traditional historicism, where "history is governed by knowable laws and, collaterally, that the discernment of them enables the design and implementation of utopian initiatives."[11] Varsava refers to Popper in arguing that, contrary to the beliefs of Auguste Comte whom Houellebecq apparently endorses, "there are no hard and fast laws which govern history because, simply enough, the conduct of people—the "human factor"—is contingent and unpredictable over time."[12] In fact, it could be argued that insofar as it lays claim to objective truth of the past, the traditional historicism of the novel is animated with the same prevalent naturalism that informs much of the novel's determinism. Like Zola's own misguided predispositions, *Elementary Particles* similarly promotes a rather naïve view regarding the irrefutability of scientific discourse; a prevalent nineteenth-century viewpoint inherited from the Enlightenment that considered the concepts of truth and knowledge to be absolutes.

In the second half of the twentieth century, poststructuralist thinkers demonstrated that all knowledge, like truth, is situated, a perspective with which many scientists would agree, and this is especially applicable to history from a historiographical perspective. This view, of course, stands in sharp contrast to *Elementary Particles'* determinism, and it is not surprising that, as a consequence, the text draws an ideological critique of poststructuralist philosophy. In one notable instance among many, the narrator claims, "The global ridicule in which the works of Foucault, Lacan, Derrida and Deleuze had suddenly foundered, after decades of inane reverence, far from leaving the field clear for new ideas, simply heaped contempt on all those intellectuals active in the 'human sciences'" (262). In this sense, the novel's ideological affiliation is concurrent with the reactionary stance of the *Nouveau Philosophes* who have succeeded the generation of Foucault and Deleuze in France.[13]

In particular, the novel addresses two strands of the genealogy of poststructuralist/counter-enlightenment thought: the Marquis de Sade's philosophy of sexual freedom and the legacy of Nietzsche's concept of the Dionysian. While Nietzsche's philosophy is disparaged through Michel's violent rejection of his ideas, as will be explored later, Sade's legacy is criticized through Bruno's reading of a conservative critic's book on David di Meola (inspired by the likes of Charles Manson), whose estate Bruno and Christiane both visited with their parents in the seventies. According to Bruno's "cynical, hard-bitten, typically masculine view of life" (170), di Meola's Satanist acts were mere decorum: "In fact, like their master the Marquis de Sade, they were pure materialists—libertines forever in search of new and more violent sensations" (174). I would contend that if the actions of di Meola are to be considered from this perspective, then the narrative performs a biased and conservative reading, if not a grossly decontextualized misreading, of Sade's oeuvre in an attempt to deride its philosophical pertinence. Whereas Georges Bataille's reading of Sade emphasized the illuminating possibilities revealed by Sade's sexual poetics—a position later picked up by Foucault and the Tel Quel group—other writers such as Pierre Klossowski, whose influential reading runs similarly deep among the ranks of continental philosophers, considers Sade's philosophy of free will as a reaction to the materialism of the Enlightenment. The conservative reading of Sade performed by Bruno specifically aims to further criticize the humanistic ideals of freedom and individual agency adopted by many French intellectuals of the twentieth century. Therefore, it could be argued that in allegorizing the ways in which Sade's politics of sexual freedom quickly degenerate into ritualized murder, the novel vouches for and bears witness to a symbolic return to the more conservative values of a school of empiricist thought. Jack I. Abecassis suggests that "[i]n reading Houellebecq, you know that you are, at heart, in the presence of a *Moraliste* of the French Augustinian variety (Arnault, Pascal, La Rochefoucauld)."[14] This *Moraliste*, I would claim, is a conservative reactionary; he abhors the ideals of individual freedom promoted by the postwar generation because his text specifically yet mistakenly situates the root of the current state of moral decline in their egotistical endeavors for libidinal wish fulfillment.

The reactionary ideology of the novel is introduced as reverence to the figure of Michel's conservative grandmother, who embodies the archetypical model of self-denial and stoicism of "the generation who as children had suffered the hardships of war" (42), and whose traditional, catholic values regarding gender roles, sex, and marriage have been shrugged off by their children. Most expressively manifested in the contempt she expresses toward her daughter-in-law, the criticism of liberal mores is anchored in the belief that the libertine generation embodied by the couple Janine/Serge is more preoccupied by the unrestrained pursuit of individual freedoms than by securing the well-being of their offspring. Consequently, their carefree and egotistical attitude has adversely affected their progeny, who suffer from neglect and abuse.

Following Varsava's earlier observation, the text is quick to point to the faults of a generation it deems responsible for contemporary society's generalized state of despair without considering the larger context. Such judgment appears impulsive at best and is not the fruit of objective critical observation because it entirely disregards the sociopolitical achievements of the historical period. For example, whereas women have acquired more social and political rights vis-à-vis the dominant patriarchy as noted earlier in the introduction, the novel responds by reducing the social position of the female population to traditional gender roles of subservient domesticity and deriding feminism as a whole: as Christiane tells Bruno "I think that feminism has hit [women] harder than they like to admit" (117) since it "managed to turn every man into an impotent, whining neurotic," and led women to complain that "there were no real men anymore" (121). To that effect, Varsava aptly observes:[15]

[t]he epilogue of the novel proclaims loudly that "THE FUTURE IS FEMI-NINE," with the "feminine" defined by the naively gender-stereotyped qualities of general benevolence and self-abnegation. As Frédérick Hubeczjak,

Michel's follower, tells us, cloned humanity takes solace in a utopian realm that is "as round, smooth, and warm as a woman's breast." (259)

In consideration of these sexist overtones, a more careful reading between text and context would contend that, contrary to *Elementary Particles'* argument, greater individual freedoms are not incompatible with social progress or gender equality even if they may impact traditional male privilege.

Houellebecq's novel is grounded in a conservative, pseudoscientific determinism that permeates the narrative and its characters. As the engineer of a future race of humanoids devoid of humanity's passions, Michel's philosophical allegiances are directly positioned in the positivism of Auguste Comte. More indirectly, however, his ideological dogmatism can be traced to the moral imperative expressed by Zola as part of the naturalist endeavor.[16] Zola believed that in its existential mapping of the human psyche, the experimental novel could help determine the ways in which abhorrent behavior patterns could be corrected and that, consequently, it could serve political means in its pragmatic attempt to establish the guidelines for a healthy society.[17] Michel, like Zola, believes in the potential of the experimental model to produce irrefutable knowledge that is immutable, a guiding principle for the achievement of his (anti)ontological project.

Concurrently, Michel's philosophical ideology rejects Nietzsche's relativism in favor of Kant's absolutism of reason and morality, and in particular the idea that "perfect morality is unique and universal" (28), which he considers to be the pillars of a healthy, happy, and long-living society. For Michel, the belief in science as an irrefutable knowledge base for ontological experiences is unequivocal, and the novel's own narrative raison d'être advocates the triumph of Michel's scientific project as the result of his philosophical vision, a vision that categorically rejects a genealogy of Western relativism which finds its primeval expression in Nietzsche's writing.

Nietzsche particularly despised the religious and cultural imperatives of the Enlightenment that perceived that truth and knowledge could be attainable solely in a state of highest morality. He considered this belief "*la niaiserie religieuse par excellence*" [the utmost religious foolishness (translation mine)],[18] claiming that "morality in Europe at present is a herding-animal morality."[19] Nietzsche shows contempt for the boundaries beset on intellectual freedom by morality and argues that truth is not merely to be contained within the narrow limits of righteousness. Quite the contrary, he contends that knowledge and erudition can also be found in a "radical other": "severity, violence, slavery, danger in the street and in the heart, secrecy, stoicism, tempter's art and devilry of every kind,—that everything wicked, terrible, tyrannical, predatory, and serpentine in man, serves as well for the elevation of the human species as its opposite."[20] In parallel, Nietzsche's call for the Dionysian in man implies to some degree the expression and affirmation of instinctual drives and desires that transgress the morally permissible at that limit which separates human from animal, forces that can be both revolutionary and cataclysmic, or, as Bataille has emphasized in his subsequent readings, both elevating and liberating.

The epigraph from Orwell's *1984* encapsulates both Sade's philosophy of sexual transgression as revolutionary and Nietzsche's argument regarding the liberating potential of desire in the Dionysian. Yet, this call for a return to a more elemental state of natural desire is also sharply criticized in *Elementary Particles*. Whereas in *1984*, Winston yearns for a return to the pure expression of desire as the pathway to social and political emancipation, Houellebecq's novel identifies therein the problematic root of the economies of desire in contemporary consumer society for which the spread of both Nietzsche's and Sade's ideas are ostensibly complicit.

According to dualist and transcendental perspectives, Michel finds particularly despicable the inherent violence of the animal kingdom, which he perceives as a rationale for "nature [deserving] to be wiped out in a holocaust—and man's mission on earth was probably to do just that" (29). Furthermore, the connection between the "dominance and brutality" (38) of the animal kingdom and Nietzsche's philosophy is literalized in the figure of Jean Cohen, the housemaster of the school where Bruno as an "omega male" is violently bullied and "psychologically scarred for life" (39). Considering Bruno's trajectory henceforth, the implicit argument is that the natural order of the libidinal economy of desire replaces the hierarchy of the class system by a much more oppressive and despotic hierarchy of social dominance established through strength in combat.

In a praising review of *Elementary Particles*, Abecassis argues that, following a perspective already advanced in *Whatever* (Houellebecq's first novel, published in 1994 as *Extension du domaine de la lutte* in France), the novel draws a correlation between unrestrained sexual expression (or "sexual liberalism," see below) and economic liberalism, whereas the production of sexual desires and their fulfillment replicates quite faithfully the economic model of advanced capitalism. Quoting from *Whatever*, Abecassis notes that "the extension of liberty to sexuality is poisonous, for the more you extend liberty, the more you risk and eventually lose."[21] He then uses this idea as a lens to consider *Elementary Particles* as a discursive extension of the same sociohistorical critique of sexuality:

> In economies as in sex, free competition ("libéralisme") must thus necessarily bring about the pauperization and alienation of the majority. Consequently, "libéralisme sexuel" returns in late twentieth century to the baboon state: it is the winner-take-all world of the alpha male, which in Houellebecq's world is the Dionysian male rock and roll star.[22]

My main contention, however, is that the equation that underlines much of Houellebecq's critique of poststructuralist philosophy as well as the sexual revolution of the 1960s and the supposed "sexual liberalism" that ensued is based on a faulty conjecture derived from a very selective and narrow reading of evolutionary psychology, social history, and contemporary philosophy. While it is undeniable that contemporary sexual mores are considerably less restrictive than they were at the beginning of the twentieth century, there is very little evidence to support the fact that the ideals of freedom advocated by the sexual revolution were actualized and that libidinal desires have been "liberalized" to the extent that Houellebecq's text presupposes. Rather, I would argue that in this particular context sexual "liberty" is a mere illusion; the fabrication of a disciplinary society whose mechanisms of power have been clearly mapped out by Foucault.

In *The History of Sexuality*, Foucault traces back to the eighteenth and nineteenth centuries the explosion of discourses on sexuality, where sex talk penetrated all levels and all classes of society: "[t]here was installed rather an apparatus for producing an ever greater quantity of discourse about sex, capable of functioning and taking effect in its very economy."[23] He is careful to link the proliferation of sexualities to discourse, a system of language, because it provided the necessary means for the disciplinary society to further classify all aspects of human existence, and hence to further regiment it. Modern society creates the desires it supposedly abhors by naming them and classifying them only to exert better control over its members; this is why Foucault contends that in creating names for perceived perversions (such as homosexuality, fetishism, etc.) beyond the category of the taboo, society "is in actual fact, and directly, perverse."[24] The supposed liberalization of sexuality, the multiplication of sexual practices linked to their *recensement* or census, had the perverse effect to implement an even more pervasive and wide-ranging structure of power and control. In other words, for Foucault the exponential growth of identifiable sexual practices in the last two centuries does not equate greater freedom. Quite to the contrary, this discursive cartography allows for a more efficient exercise of surveillance. To go back to *Elementary Particles'* contextualization of modern society, it is not that a model of sexual liberalism (or economic liberalism for that matter) replicates the law of the jungle,[25] but rather that it juxtaposes a multitude of sites "where the intensity of pleasures and the persistency of power catch hold, only to spread elsewhere."[26] Thus, far from having returned to the "baboon state" as Abecassis claims by way of Houellebecq, we have further sublimated our natural drives and instincts by mediating them through discourse and by providing the existing power structures the opportunity to map them out more accurately.

With regard to the sexual liberties of the individual subject, the so-called "libidinal economy," the question is not whether contemporary sexual mores replicate the liberal economic model of advanced capitalism, but whether present social conditions preempt the existence of such liberties. The emergence of diverse sexual practices may point to the illusion that there is a greater sense of sexual freedom, but in fact, as Foucault puts it, it merely implies that they are being categorized and classified and thus, disciplined and regimented. While the novel may pretend that sexual liberalism is an established fact, in actuality freedom of sexual expression has more accurately undergone a potential shift from that of the "real" to that of the simulacrum, a sign that marks the very absence of what it signifies,[27] and it is specifically in its property as simulacrum that it can be regarded as coercive.

## From the Disciplinary Society to a "Society of Control"

While the discursive strategy of *Elementary Particles'* ideological criticism is flawed and misdirected, the equation drawn between an economy of sexual desire and a market economy merits our attention. The comparison is significant because it exposes quite appropriately how the mode of spectacular production that characterizes modern consumer society has hijacked the ideals of the sexual revolution both to perpetuate class hierarchies and to impose an impressive regimen of control at both ends of the market cycle, from the production to the consumption of objects of desire both material and immaterial.

Interestingly, the novel introduces the reader to the *système des objets* theorized by Baudrillard[28] as it relates to consumer objects of desire in a rather subtle way, which undermines to some extent the overwhelming determinism of the oedipal narrative structure. The title of chapter ten of the novel's first part announces "Caroline Yessayan is to blame for everything." However, at the conclusion of the episode where Bruno fails to connect with his classmate because of his misdirection (he touches her thigh rather than her arm), the text reveals that "Caroline Yessayan's *miniskirt* is to blame for everything" (emphasis added by author, 46). The narrator even admits that Bruno's childhood experience would have shifted if he had not been so clumsy since the young girl would have welcomed Bruno's attentions. Following how the displacement of the blame from human subject to consumer object acts upon the structure of the narrative, the conservative determinism of the novel can be deconstructed. In other words, the text's ideological critique may *not* be directed toward human agency or the open sexuality of the 1960s generation but rather, following Foucault, Baudrillard, and Debord, toward a political economy and a system of objects that regiment and manipulate individuals through a spectacular mode of consumption.

Following Foucault's work in "Postscript on the Societies of Control," Gilles Deleuze observes that in the late twentieth-century era of advanced capitalism, the continuous (in)corporation of human existence, "the different determinant spaces of enclosure through which the individual passes" mark the transition from a disciplinary society to a "society of control." Deleuze argues that in an age where the corporation has replaced the factory "enclosures are *molds*"; they are dynamic entities that exert control as *modulation*.[29] In situating the crisis of desire in society in the petit-bourgeois corporate technocratic and bureaucratic lifestyle, both *Whatever* and *Elementary Particles* are noteworthy illustrations for such sociopolitical theorization, especially with regard to how various corporations *modulate* desire as a means to control it.

In chronicling the rise of consumer culture when "mass-market entertainment from North America (the songs of Elvis Presley, the films of Marilyn Monroe) was spreading all over Western Europe" (47), the narrator clearly posits how the media and the "liberal press" exert a very early influence on the human understanding of sexual desire, and consequently, how human beings internalize the canons of beauty and "the ideals of the entertainment industry" (47). Bruno's fetishization of youthful female bodies—like that of Lurie in *Disgrace*—as well as the simulation of sexual practices directly inspired by hardcore pornography are testament of these processes of mediation. In a first instance, at the "aging" nudist retreat where Bruno will eventually meet Christiane, he is "taken aback to see teenagers," as he finds "The scene indescribably graceful and erotic" to the point of dizzying arousal (87). Later, at the swinging clubs he frequents with Christiane, "couples quickly abandoned their search for pleasure . . . in favor of prodigal sexual abandon . . . lifted directly from the gang-bang scenes in the fashionable porn movies shown on Canal+" (201).

As I have already alluded in the introduction, in *Society of the Spectacle* Debord considers that society has become a "spectacle" to the degree that "[e]verything that was directly lived has receded into a representation," thus affecting how society functions as a whole: "[t]he spectacle is not a collection of Images; it is a social relation between people that is mediated by images."[30] This hegemony of representation over reality, or, in Saussurian terms, of the sign over the referent, goes beyond the mere affluence of images in the media; rather it pertains to a world-vision that is objectifying, explains Debord, extending itself in such a way that "the spectacle is an *affirmation* of appearances and an identification of all human social life with appearances."[31] In congruence with Debord's views, Jean Baudrillard argues in *The Consumer Society* that under the spectacular mode of production and consumption, goods and services are assigned *sign-value*—as opposed to *value* or *exchange-value*—which can be read as either signifying processes of communication or differentiation. From the latter perspective, the homogeneously heterogeneous patterns of consumption across the various social classes can be read as signs of *distinction*, whereas individuals covet and acquire objects (of desire) that correspond and are made accessible to their respective economic status. Accordingly, I would argue that, in lieu of following the deterministic logic promoted by *Elementary Particles'* scientific discourse on natural selection, the access to objects of sexual desire and the very fulfillment of that desire is likewise regimented by specific signs of distinction, which is determined by a set of sign-values attributed to their appearance, attributes, and material possessions. As long as individuals belong to the privileged sexual class—the individuals who embody the canons of youth, beauty, wealth, and power propagated by the images of the media industry—they will be given the opportunity to fully realize their libidinal wishes through consent or coercion, an idea that is further explored in the discussion of *American Psycho* in chapter three. The vast majority; that is, the average-looking, poor, old, unhealthy, and inadequately equipped underclass, will continue to feel alienated by a system that mediates their desire for objects of consumption that remain out of their reach, therefore underlining the Lacanian idea that in late capitalism, desire mostly operates as a "lack."

Deleuze carries over the idea of Foucault's biopolitic by reminding us that, in the disciplinary society, power exerts control over the body *as* a body "at the same time power individualizes and masses together," but that in the society of control, society is outdoing the politics of inscribing individual bodies: "we no longer find ourselves dealing with the mass/individual pair . . . Individuals have become '*dividuals*,' masses, samples, data, markets, or '*banks*'."[32] Under this light, Michel's assessment of Bruno cited in the early pages of this chapter can be read more allegorically. Taken out of the perspective projected by the determinist discourse that immediately follows it, rather than being considered as the human equivalent of a "thwarted animal" (148), Bruno can be perceived as a representative of that individual mass representing a specific "target market" on whom society exerts control by producing homogenized forms of desires. What is clear from this perspective is that, far from a "natural" model of competition

(Abecassis's "baboon state" cited earlier) where, following Lacan, sexual desire is pursued as need-fulfillment, the spectacular consumer society has *mediated* desire by sublimating instinctual drives and imposing a signified system of distinction.

Read literally as a work of naturalism, Houellebecq's *Elementary Particles* fails as a global, determinist critique of the liberalization of sexuality. On the one hand, the problematic of desire is not only embodied by characters such as Bruno and, to a lesser extent, Michel, whose pathologies and anxieties are clearly situated in the very individuality of their psychological portraits drawn by their respective biographies, as will be explored below. On the other, it makes an erroneous historical assumption regarding the possibility for sexual freedom in a modern consumer society wherein subjectivity and desire are mediated by the sign-value of images. Even if the novel falls short of responding to the challenge posed by Winston in Orwell's epigraph, it nevertheless provides for an insightful, if not compelling, illustration of the political economy of late capitalism as a Deleuzian "society of control."

## The Determinist Experiment: The Pathos
## of Oedipal Desire as Male Prototype

In exploring the intertextual map drawn by the novel, it is impossible to miss the direct and indirect references made to Emile Zola, to whom I alluded earlier. What is most interesting as a form of indirect referentiality is the particular ways in which the novel re-enacts some of the methods articulated in *Experimental Novel*, Zola's foundational piece on the theory of the naturalist novel. As an avid if not naïve admirer of the scientific method of experimentation, Zola argues that a similar methodology could be applied to novels in order to trace the intellectual and emotional reactions of living beings to specific social phenomena as a means to unearth scientific truths underlying human behavior. Zola bases his theory on the belief there are both genetic and environmental causes to explain human behavior and that given specific information, one can determine the outcome of particular phenomena.[33] And so, in providing ample detail on paternal lineage and sociocultural context, *Elementary Particles* makes similar claims pertaining to how behavior patterns of its main protagonists can be determined by these preconditions. Yet Houellebecq also provides an extension to Zola's theory by providing direct scientific commentary to the narrative structure as a means to reinforce this deterministic viability. Regardless of whether the scientific discourse that informs the novel is accurate, it procures a reliable alibi in producing what Roland Barthes has dubbed "The Reality Effect," thereby substituting the signified with a referent "at the very moment when these details are supposed to *denote* reality directly" (emphasis his).[34] Hence, the scientific discourse that informs *Elementary Particles'* naturalistic determinism aims to bestow an aura of empirical irrefutability to how it situates the crisis of contemporary existence in the liberal economies of sexual desire, whose anxieties are most remarkably personified in Bruno.

The narrative heteroglossia presents the figure of Bruno as an archetype of the modern male subject, arguing that even though his biological being was particular to him and differentiated him from others, "his motives, values and desires did not distinguish him from his contemporaries in any way," as Michel notes (148). Although there is some definite value in this observation, I would argue that because of the determinist subtext that informs the novel, the reader is compelled to resist this generalization as it is articulated (through free indirect discourse) by Bruno's brother, who is an equally psychologically scarred character and thus, a highly subjective and partly unreliable narrator. By paralleling Bruno's sexual frustration to that of a "thwarted animal" incapable of fulfilling a basic need, Michel not only wrongly compares animal need to human desire,[35] but also mistakenly conflates the complexities of human *mediated* sexual desires—the production of which is the result of a complex psychosexual development nurtured socially—with an animal's basic and *unmediated* instinctual drives.

As noted above, determinism takes into account both genealogy (the biological buildup of the subject, its sex, and genetic relation to its parents) and the material conditions of the environment as the forces that shape the individual's emotional and intellectual response to a wide range of social phenomena. Whereas Bruno can represent a prototype of heteronormative masculinity as shaped by his environment, he remains nonetheless a strongly individuated male figure whose genetic buildup is more particular than it is general, and whose psychological pathos is largely determined by his relation, or lack thereof, to his parents. In other words, Bruno cannot be considered as an archetypical subject of contemporary Western society because in retracing his specific genealogical inheritance and by recounting the formative years of his childhood, the narrative individualizes, rather than generalizes, his subjectivity. The rationale for his uncontrollable and insatiable sexual desire and his castrated inability to fulfill his libidinal wishes are the direct results of the combined characterization of his parents as well as his individuated failure to resolve the pre-oedipal and oedipal stages of sexual maturity. Consequently, the veracity of the novel's critique is greatly diminished because it rests on a highly specific heterosexual pathology derived from Bruno's genetic blueprint and sexual development. Even within the very narrow confines of the heteronormative perspective it presents, *Elementary Particles* falters as a general critique of sexuality and sexual desire because the psychological portrait[36] of Bruno as an individual subject cannot be considered as representative of contemporary society as a whole.

In a surprising pastiche of the modernist trope of self-awareness, the text draws particular attention to the genealogies of its two main characters, Michel and Bruno, by manifesting its subjective presence as the clear manifestation of the narrative "eye/I" (19) in the novel. In one instance, the narrator reveals the *necessity* to recount the "singular destiny" of Martin Ceccaldi and his daughter Janine, whose characteristics are *not* symptomatic of her sociohistorical context. Quite to the contrary, the narrative dubs her a "precursor," an intelligent and independent freethinker with a clear inclination for sexual promiscuity, but also a "catalyst . . . of some form of social breakdown" (26). As half brothers, Bruno and Michel share rather unequally their mother's characteristic traits since it appears the younger brother inherited none of her libidinal drive, whereas Bruno seems overburdened by sexual desire. The narrator implies that Marc Djerzinski rescued his son at the age of three from the perceived negative influence of his mother. Described as a brilliant yet solitary and introverted character, Michel inherited most of his father's intellectual and physical characteristics. He was then placed in the relatively safe and healthy environment inhabited by his conservative and stoic grandmother, an idealized feminine model of self-sacrifice, "who has literally given [her life] for others, out of love and devotion" (77).

Whereas Michel's birth is narrated from the perspective of his father, Bruno's is considered from the onset as a mistake. His presence is almost immediately perceived to be a nuisance to both his parents, who "realized that caring for a small child was incompatible with their ideals of personal freedom" (22). As the result of this unwanted pregnancy, Bruno is sent to his grandparents in Algiers. Witnessing their death at a very early age and losing any sense of security they may have provided, he subsequently suffers the various humiliations endured by the "omega male" as a physically disadvantaged boy in boarding school (43–47). Unlike Michel's secure upbringing, whose grandmother provides both solace and security in an Edenic setting, Bruno suffers tremendously in the early stages of his psychological development from the irreparable consequences of the absence of any notable mother or father figure, as well as from the lack of a stable and safe environment.

It is well known that in Freudian psychoanalysis, the oedipal stage is regarded as a critical phase of psychosexual development wherein male children[37] simultaneously experience sexual desire for the mother and the desire to kill the father because they consider him a rival for the exclusive love of their mother. Freud considered the triangular structure to be fundamental in adult heterosexual development, and believed that the successful resolution of this conflict was the key to successful sexual maturity. As a consequence of the rivalry with the father, the male child experiences castration anxiety, which is resolved when the child is capable of accepting the presence of the father (or "internalizing" the patriarchal "law," as Lacan would later elaborate), identifying with him, and deflecting his libidinal attention to other female objects of desire, most notably during puberty.

In the absence of both his parents, Bruno was not able to adequately undergo the various stages of psychosexual development as determined by Freud. The classical oedipal triangle of son-mother-father never took shape because on the one hand, his mother as the sexualized other only makes her appearance later in his formative years, and on the other hand, the presence of his father was substituted by Jane/Janine's various lovers: a multitude of male rivals each competing for access to the mother. In other words, Bruno was unable to resolve the oedipal complex and thus reach sexual maturity, since not only did he not experience the awakening of sexual desire through the figure of his own mother, in the presence of an ever-morphing and continuously changing substitute male figure, he was also unable to identify with the father figure. This particular scenario is at the origin of Bruno's castration complex, an anxiety which manifests itself most notably in his own depreciation of his penis—its perceived inadequacy to provide sexual pleasure due to its comparatively diminished dimension—and possibly, his fear of vaginal intercourse. The latter is manifest in both his abjection for female genitalia because of the repeated visualization of his mother's (51, 60, 117) as well as his preference for fellatio and other types of nonvaginal intercourse (87, 141, 146), which can be read as the various signs for his fear of intimate contact and his incapacity to fulfill his desires.

Certain critics of Freud consider that the Oedipus complex is not the sole key determining factor to the child's development. Rather, the pre-oedipal period focuses on mother-child relationships that run prior to the ages at which the child is able to identify the sexual difference between his two parents. This phase is crucial in allowing children to identify various objects of desire, whether they are parts of their own body or of their mothers, or whether they are other "transitional objects" such as toys (which are neither). In the present case, however, since the narrative does not disclose an account of this stage of his childhood, it would be difficult to accurately trace how the lack of maternal presence in his early existence has affected Bruno's psychosexual development. Yet, there is one particular instance that describes Bruno's joy in riding his tricycle in his grandparents' house that is particularly insightful:

His grandparents lived in a beautiful apartment . . . A central hall, twenty meters long, ran the length of the apartment, ending in a drawing room from whose balcony the whole of the "White City" was at one's feet. Many years later, when Bruno was already an embittered middle-aged cynic, he could still remember himself, aged four, pedaling furiously down the dark hallway toward the shimmering portal of the balcony. It was at moments like this that he had come closest to happiness. (31–32)

This memory stands in sharp contrast to the opening line of this chapter that claims "Bruno's earliest memory was one of humiliation," as it details he cried out of anger for being unable to participate in one of his nursery's school mating games (31). It is quite evident that this entire passage can be read as a metaphor for Bruno's own birth: the long dark corridor, the "furious" effort, the eruption into the "shimmering" white light of the day. When he later reconstitutes the episode, it is revealed that the moment at which he felt closest to his mother was the moment of his birth,[38] which, in consideration of the subsequent anxieties he suffered due to her devastating absence, can perhaps be regarded as the most joyous moment of his life. This explains how Bruno's childhood neuroses shape his encounters with his mother's sexuality and that of female others, and how separation anxiety is subsequently transferred to castration anxiety and his generalized fear of penetration.

In fact, Bruno's case offers an exemplary literal model to explore Jacques Lacan's concept of desire experienced as a "lack." Heavily influenced by Ferdinand de Saussure's structural linguistics, Lacan first configures the subject as a linguistic sign (S/s), whose wholeness is split along the "bar" of repression between the conscious and the unconscious, or within the perspective of heterosexual pathos, the "dehiscence" that establishes sexual difference. Concurrently, Lacan argues that the subject is constituted by something missing, a "lack" which creates desire and which the subject will try to recover. The split can be configured as that of the infant who is separated from its mother and seeks to reconstitute itself through the desire to recover its "whole" or, as Judith Butler asserts from a historiographical definition of desire, to "return to an impossible origin."[39] Bruno is a subject whose neurosis is derived not only from the separation with his mother's body, but the impossibility to prefigure or contemplate the recovery of its wholeness by its very absence.

Under this perspective, we can start to understand Bruno's anxieties stemming from the reconstruction of the birth metaphor cited above as an ontological beginning, the moment at which he is separated or projected from his mother's "(w)hole." All wordplay aside, Lacan's structural topography also configures the dynamics of Desire as a series of linguistic signs. Desire is that signifier "S" that never changes but that remains unfulfilled because it can never cross the bar (repression) that marks its separation from the desired object, the signified "s." Set within a chain of signifiers, Desire will continuously be displaced to (an)other signified(s). From this specific angle, the lack or absence of a foundational object of desire (the mother) causes Bruno's desire to be constantly deferred in the guise of desirable others. As we have seen, however, the possibility for Bruno's desire (Signifier) to reach other objects of desire (signifieds) is also problematic due to the castration anxiety attributed to the inadequate size of his penis. In sum, Bruno's oedipal stage is unresolved because the lack he experiences as a subject is further problematized by the fact that he lacks a signifying "phallus," and is thus unable to successfully substitute the desire for his mother by other objects in the signifying chain. It is only when Christiane enters his life, as both mother figure and lover, that Bruno is capable of overcoming his oedipal fixation by literally doing away with the image of his mother's "thin, crumpled vagina" (141) and consequently, fulfilling his libidinal wishes, if only for a brief interval.

The particularity of Bruno's psychosexual development as determined both by his relationship to his parents and by specific sociohistorical conditions presents him as an unsuccessful prototype, not an archetype, of male heteronormative sexuality. And so, within the naturalistic discourse of the novel, insofar as Michel considers Bruno to be a normativized subject of scientific study, the logic behind his endeavor to conceive a human model in which pleasure is dissociated from sexual desire makes perfect sense. Yet, as noted above, Michel's error is to regard Bruno's heavily pathologized, heteronormative, and somewhat sexist predisposition as a comprehensive topography of human desire. Not only is Michel mistaking Bruno's psychosexual disorder for that of an entire society, but he also seemingly ignores the vast pluralities of forms and traces under which sexual desire is manifested and experienced across a much wider and more comprehensive array of subjective individualities.[40] Although the novel presents itself as a naturalist portrait of society, my contention is that any attempt to represent the problematics of sexual desire from this vantage point yields individuated results that can only be applied selectively and not to the general population as a whole. A case in point would be the episode where the narrative contrasts the sexual fiascos of Bruno with the success rate of Patrick, one of his peers, who "succeeded in fucking thirty-seven girls in the space of three weeks" while they both assisted a language course in Germany. As the text indicates the difference could not be accounted for by their distinct socioeconomic conditions, since they were both "from a respectable family, and their career prospects were almost identical" (64), it becomes clear that Bruno's sex issues are more particular than they are general.

Since the narrative voice clearly insists on tracing the destinies of its main protagonists as the result of their distinct genealogies, *Elementary Particles* fails as a global, general critique of a modern model of personal liberties, precisely because the text masks the location and the particularity of these discursive agents even as it draws highly subjectivized and individuated portraits of its main protagonists. The anxieties experienced by Bruno cannot be considered to represent a predominating or archetypical situation of sexual neurosis for all of contemporary society because the novel specifically situates these anxieties in a male heteronormative subject whose psychosexual pathologies are remarkably situated both in his genetic predisposition and as the consequence of parental abandonment. Similarly, Varsava compares what he judges to be Houellebecq's narrow and one-sided representation of specific European men to its referent, the larger picture of Western European society. Considering both the blatant oedipal plot and the various improvements achieved by that very model of "social democracy" that the text criticizes, he concurs, *"The Elementary Particles* says very much more about insecure, sexually-obsessed European men in early middle age than it does about European society at large."[41] It is precisely this type of grand narrative of social determinism inspired by the oedipal model of subjectivity that Deleuze and Guattari vehemently undermine in *The Anti-Oedipus*. Consequently, by providing a gripping portrayal of the pitfalls of male desire in the consumerist mode of capitalistic production, *Elementary Particles* highlights the rather logocentric and sterile, reterritorializing pathos of the traditional Western (Lacanian) configurations of desire as "lack," which stands in striking contrast to the more emancipating, regenerative potential offered by Deleuze and Guattari's concept of "desiring-production."

# 3

# Extreme Desires in Bret Easton Ellis's *American Psycho*

> It is known that civilized man is characterized by an often inexpli-
> cable acuity of horror.
>
> —Georges Bataille, "Eye"

In recent US publishing history, few books have been received with the level of outrage that characterized the release of Bret Easton Ellis's *American Psycho*, a 1991 novel about a Wall Street serial killer. Reviews deplored its extremely graphic content that dispassionately offered up scenes of sex, mutilation, and murder to punctuate the toneless blather of the Yuppie lifestyle. Various groups and individuals campaigned for a national boycott of the novel because of the acts of misogynistic and pornographic violence it portrays, while in other countries, authorities attempted to ban the novel.[1]

The protest against *American Psycho* closely echoes debates those regarding the potentially harmful effects of the displays of sex and violence in the media. For its part, the general public appears unperturbed by such concerns and has embraced the representations of sex and violence as they appear in movies, magazines, videogames, and television, seeing them as highly stylized forms of entertainment. The recent trend of "torture-porn" bears witness to the fact that audiences are indeed fascinated by the images of graphic

An earlier version of this essay appeared in *Revista Atenea* 24, no. 1 (June 2004) and portions of this chapter appeared in "Visual Poetics, Intertextuality, and the Transfiguration of Ideology: An 'Eye' for an 'I' in Mary Harron's Cinematic Adaptation of Bret Easton Ellis's 'American Psycho'," *ILS* 11, no. 1 (Fall 2009).

violence offered by the entertainment industry.[2] Given the turn toward an increasingly pornographic aesthetic[3] wherein representations of violence are pushed to their extreme—as violence is perceived to be sexy and sex becomes another form of violence—it would seem surprising that a work of contemporary written fiction could have generated such outrage.

*American Psycho* is a fictional novel set in New York City in the late 1980s. Patrick Bateman, its protagonist and narrator, is a Wall Street golden boy who is also apparently a brutal psychopath and gruesome murderer. The novel does not offer any continuous, linear plot; the various chapters of the book—whose titles are often repeated—are a collage of scenes or episodes wherein the totally uninflected first-person narrative unfolds in a precise, detailed, and seemingly objective fashion. All traces of affect and any references to feeling are stripped away from Bateman's voice, a voice that reproduces the language of consumer product advertisements; music, restaurant, and fashion reviews; and pornographic and horror fiction. What is particularly remarkable, and perhaps even shocking or disturbing, is that Bateman displays the same matter-of-fact affective filter to describe in detail grooming and exercise routines, music albums, clothing, and restaurant scenes as he displays for his barbaric acts of mutilation and murder. The disjointed and unsettling quality of the narrative is amplified by the ambivalent relationship between reality and fiction that characterizes the novel, an ambiguity that becomes particularly prominent and mystifying at various moments throughout the text.

In *American Psycho*, Ellis draws an extended metaphor for the passive, almost vegetative state that characterizes the contemporary white-collar existence where the need to fulfill one's instinctual drives has been supplanted by a voracious appetite for a variety of consumer products: clothes, cars, home electronics, music, and Hollywood blockbusters. This superficial, consumerist lifestyle is plagued with ennui and dissatisfaction, and the text suggests that the only relief from an existence defined by "surface, surface, surface . . . all that anyone found meaning in" (375) is found by indulging in violence, whether fictional or not, real or simulated.

This chapter begins by providing a brief overview of Ellis's text and the controversy surrounding its publication before discussing the ways in which the novel's visual poetics[4] function as visceral critique by transfiguring the aesthetics of sexual violence into a symptom of contemporary consumer culture.[5] In part, I demonstrate that contrary to Houellebecq's more distanced, third-person critique of sexual politics and consumer culture in *Elementary Particles*, in *American Psycho* the critique is viscerally actualized through a narrative process of subjectivization.

A subsequent section addresses the hyperrealist aesthetic of the novel as well as contemporary discourses on capitalism and desire. Considering *American Psycho* in relation to the concepts of simulacra and schizophrenia articulated by Jean Baudrillard and Fredric Jameson respectively, I point to the possible ways in which the text reterritorializes male heterosexual desire within the consumerist pathos of the society of the spectacle. From there, I transition to a comparison between Ellis's text and Mary Harron's 2000 film adaptation. The film is quite faithful to the critique of consumer capitalism provided by the text's representational qualities even though it chooses to bypass the dynamics of the visceral poetics at work in the novel. Whereas the novel aims to shock its audience in order to provoke ontological reflection, by "neutering" the text and turning it into a satirical comedy and hence a more straightforward parody, Mary Harron's film produces a distanced and detached critical social commentary. Consequently, this difference in poetic strategy prompts a number of questions regarding the politics economies of visual translation, language, and the gaze, as well as the ways in which we address the violence of late stage consumer capitalism as a collective cultural phenomenon or as an individual pathological disorder. The chapter ends with a discussion that focuses on the novel's contextual implications by reconfiguring the most salient themes in relation to cultural discourses of national consciousness and ideology.

### Shock and Scandal: *American Psycho* as Postmodern Pastiche

Because of its matter-of-fact descriptions of graphic violence, *American Psycho* was surrounded by public outrage even before its release in 1991 by Vintage Contemporaries. Upon receiving the manuscript, Simon & Schuster, the publisher of Ellis's previous books, withdrew from its engagement (and forfeited a $300,000 advance) to publish and distribute *American Psycho*, fearing a national uproar over the novel's overtly explicit scenes of sexual violence. The novel's meticulous and uninflected prose was construed by a considerable contingent of readers and reviewers as reflecting a total lack of decency and morality. Some of the most controversial excerpts of the book had been leaked from the publishing company and it was quickly labeled as sadistic, pornographic, misogynistic, and loathsome,[6] creating a stir equivalent to the release of Vladimir Nabokov's *Lolita* almost half a century earlier.[7]

Contingents of readers and reviewers were appalled by how the explicit depictions of sex and violence and the absence of moral framework would affect their respective readers. Roger Rosenblatt of the *New York Times* called for his audience to "Snuff this book!," and Tammy Bruce of the Los Angeles chapter of the National Organization for Women (NOW) urged the public to boycott the novel based on her perception that Ellis's book acted as a misogynistic manual of sexual torture and mutilation. In what seems to be a misconception of the properties of art and authorship as well as an apparent failure to distinguish between narrator and author, and between fiction and reality, Tara Baxter, among others, assumed the acts of sexual violence perpetrated by Patrick Bateman, the narrator and main protagonist of the novel, were a projection of the author's own vicious desires.[8]

Interestingly, as in any contemporary case of public outcry and censorship, the protests and scandal only contributed to the novel's notoriety as a succès de scandale; *American Psycho* quickly became a bestseller (even as the *New York Times* decided not to include it on its bestseller list), a fact that speaks eloquently of the twisted ethics of consumption of the public at large. However, what is quite disconcerting in this public outcry is that the outraged contingency grossly misread and misinterpreted *American Psycho*. Critics appeared blind to the novel's satirical character, missing the fact that Ellis's book actually condemns the very same acts they believed it glorifies. Since publication, the novel's validity as a literary satire has been reassessed; while some may consider the text to be a satirical, postmodern tour de force, others still perceive it as indisputably gross and contemptible, a worthless piece of subliterary junk.[9]

For instance, Alberto Manguel contemptuously argues that *American Psycho* is not a novel of literary claims. He bases his view on the idea that even if the text had been meant to be read as a social satire, Ellis's minimalist style and the novel's grotesqueness pre-empt the possibility of it being seriously considered as such: "Ellis's prose does nothing except copy the model it is supposed to denounce."[10] He also claims that the novel's "pornographic horror"[11] literally made him feel sick.[12] In other words, according to Manguel, *American Psycho* does not offer any form of distancing from its subject, a distance that would allow for a type of intellectual reflection; contrary to other shocking or controversial works of previous epochs, he suggests the novel eludes satirical consideration because it lacks a discernible framework to do so.

Although Manguel is correct in pointing out that Ellis's novel does not allow readers to distance themselves from the text and contains passages of "pornographic horror" capable of producing a strong visceral response, many of his conclusions are either misconstructions or misunderstandings. For one, it is bewildering that Manguel claims *American Psycho* cannot be read as a social satire, since it faithfully corresponds to various definitions of satire, starting with Bakhtin's description of Menippean satire.[13] Ellis's text is gruesomely crude and at times extremely shocking, a point with which Manguel does not disagree, but not only because it is graphically explicit. The "zone of crude contact" of which Bakhtin speaks is most notably produced by the various literary strategies deployed in the book as they aim to reduce the distance between reader and narrator. In addition, *American Psycho* shares the same purpose of the Menippean satire, which is, as Bakhtin points out, "to put to the test and to expose ideas and ideologues." It is specifically the perverse and violent ideologies of consumer capitalism that are challenged in Ellis's novel.

Accordingly, Price[14] aptly argues that in the nature of Bakhtin's concepts of heteroglossia, the grotesque body, and the carnivalesque,[15] *American Psycho* is a parody of mass consumerism and capitalist greed; tenets of neoliberal ideology that were prevalent not only in the historicized period of the novel's 1980s setting, but have increasingly asserted themselves in contemporary US society. In *American Psycho*, heteroglossia is manifest in the interweaving of multiple discourses, from the inner projections of the main character to the extensive descriptions of consumer goods as quotations from instruction manuals and magazines. The concept of the grotesque body figures predominantly in the explicit depictions of sex and violence spread throughout the novel. At another level, Bateman's body is also grotesque in an especially modern way: so fetishized ("transformed" or "modeled" by body-building, grooming, and label-wearing) as to become grotesque (24–30).

A satire in both the classical and the medieval senses as defined by Bakhtin, *American Psycho* can also be read, following Fredric Jameson, as a postmodern pastiche of spectacular consumer society. The focus of Ellis's satire corresponds to the conceptualization of the postmodern as that which criticizes the underlying strictures of late-stage capitalism. The heteroglossia that characterizes the novel and the seamless integration of popular discourse and imagery illustrate the feature of postmodernism that erodes the boundaries between the high and the low, art, literature, film, and popular culture.[16] The text criticizes consumer capitalism at large and in doing so, it addresses several aspects in particular. For one, it denounces the fetishization of material goods as well as the overwhelming importance conferred upon monetary wealth and physical appearance as measures of success, where identity becomes the sum of product labels with which the body is adorned. Secondly, *American Psycho* addresses the overpowering presence and influence of media images in contemporary existence, thereby exemplifying the salient characteristic of the postmodern as defined by Baudrillard in "The Precession of Simulacra"[17] wherein the real has been replaced by simulacra. Moreover, Ellis's novel condemns the de facto violence of the dominant socioeconomic class for carrying out acts of violence, both directly and indirectly. And most flagrantly, the novel deplores Western society's objectification of human existence and the twisted ethics of consumption as individuals shamelessly indulge in a wide array of voyeuristic goods that are linked to a perverse fascination with gore and pornography.

**Pornography and Horror: The Politics of Sexual Violence**

*American Psycho* mimics pornographic language to exemplify how consumer culture objectifies human sexuality and how the public at large endorses this practice by indulging in its various representations, from suggestive displays of sexual behavior to hardcore porn. Underlining the absence of emotional content in *American Psycho*, Murphet observes that the women with whom Bateman has sex are paid and suggests the act is merely another consumer good in the novel, another product of a capitalist society for which Bateman is the figurative embodiment. It is to this particular equation that the entire billion-dollar porn industry owes its success, an industry whose print and visual media typically enclose accounts of sexual acts that Ellis's novel reproduces. While pornography may have traditionally been marketed to a predominantly male audience, female viewers also form an integral part of the consuming public.[18] And while the point of view of the novel is undeniably male, it is irrefutable that both males and females are active participants in the materialist society for which Bateman constitutes the perfect poster boy: an image of flawless beauty and financial success to which males aspire and females are supposed to desire, especially from the privileged white male point of view of the narrative (53, 90).

In the novel, heterosexual intercourse is primarily depicted through a pornographic lens, suggesting that both sexes are only capable of *using* each other by relating on a superficial, nonintimate level that is both selfish and impersonal. In addition, the fact that pornography is a consumer product implies that it is only through a marketable transaction that humans are able to communicate. Julian Murphet points out that tangible—that is, "real"—sexual relations between female and male characters in *American Psycho* are nonexistent or doomed to fail, for "men and women in this textual world exist on parallel, untouching planes of reality; each sex satisfies for the other only preconceived and fixed expectations."[19] By consenting to have sex with Bateman—and accepting money in exchange in most cases—the female characters of the novel enter the process of objectification imposed by prostitution and pornography in accepting the contractual terms of the transaction. In other words, there exists no possibility of actual intimate contact—whether physical or emotional—between male and female characters. This idea is illustrated on numerous occasions, such as in the romantic-turned-parody vacation Bateman spends with Evelyn in East Hampton (278–82), or in his inability to have a relationship with Jean, his secretary, the only female who seems to somewhat elude the surface materiality of the other characters in the novel. In one instance, Jean casually asks him if he wants to go up to her apartment; he eventually declines, telling himself, "pornography is so much less complicated than actual sex, and because of this lack of complication, so much more pleasurable" (264). To "actual sex," Bateman prefers the unrealistic, seemingly flawless, virtual sex portrayed in pornography where emotions are nonexistent and women mostly exist to satisfy men's desires.

The source of pornographic pleasure is scopophilic and thus an act of voyeurism, of enjoyment at a distance. But the void of emotions prevalent in pornography initiates a process of transfiguration and fetishization, wherein the absence of a discernible subjectivity from the participants allows the ego to project itself into the action, on page or on screen, and take possession of the sexualized object. There is a way in which the aesthetics of pornographic pleasure folds into the ideology of consumption as driven by media advertising, for they both aim (and succeed) in continuously arousing desire by promising its fulfillment, even as the elation is only ephemeral at best. Bateman fully submits to this mode of operation; not only does he avidly consume various products and services (including prostitutes), but he also proceeds to accumulate them endlessly in the pursuit of the ever-evasive possibility of consumer bliss.

The pornographic aesthetic that informs the sexual relationships of the text illustrates the commodification of existence in postindustrialized society. The pornographic gaze not only commodifies and fetishizes women (and men) as sexual objects but also sees the body as fragmented, as separate and detachable pieces of anatomy—a breast, a leg, a foot, a mouth, a penis, a vagina—as if each could easily be severed from the unified entity of the body in its entirety as a three-dimensional subject (i.e., as a "whole" and not merely a hole, pardon the pun). In fact, one of the direct effects of such processes of objectification as it is imposed by the prevailing condition of consumer capitalism present throughout the entire novel is to erase individual subjectivity. When people are turned into objects, they have stopped existing as subjects and consequently their lives is considered to hold little or no value beyond their usefulness to the consumer, which, in the novel, translates into being sexually used and abused by Bateman. This concept is perfectly exemplified in *American Psycho* where, as Murphet notes, "the most disturbing thing about Bateman's sexuality . . . is that it segues into the most excruciating violence of the book's most notorious passages."[20]

As the novel unfolds, the protagonist is increasingly portrayed as a cold-blooded and brutal murderer who kills indiscriminately and on impulse. In the span of the text, his list of victims include a homeless person (129–32), a dog and its queer owner (167), a stockbroker (217), a number of different female "pick-ups" and prostitutes (245, 289–90, 304–5, 328); a child (298), and a street musician (347). However, it is important to note that apart from the stockbroker (and perhaps the child), all of these victims constitute social "others": what liberal capitalism and patriarchal society consider "inferior" beings leading pointless existences. At one point, Bateman goes so far as to call a vagrant "a member of the genetic underclass" (266), but this contempt is perhaps best exemplified in the scene where Bateman coldly gauges the vagrant's eyes after teasing him by waving a five-dollar bill in his face, insulting him because he is unemployed, and telling him they have nothing in common (131). Interestingly enough, as women accept becoming consumer products, as explained earlier, so do the homeless. After Bateman brutally mutilates the bum, the latter realizes he can exploit the situation by claiming he lost his sight through war injuries (385), a satire of conditioned victimization.

The acts of violence toward social others prompt Price to observe, "in Patrick Bateman's world, there is no contradiction between being a Wall Street hotshot and a serial killer because the ideology of the culture obscures such a contradiction."[21] This parallel between the individual violence of the main protagonist and the collective violence of capitalism is displayed when someone asks Bateman what is his line of work. Bateman answers, "murders and executions," but his answer is assumed to be "mergers and acquisitions" (206).

In contrast to some critics in the vein of Manguel who may contend the book's violence overshadows the satire, I would argue that in fact the violence only adds to the critical discourse of the novel by laying bare the excesses of the system it criticizes. Although most killings are markedly graphic, the most telling passages are the ones that combine sex and violence, particularly where, as the novel progresses, one inevitably leads to the other. In Ellis's novel, the relationship between sex and death, or Freud's concept of Eros and Thanatos, is taken to its literal extreme, thus establishing a direct link between pornography and violence as it metaphorically signifies the mass media objectification of sexuality and the economic cruelty of late-stage capitalism. This next excerpt is taken from one of the two chapters titled "Girls" where Bateman hires two escorts and takes them to Paul Owen's apartment, a colleague he recently murdered, which he decides to use as the venue for his sexual adventures and gruesome murders. While the sexual encounter is depicted in precise pornographic fashion (303)—as the majority of other sex scenes in the novel—Bateman eventually fails to be aroused, and thus, decides to find an alternate way to reach an orgasm:

> . . . finally I saw the entire head off—torrents of blood splash against the walls, even the ceilings—and holding the head up, like a prize, I take my cock, purple with stiffness, and lowering Torri's head to my lap I push it into her bloodied mouth and start fucking it, until I come, exploding into it. (304)

Bateman's capacity to reach climax is closely correlated with the acts of mutilation and torture he carries out on his victims. In thus noticing there is a gradual increase of these acts both in incidence and intensity, the reader sees that violence becomes progressively the only way in which Bateman is able to fulfill his sexual drive. This brings us to the conclusion that the sadistic traits of both the main protagonist and the narrative are increasingly reinforced not only through the repetition of acts of viciousness and murder, but through their increasing intensity as well. Violence in *American Psycho* not only serves to illustrate the violence and savageness of capitalism—epitomized by Bateman being both a relentless and successful Wall Street stockbroker and a seemingly equally successful and relentless murderer—but the misogynistic aggression of the male pornographic gaze as well. And for Bateman, sex and violence as sources of physical pleasure are closely intertwined through the same processes of increasing explicitness and repetition.

Even though this and other similar passages occur late in the novel, they have prompted critics such as James Gardner to deem them "excessive" and, in more senses than one, they are. While these scenes are responsible for provoking the most vehement reactions to *American Psycho*, they are not the perverse projections of a deranged author, nor are they designed solely to fuel the misogynistic fantasies of a small contingent of male readers as some critics hastily decried. They are the result of careful crafting and serve a precise and specific aim: by remaining in step with the overall first-person narrative style of the novel, these scenes project the reader to the forefront of the action and intend to provoke a sensation of unadulterated horror while simultaneously laying bare the violent ideologies at work in contemporary media consumption.

As I argued elsewhere, the power of horror lies specifically in its propensity to trigger a strong affective response in the reader and, in doing so, assault the reader's sensibility.[22] By narrowing the distance between the text and the reader, horror creates a rapprochement between reading as an intellectual activity and reading as a physical experience. As Georges Bataille argues in his theories of eroticism (*erotisme*) and transgression, it is the visceral response created by this rapprochement that allows the author to fully unleash the ontological possibilities of language.[23] In the case of *American Psycho*, the power of horror lies specifically at the point where reading the text becomes a visceral experience, where the aesthetics of horror cause a somewhat expected "revulsion of the gut," as Manguel describes it.[24]

Within the same line of thought, one can compare the experience of horror to that of pornography insofar as they are both "body genres," as Linda Williams calls them.[25] While sexual content aims merely to titillate the reader, pornographic displays aim to arouse, to trigger a bodily sensation of physical pleasure. Although the reactions elicited by horror and pornography contrast in the sense that the response to horror may be repulsive and the reaction to pornography is mostly pleasurable, as language and experience conflate, both are corporeal responses. Ellis utilizes this uncanny alternation between revulsion and fascination to put the reader's sensibilities to the test.

In the absence of a real plot, this vacillation of bodily responses to the content becomes the focal point of the reading experience of *American Psycho*. Even as the text suggests the acts of sexual violence are the product of the main character's imagination (375), the violence does happen *textually*. Paradoxically, while these accounts may be particularly appalling for the reader, they also become inescapably appealing. The stylistic devices employed by Ellis compel the reader to long for the scenes of sexual violence as they become the sole plausible point of interest and the unique avenue for catharsis. *American Psycho* not only plays with the reader's feelings of revulsion and fascination to exert control over the reader's affective response; it also further conditions these responses by condensing the narrative point of view and using boredom as a political and aesthetic strategy.

Audiences of horror films can experience a spectrum of emotions associated with sadistic and masochistic positions of male perpetrator and female victim, positions they are able to assume invariably of their own gender identity.[26] But even as the classic horror film elicits bodily responses to the action on screen, it also permits the viewer to distance themselves from the characters,[27] an escape route that is not on offer in Ellis's novel. Bateman is the sole narrative voice of *American Psycho* and as such, it does not allow readers to distance themselves from the events on the page and coerces them to assume the role of participant, either as victim or executioner. However, adopting the victim's point of view becomes increasingly unpleasant, if not unbearable, and consequently, the reader quickly assumes Bateman's perspective, as deranged as it might be. Bateman's voice is uncontainable: it becomes overwhelming as it assumes total control over the text. To that effect, Elizabeth Young aptly argues:

> From the first line, "Abandon all hope ye who enter here," to the last, "This is not an exit," we are *signed*, we are entered in to what is really a *circle* of hell. Once we have given ourselves up to the text, made the choice to "abandon hope," we have no way out. It is a closed system. These imprisoning, claustrophobic qualities are deftly manipulated in order, not only to force us to live as close to Patrick as possible in a fictional sense, but to imprint the reader with such force that we cannot ever get out. This is an act of great aggression and confidence on the part of the author revealing a controlling ego which asserts its rights over both characters and readers.[28]

This control is further implemented through what critics define as Ellis's "aesthetics of boredom,"[29] in referencing the "boring" passages of *American Psycho*: the endless name-dropping, label-listing, descriptions of household items, cataloguing of grooming and exercise routines (24–29, 69), dining guide blurbs, the typical *Rolling Stone* or *Billboard* pop music reviews (252–56), and the empty, senseless dialogues between characters (108–9) that are so superficial and so seemingly alike that their identities are constantly being mistaken. Yet these uneventful passages, which represent the majority of the text, work as "a carefully considered foil to the violence," Murphet argues.[30] While Manguel identifies them as a sign of Ellis's lack of style confirming the book's subliterary status, he ignores the fact that, quite to the contrary, Ellis has structured *American Psycho* meticulously, and that the purposes of the novel are in part executed by his stylistic choices. To that effect, Murphet explains that the violent incidents are "so confronting and disturbing partly because they have been so long in coming . . . and partly because what had remained latent behind the surface banality is here given such swift and explicit expression that we are simply unprepared for it."[31]

What is most disconcerting is that both the boring and the violent passages are syntactically very similar, which increases the potential shock effect when the content shifts from one to the other. Thus, the two are interdependent in a way that each accentuates the other, and this dialogism works to maximize the effect on the reader. In the face of the extensive boring passages, the reader starts longing for something to happen: in the text, however, the only thing of remote interest that ever happens is the sex and the violence, even if the plausibility of these events may be contested.

As both the premise and promise of the text (how can there be a psycho without bloody murder?), the violence raises the reader's expectations, but also hijacks the reader's desire to read the novel, exposing and exploiting their scopophilic tendencies. This was mostly put in evidence during the scandal surrounding the novel's release, which also contributed to creating its main appeal. The knowledge that the novel contained gruesome depictions of sexual aggression did not intimidate readers. Quite the contrary, readers—and possibly some who would have never bought the book if they had been unaware of its content—were eager to acquire the novel and fulfill their expectations by experiencing the blatant depiction of pornographic horror that the media reviews publicized. Ironically, the mechanics of controversy work rather well with the overall premise of *American Psycho*, for it is partly this type of twisted fascination for gore and pornography that the

novel denounces, further implicating the reader within the cycle of voyeuristic consumption.

By actualizing the affective dimension of the text through the visceral
aesthetics of pornography and horror and by implicating the reader in the
violent ideologies of consumer culture through a carefully orchestrated
textual strategy, *American Psycho* unleashes its potential as a text of social
criticism. While it could be argued that if the objective of the text was to
illustrate metaphorically the misogynistic violence of the male gaze in particular and patriarchal society in general on the one hand, as well as the
perverted *collective* violence, direct or indirect, of late stage capitalism on
the other, the point would have been made more succinctly by avoiding the
accumulation and repetition of scenes of gore and pornographic violence.
This argument is flawed, however, for it again fails to take into account the
overall premise of *American Psycho* being a meticulously crafted satire. As
Linda Williams argues, far from being merely gratuitous displays of excessive sex, violence, and emotions, the pornographic and horror genres serve
specific cultural functions related to the problematics of sexuality, gender,
and identity. And so, the perceived "excesses" of the text are by no means
gratuitous; as the subject of the novel's attacks are consumerism and the
neoliberal tenets of American society, the excessive violence illustrates the
excesses of commodity fetishism that form an integral part of consumer
culture and liberal capitalism.

## Postmodern Spectacle: Simulacra and Schizophrenia

As postmodern pastiche, *American Psycho* is cluttered with direct references
to popular print media (the *Wall Street Journal* and *CNN*, *GQ*, and *Rolling
Stone*), horror and pornographic movies such as *Body Double* and *She-Male
Reformatory*, or the "Patty Winters Show" as a stand-in for daytime celebrity
television shows. Bateman's narration faithfully reproduces the language
of these various outlets: whether it pertains to grooming and style advice
(29, 277–78), music reviews (133–36, 252–55, 352–58), or image-conscious
political speeches (15, 199). As a white affluent male, Bateman's demeanor
is an indication of his desire to "fit in" (297) as prescribed by what one
should wear, think, act, or buy, dictated by advice columns and product

reviews. Popular opinion shapes Bateman's perceptions even on the smallest of subjects. He decides that he likes the pizza at Pastels because McDermott shows him a *New York Times* review that indicates that Donald Trump thinks they serve the best pizza in New York (109–10). His possessions are a collage of pictures taken from luxury product publications. The description of his upscale Manhattan apartment is a feature article in *Elle Décor* or *Architectural Digest*: "A polished white oak floor runs throughout the apartment. On the other side of the room, next to a desk and a magazine rack by Gio Ponti, is a complete stereo system (CD player, tape deck, tuner, amplifier) by Sansui with six-foot Duntech Sovereign 2001 speakers in Brazilian rosewood" (25). In the image-obsessed world of the status-conscious Wall Street executive, existence is valued by how well one can duplicate life depicted in the glossy pages of magazines and other visual channels of mass communication.

This logic of replication is exacerbated in the seamless integration of these discourses in the narrative voice, thereby suggesting that Bateman's consciousness, his desires, thoughts, and perceptions, are an assemblage of the various linguistic and visual signs encountered in the media. This is particularly prevalent in the discursive construction of masculinity that informs the narrative point of view. Mark Storey observes that Bateman, "as an exemplar of traditionally male language systems (violence, pornography, the media, fashion, commerce) taken to their extremes," creates an "artificial identity that is formed entirely by the culture that surrounds him."[32]

Following the phallogocentric codes of patriarchal culture, Bateman and his colleagues systematically evaluate women according to their physical attributes; their taste consists of the paradigmatic male fantasy of a playboy centerfold behaving like an uninhibited porn star on a movie set. Synthesizing the female ideal of this misogynistic mindset, George Reeves details, "A good personality . . . consists of a chick who has a little hardbody and who will satisfy all sexual demands without being too slutty about things and who will essentially keep her dumb fucking mouth *shut*" (91). Interestingly, these "business lunches" are occasions for Bateman and his cronies to engage in senseless conversations about the latest male fashion trends and gawk at the "hardbodies" in the room: no actual business is ever conducted.

In fact, Bateman never seems to be doing any *work*. Rather, his days at the office are spent planning his busy social schedule (64), and if he is not securing a reservation at an exclusive restaurant, he is listening to music and reading magazines (65–66, 266). He also uses "work" as an excuse to conveniently slip away from situations he finds uncomfortable. In one instance, when Evelyn wants to make dinner plans with him, he responds that he cannot because he is working, to which she responds, seemingly vocalizing the thoughts of the reader, "What work? What work do you do?" (221). For Bateman, "work" is another accessory to his wardrobe; he plays the part because it fits the image.

Appearances supersede everything in this society of the spectacle, where, as Guy Debord famously argued, an objectifying world-view is so prevalent that "the spectacle is an *affirmation* of appearances and an identification of all human social life with appearances."[33] Accordingly, Bateman is consumed by his appearance; he takes extremely good care of himself through an obsessive regime of beauty products and regular visits to the spa and the gym. His sense of being is based on how others perceive him. Bateman constantly checks his reflection and blatantly admits, "All it comes down to is this: I feel like shit but look great" (106). When the boardroom is in fact a catwalk (108–11), the spectacle becomes the site and the means through which individuals and relatives, citizens and public institutions, consumers and corporations inform and interact with one another.

As alluded to in chapter two, in "The Precession of Simulacra," Baudrillard takes Debord's concept of the spectacle to its paroxysm by arguing that in modern consumer society, which promotes the gradual eradication of nature by culture, the sign (i.e., images and representations) has replaced reality. Typically, individuals privilege the sign over things signified and substitute "signs of the real for the real itself."[34] The purpose of the sign has become what Baudrillard calls a "simulacrum," which he differentiates from representation in the sense that a simulacrum marks the absence, not the existence, of the objects it is supposed to signify.[35] Consequently, the world as we experience it is "hyperreal": we simulate models of who and what we are supposed to be, following social constructs and conventions propagated through various forms of mass media. In the hyperreal world of *American Psycho*, subjectivity is reduced to the designer labels and brand names of the material goods one possesses.

In Ellis's novel, the logic of simulacra is pushed to the point of circular referentiality. Not only do people become the sum of the labels they wear and the goods and services they consume, but they also become carbon copies of each other. At the onset of the narrative, Bateman notes that both his girlfriend (Evelyn) and his mistress (Courtney) are wearing exactly the same outfit, "a Krizia cream silk blouse, a Krizia rust tweed skirt and silk-satin d'Orsay pumps from Manolo Blahnik" (8, 9), begging the question whether Bateman's simultaneous involvement with both of them is rooted in their identical fashion sense. Under this predicament, individuals are constantly mistaken for someone else. In the boardroom, for example, Paul Owen mistakes Bateman for Marcus Halberstam, which, interestingly, does not seem to upset Bateman because Halberstam shares the same taste in clothes and they go to the same barber (89). In another instance, Bateman is able to leave an announcement on Paul Owen's answering machine because his "voice sounds similar to Owen's and to someone hearing it over the phone probably identical" (218). The obsession with surface materiality begets uniformity and conformity to the extent that no one can be distinguished from anyone else. After Evelyn's dinner party, Bateman asks Evelyn if she is interested in Price:

> "He's rich," I say.
> "*Everybody's* rich," she says, concentrating on the TV screen.
> "He's good-looking," I tell her.
> "*Everybody's* good-looking, Patrick," she says remotely.
> "He has a great body," I say.
> "*Everybody* has a great body now," she says. (23)

Characters are interchangeable because they are *mediated*; that is, manufactured by the media, and like consumer products from the same assembly line, they are all alike and replaceable.

In the world of copies and simulacra that Patrick Bateman inhabits, looks are reproducible because in an existence defined by material possessions, human subjects become objects, and all authentic sense of personal identity and self-consciousness vanishes as people do not recognize or care for one another. Bateman is well aware of this fact as he realizes, "If I were to disappear into that crack . . . the odds are good that no one would notice I was gone. No . . . one . . . would . . . care" (226) and later confesses,

> . . . there is an idea of a Patrick Bateman, some kind of abstraction, but there is no real me, only an entity, something illusory, and though I can hide my cold gaze and you can shake my hand and feel flesh gripping yours and maybe you can even sense our lifestyles are probably comparable: *I am simply not there.* It is hard for me to make sense on any given level. My self is fabricated, an aberration. I am a noncontingent human being. My personality is sketchy and uninformed, my heartlessness goes deep and is persistent. My conscience, my pity, my hopes disappeared a long time ago (probably at Harvard) if they ever did exist. (Emphasis in the text, 376–77.)

There is no real Bateman because hyperreal society is dominated by simulacra, wherein everyone simulates models of who and what they are supposed to be following societal ideas of prefabricated identities.

Bateman's expressions of conformity allow him to exist in the "reality" of the consumerist pathos. As long as he is dressed according to accepted standards of style, maintains a healthy physique, and has flawless skin—in other words, as long as he fits in and is "GQ" (90)—the people around him do not care about (or pay attention to) the fact that he is (or believes he is) a " fucking evil psychopath" (20). In one instance, Bateman tells Helga, his skin technician,

> Did I ever tell you I want to wear a big yellow face mask and then put on the CD version of Bobby McFerrin's "Don't Worry, Be Happy" and then take a girl and a dog—a collie, a chow, a sharpei, it doesn't really matter—and then hook up this transfusion pump, this IV set, and switch their blood, you know, pump the dog's blood into the hardbody and vice versa, did I ever tell you this? (116)

Yet Bateman's confession does not faze Helga, as she and her assistant continue providing him with a facial and a pedicure and compliment him on his complexion. Similarly, people around him are so engrossed in their own superficial and egotistical lifestyles that they don't "hear" when he tells them "I'm into murders and executions," (206) or "I'm utterly insane . . . I like to dissect girls" (216). Paradoxically, it could be argued that Genesis's "The Man on the Corner" is Bateman's favorite song because even though it is apparently about "a bum . . . a poor homeless person" (134), he relates perfectly: "When he shouts, nobody listens / where he leads, no one will go . . . Nobody knows him, and nobody cares."

In this sense, his killing spree is perhaps a means to be recognized for the individuality of his actions, and his telephone confession to Harold Carnes, his lawyer, is a desperate call for attention (352). However, when Bateman brings the matter to Carnes when he sees him, Carnes confuses him with a man named Davis and then proceeds to deride his confession as a practical joke (388). Truth is, "Inside . . . *doesn't matter*" (397), because appearances are *all* that matter, and as far as his entourage is concerned, Bateman is "the boy next door" (9, 16, 18, 35).

Whether it pertains to dressing like a model in a *GQ* spread, obtaining a reservation at a restaurant recommended in the *Zagat* guide, having pornographic sex with various "hardbodies" as detailed in *Hustler*, or mutilating and killing others according to the ways in which people are brutally murdered in horror movies, Bateman's existence is a media-induced "reality." Accordingly, by drawing extensively from cinematic techniques, Bateman narrates his life as if it were a movie (1, 59, 164, 243, 286, 292, 343, 348). In this spectacular, hyperreal existence, the distinction between fact and fantasy is extremely amorphous, and although Bateman's voice and his thoughts are real, the actuality of his actions remains uncertain.

The most graphic scenes of the text are the faithful reproduction of scenes scripted in countless pornographic videos and horror movies. For example, Bateman's desire to viciously mutilate women with a power drill (303, 326) is without a doubt inspired by the movie *Body Double* (113), which he has rented and reportedly seen over a dozen times. The cartoonish quality or the grotesqueness of the violence depicted in *American Psycho* renders it entirely or partly *invraisemblable*, which makes it unclear whether the murders actually take place, or whether they are merely the verbal expression—a *projection* rather than an *actualization*—of the protagonist's repressed desires. Max Horkheimer and Theodor Adorno have famously argued that "the culture industry does not sublimate; it represses"[36] and the blurred lines between Bateman's conscious reality and his (unconscious? imaginary?) projections of sexual violence are indicative of a continuous internal discourse between the expressed and the repressed. As readers, we are left to ponder whether Bateman's murderous rampage actually ever took place. Not only is Owen reportedly still alive (388), but there is no validation for any of his crimes: when he returns to Owen's apartment to see what has happened to the body of the two prostitutes he maimed there, the building and the guard look different, his key doesn't fit, and there is absolutely no trace of what transpired (366–70). This continuous ambiguity between narrative and textual reality persists throughout the novel and constantly sends the reader questioning not only the authenticity of the events described but also the nature and extent of the protagonist's psychotic disorder.

In a world where the spectacle has hijacked all aspects of human existence, Bateman is as much a representation of a mediated reality as he is a victim of it. In the absence of individuality and authenticity, whereby reality is shaped by the external perceptions communicated through media culture, all layers of subjectivity are gradually stripped away:

> There wasn't a clear, identifiable emotion within me, except for greed and possibly, total disgust. I had all the characteristics of a human being— flesh, blood, skin, hair—but my depersonalization was so intense, had gone so deep, that the normal ability to feel compassion had been eradicated, the victim of a slow, purposeful erasure. I was simply imitating reality, a rough resemblance of a human being, with only a dim corner of my mind functioning. (282)

Bateman imitates the reality configured by the omnipotence of media images flooding the sociocultural landscape. The precession of simulacra has turned him into "a rough resemblance of a human being." But it would be incorrect to assume that Bateman is alone in this predicament: his "depersonalization" is an intrinsic characteristic of postmodern subjectivity. In fact, referring to Thomas B. Byers' concept of "pomophobia" (a series of fears associated with the postmodern era of late capitalism), Storey argues that "even the concept of identity is in the process of redefinition."[37]

In "Postmodernism and Consumer Society," Jameson periodizes postmodernism in relation to consumer capitalism and argues that the existential condition created by the omnipotence of media culture in the late twentieth century is akin to the schizophrenic experience.[38] Drawing from Lacan's theorizations, Jameson explains that the schizophrenic has no sense of personal identity because he is unable to understand his relationship with the outside world in terms of the continuity of time as experienced through language (118–19). Jameson explains, "The schizophrenic experience is an experience of isolated, disconnected, discontinuous material signifiers which fail to link up into a coherent sequence," and he qualifies it as being particularly unpleasant.[39] In a number of instances, Bateman's narration follows the disembodied, fragmented, and disjointed flow of the schizophrenic experience. The linearity of events is randomly disrupted within (85–86, 177–79) and between chapters (148–53), and his voice often breaks off incoherently, thereby reflecting the flickering screen of channel surfing or MTV-style rapid-fire editing (80–81, 342–43). Moreover, the uncertainty, discontinuity, and magnitude of detail that informs the text's most sensational scenes confirm Jameson's idea that "as temporal continuities break down, the experience of the present becomes powerfully, overwhelmingly vivid and 'material': the world comes before the schizophrenic with heightened intensity, bearing a mysterious and oppressive charge of affect, glowing with hallucinatory energy."[40]

In *American Psycho*, the repetitive and increasing occurrence of delusional episodes and hallucinations reinforces the text's schizophrenic character. For instance, the chapter entitled "Chase, Manhattan" (347–52) morphs into an action movie in which "Patrick Bateman" stars as the main protagonist. Bateman's narrative "I" becomes completely disembodied as he suddenly substitutes the first person for the third person mid-paragraph:

> . . . *I lose control entirely*, the cab swerves into a Korean deli, next to a karaoke restaurant called Lotus Blossom I've been to with Japanese clients, the cab rolling over fruit stands, smashing through a wall of glass, the body of a cashier thudding across the hood, *Patrick* tries to put the cab in

> reverse but nothing happens, *he* staggers out of the cab, leaning against
> it, a nerve-racking silence follows, "nice going, Bateman," *he* mutters . . .
> (emphasis added by author, 349)

Bateman's schizophrenia is by and large induced by his media-saturated
consciousness; subjectivity never comes into being because the self fails
to "accede fully into the realm of speech and language" as Jameson would
phrase it.[41] However, it would be inaccurate to conclude that Bateman has
completely lost touch with reality. Quite to the contrary, Bateman is deeply
connected with the world around him; as he indicates, he is "in touch . . .
with humanity," but it is a humanity consumed with appearances, one that
is completely immersed in the hyperreal spectacle of simulacra.

The schizophrenic experience as theorized by Jameson and exemplified
in Bateman's hyperreal existence is distinct from Deleuze and Guattari's conceptualization of the schizophrenic as that figure which resists the inscrip-
tion of capitalist reterritorialization. Even though Bateman is not defined
by any latent oedipality—the text carefully undermines this possibility in
the chapter entitled "Sandstone"—his (male) desire remains constructed as
"lack" according to the need-based imperatives of the consumerist pathos.
In other words, rather than actualizing the desiring-production of the multiple, nomadic subjectivities of the Deleuzian schizo, Bateman's subjectivity
(or lack thereof) is deeply entrenched, on the one hand, in the repressive
regimes of a phallogocentric order, and on the other, in the crisis of established, hegemonic concepts of identity in late stage capitalism.

### From Pastiche to Parody, or, an "I" for an "Eye"

Mary Harron's 2000 film adaptation of *American Psycho*[42] provides an insightful intertext to Ellis's novel, especially if we query the critical and ideological discourses that have surrounded the reception and interpretation of both
novel and film. Whereas the release of the book was characterized by public
outrage about the overtly explicit accounts of sexual violence, Harron's film
was largely praised in part because it excised the explicitness of the original. Presumably, the excessive violence of the text was drastically reduced
to highlight its satirical qualities, even if in light of the above exegesis, it is

difficult to understand how the detractors of the novel were unable to read *American Psycho* as a satire. This directorial decision appears to have pleased the reviewers who had originally found Ellis's novel despicable. In the *New York Times*, for example, while Roger Rosenblatt[43] expressly condemned the excesses of violence of Ellis's text, Stephen Holden[44] praised Harron's directorial decision to "remove its excess fat in a kind of cinematic liposuction," claiming that she thereby "salvage[d] a novel widely loathed for its putative misogyny and gruesome torture scenes."

One might ask whether it was necessary for Mary Harron to adapt the text in order for its satirical thrust to be recovered. Perhaps it was the filmmaker's female/lesbian status that gave her a degree of immunity from the attacks that Ellis received, as Guinevere Turner, the script's coauthor, points out.[45] This is possibly one part of the explanation, but I would contend that the trajectories of both texts are equally implicated in broader aesthetic and ideological concerns that inform the politics of language and the gaze as they displace the locus of responsibility from the individual to the collective and vice versa.

In "Judgment Is Not an Exit," Marco Abel appropriately points out that in emphasizing the satirical edge of the novel (the point missed by the likes of Manguel, Rosenblatt, and Baxter), Harron unveils the book's vein of social criticism by juxtaposing it with a strong sense of irony and comedy. Yet Abel also argues that with this shift in emphasis, the director transforms the text into a "traditional" satire by preempting the possibility of the audience's responding affectively to the violence.[46] Keeping in mind Jameson's distinction between pastiche and parody, it could be argued that by reinstating laughter in Ellis's text, Harron transforms it into a more straightforward parody. Partly because of the chosen medium and partly because of Harron's directorial choices, the film does not require the same involvement—that is, the same degree of active participation in the reading/viewing process—from its audience that the novel demands from its readers. Whereas the narrative strategies deployed by the novel make a point of implicating the reader, the film seems consciously to impose a Brechtian *Verfremdungseffekt*, a "distancing effect,"[47] between the actions depicted on screen and the spectator in order to promote critical reflection over emotional involvement. While the distancing effect in Harron's work does not necessarily eviscerate the viewer's affective response—quite the contrary, it can exacerbate it by exerting control through a narrative strategy of temptation and denial—it reduces its capacity by recasting the viewer's critical attention on the representational qualities of the film.

The distancing effect also marks a departure from the ways in which Ellis's narrative strategy functions as an ideological critique. In her examination of the novel's voice as that of a serial killer, Carla Freccero notes:

> American Psycho is narrated for the most part in the first-person voice of a serial killer. The serial killer is a popular American figure of dementia, universally regarded as unthreatening precisely because of his singularity, the nonrationality of his pathology, and the individualized and eccentric nature of his violence. A serial killer is not the oppressed masses, and although his murders are usually lurid, his reach is limited. In this sense, the serial killer serves the function of a fetish in public culture: he is the means of the disavowal of institutionalized violence, while the "seriality" of his acts of violence marks the place of recognition in this disavowal. Through the serial killer, then, we recognize and simultaneously refuse the violence-saturated quality of the culture, by situating its source in an individual with a psychosexual dysfunction. We are thus able to locate the violence in his disorder rather than in ourselves or in the social order.[48]

Observing that in American popular culture the fictive individual image of the serial killer is a "consoling fantasy" which acts as a "condensation of the violence of American historicity into a singular subject who performs discrete, singular injurious acts,"[49] she concludes that Ellis's novel "does not offer its readers the serial killer as consoling fantasy."[50] As a result of the author's minimalist style as well as the absence of an expository or explicative pathological profile, Bateman escapes the singular categorization of a serial killer in the vein of other well-established and distinguishable psychopaths such as Thomas Harris's Hannibal Lecter or Norman Bates of Alfred Hitchcock's Psycho. Abel argues that Harron's film clearly portrays Bateman as a "monster" and that consequently "the audience can feel superior and thus is likely to remain uninterested in identifying with him."[51] This distancing is not only a typical response to villains, but it is also somewhat similar to the ways in which the readers of Houellebecq's Elementary

*Particles* can easily dissociate themselves from the precisely drawn psycho-pathology of its protagonists. Rather than illustrating the pathology of a singular subject, the book illustrates the pathology of a given culture: the all-encompassing, collective violence that characterizes contemporary consumer capitalism. Quite the opposite, Harron's version offers the spectator an "exit," an "escape route"; by depicting Bateman as a classic serial killer and a "consoling fantasy," the audience feels detached from the excesses of violence, pornography, and consumerism the text portrays. In Ellis's text, the distance between reader and narrator is narrowed through a forced process of identification: there is no distance between the "I" in the text and the personal "I." The position of the reader is that of an active participant; as Laura Tanner observes, "the reader identifies with (imaginatively becomes) the violator," as we are bound to project ourselves into the action.[52]

Ellis's unassuming prose coerces the novel's audience into adopting Bateman's point of view. Far from receiving any escape route, the reader is compelled to get absorbed into the narrative. The irony of Ellis's minimalist style and Bateman's unaffected tone is that they relegate the responsibility for feelings and emotions to the reader. And so, we are able to experience what apparently Bateman does not; that is, feelings of revulsion and abhorrence for the acts of sexual violence he perpetrates, even while the style suggests no such revulsion is necessary. It is the absence of affect in Bateman that produces the close, intimate space between the reader and the narrator. Without a primary filter of characterization and personality, the reader subconsciously becomes Bateman.

It is also Bateman's lack of personality, which is partly highlighted by the fact that he is constantly being mistaken for someone else, that not only compels the reader into filling the affective void by becoming the protagonist but also makes the reader long for the violence as the sole answer to the boredom which plagues the endless descriptive passages of the text. Due to the author's detailed and uninflected prose and the sudden, uncanny, difference in content between the boredom that characterizes the majority of the narrative's cataloguing of consumer goods and the unexpected explicitness of its most violent scenes, the readers' sensibilities are heightened and they are unable to distance themselves from the text. It is through both the poetics of forced participation and the structure of the novel that *American*

*Psycho* literalizes the ways in which the perverted system of consumer capitalism comes full circle: faced by the boredom that plagues our lives as consumers we seek elation through some of the highly aesthetical, glamorously violent, and obscenely perverse productions of the entertainment industry.

In Harron's film, the distance between the spectator and the character is restored. The lens of the camera acts as a physical filter, thus preventing the audience from being entirely absorbed by the text, which is rather ironic considering that the audience usually identifies with the camera through the traditional mechanics of the gaze. In this case, the narrative function is enacted as a series of shots, camera angles, and montage from a predominantly third-person point of view, and while the protagonist's voice remains present through the monologues that inform certain scenes, most of them are accompanied by a shot of the protagonist's face. In contrast to the novel's blank narrative voice, Bateman's voice is embodied by a discernable character on screen, thus allowing viewers an opportunity to distance themselves from both the voice they hear and the person they see. Contrary to the particular ways in which the structural and linguistic elements of the novel interact dialogically to create a distinctive writerly experience, the film's visual poetics produce a clearly discernible third-person perspective. The replacement of the first-person subjectifying perspective by a third-person "critical" one—the substitution of an "I" for an "eye"—allows spectators to distance themselves from the main character, thus allowing them to easily dissociate their own implication in the perverse, totalizing ideologies of consumer capitalism that Bateman personifies and the text literalizes. In other words, the reader of the novel finds itself in the position of the killer, and incidentally, guilty, whereas in the movie, the audience assumes the position of a witness, and incidentally, in a situation capable of judging the actions perpetrated on screen as that of a discernable other.

This shift of emphasis is metaphorized visually in the film in the scene where Bateman gauges the bum's eyes (131). In the novel, the description of the act is not only reminiscent of *Le Chien Andalou* (" . . . with my thumb and forefinger [I] hold the other eye open and bring the knife open and bring the knife up and push the tip of it into the socket . . . then slitting the eyeball open sideways . . ."), it also speaks eloquently of Bataille's epigraph wherein he positions civilization in close proximity to horror—a horror that is epitomized in the fear of the eye, both as an organ and as an instrument of vision. As a great source of anxiety, Bataille claims, "The eye is ranked even higher in horror, since it is, among other things, the *eye of conscience.*"[53] The eye is both the locus and the prism of horror; not only do we *witness* violence visually—as the conduit toward visceral, bodily responses—but the violence exerted on the eye is also the most horrific. The scene from the novel is guaranteed to make us cringe, as many of us have squirmed when we watched Buñuel's film for the first time. However, it furthermore works symbolically to highlight our own tendency to turn a blind eye to the horrors and vicissitudes of the perpetrator. In the film, since the act is shot entirely from above, we do not witness the violence up close; in other words, the particular positioning of the shot is blinding, preempting the possibility for catharsis even as the violence unfolds in front of us.

While the stylistic strategies embedded in the violent passages of Ellis's novel specifically aim to jostle readers out of their passive complacency through a series of sudden and unexpected visceral shocks, the frigid aesthetics of Harron's film position spectators in a state of rational self-reflection as they remain emotionally unscathed by the events that unfold on the screen; a strategy which seems to align itself with Bertolt Brecht's paradigm of critical distance and Laura Mulvey's politics of deconstructing the gaze through passionate detachment.

In sharp contrast to Ellis's aesthetical choices of laying bare the violent ideologies of scopophilia in consumer culture, Harron not only decided to trim the "excess fat" by removing and sanitizing the scenes of sexual violence, she also made the directorial decision to return the male pornographic gaze onto its subject. The camera makes a point of focusing on Bateman's fetishized body in the illustration of his exercise routines, his bathing and grooming rituals, and more compellingly, in the representation of the sex scenes. More tellingly, in the depiction of a sexual encounter between Bateman and two prostitutes, which he names "Christie" and "Sabrina," in lieu of focusing on the fragmented sexual organs of the two girls as in the pornographic description contained in the novel (173–76), the camera, alternatively representing both Bateman's gaze and Christie's, focuses predominantly on Bateman. It appears that this particular scene underlines the feminist politics of the film. On the one hand, the play of mirrors emphasizes

the narcissist component of mainstream pornography whose codes of scopophilic pleasure have been embraced by the visual media industry. On the
other hand, the strategy of returning the gaze specifically aims to denounce
and subvert the male gaze that has dominated the visual codes of traditional
narrative cinema.

The film certainly provides a telling critique of these two components
in contemporary consumer culture, yet I would contend that in this particular instance it works against the more compelling stylistic strategies at
work in the novel for it merely confers on the spectator another opportunity to "exit" the text. What is particularly revealing are the ways in which
the visual narrative creates an even greater distance by using a wide shot
of the prostitutes and Bateman through the perspective of a second camera, the camera that Bateman uses to tape the threesome. The audience
now finds itself behind two screens, two filters, two frames of reference
or discernment looking at the blurry, colorless, and considerably smaller
figures of the three characters. Following the point made previously, the
critical "eye(s)" of the camera permits spectators simultaneously to dissociate themselves from the perverse vicissitudes of scopophilic consumption.
In contrast, the novel's subjectifying "I" does not allow readers to remove
themselves from the objectifying discourses that characterize consumer
culture. Whereas the film privileges the sanctity and dignity of the audience, the novel violates the reader's privileged intimate space to the same
extent that the text violates its various subjects. The film diffuses the potentially disorientating or shocking effect of the text's sexual violence, while in
the novel, echoing Bataille's theories on language, *erotisme*, and transgression, it is deployed as a major stylistic strategy. To that regard, Ellis explains
in an interview for *MetroWeekly* why he thinks the movie adaptation may
have misinterpreted the novel:

> . . . it's a movie I admire—I am by no means embarrassed by it and I liked
> it a lot. I just thought it didn't really capture the sensibility of the novel.
> It was too chilly, too elegant. I thought the novel itself was a lot wilder
> and crazier. Director Mary Harron placed the movie within a feminist
> context and put quotation marks around it and I don't think the movie
> needed that.[54]

By stripping the excessive displays of gore and pornography and abiding by Mulvey's feminist strategy of returning the gaze, Harron does not investigate the ways in which, as Williams points out, these "excesses" might function as ideological critique.

## The Politics of Adaptation: Poetics, Intertextuality, and Ideology

Marco Abel contends that by privileging satire over violence, the film stresses the "representational" qualities of American Psycho, and in doing so it reflects a "tendency to judge a work of art in terms of its truth value"[55] but diminishes the text's potential in exploring the possibilities of writing at the "frontier" experienced through representations of violence.[56] In excising the visual poetics of sexual violence and transforming the gaze, Harron transforms the potential impact that American Psycho's transgressive style of criticism produces because the film's spectator does not respond on the same visceral level as the reader of the book. The shocking effects of pornographic horror are clearly absent from the film, because on the one hand, the poetics of the camera allow the spectator to remain at a safe distance from the events depicted on screen and on the other, the few violent scenes are predictable and undisturbing[57] and they do not replicate the series of uncanny shocks produced by Ellis's aesthetical choices.

The narrative style of the novel, the first-person disembodied blankness, coerces the reader to assume the position of the protagonist: the voice that readers hear in their heads when they read the book are their own. Due to the absence of any feelings and emotions in the narrative voice, the reader is compelled to respond affectively to the gruesome acts of violence it depicts. At the same time, the spectacle of sexual violence is what drives and links the various parts of the narrative. There is, at least affectively, no way out of this vicious circle: the narrative is plagued by the boredom that informs the long-descriptive passages of the novel, only to be interrupted, or perversely relieved one could argue, by the episodes of violence that punctuate the narrative. The visual poetics fold into the immediacy of the novel, we are active participants in the economies of spectacular consumption the novel decries, and hence the thoughts and desires of the protagonist are actually our own. In the movie there is an actor whom the audience sees and recognizes as a discernable person, a distinct other, and the thoughts and desires of the killer are heard in the voice of that actor. As an audience, we dissociate ourselves from the events on screen set in a distinct time and place,[58] and thus, we are clearly repositioned in our seats.[59] As a result we can easily draw the line between the character/actor and ourselves, between the psychopathology of a serial killer and that of our entire culture.

In psychoanalytic terms, the novel's narrative blurs the boundaries between the conscious and unconscious modes of expression. In so doing, it subverts the reader's unconscious desire for both a secure subjective position and a subject of self-recognition by delivering an ego-ideal that acts as a symbolic symptom of the perverse ideologies guiding spectacular consumer culture. In contrast, there is no such symbolic dimension in Mary Harron's adaptation, for the critique of consumer culture is to be read on a more literal level. The narrative structure of the film represents a more or less stable subject (an archetypical serial killer) that is easily recognizable as a discernable other, a subject the audience can distance itself from because of its otherness: a "secure" subject in the sense that the security of the subject-position of the audience vis-à-vis the character is preserved, thanks in part to the third-person perspective of the camera's eye.

Yet, from a slightly different perspective, it could be argued that in reproducing textually the visual aesthetics of pornography and horror films, Ellis embraces the postmodern rhetoric of undermining the high/low dichotomization of critical discourses surrounding literary and popular culture. Conversely, it could also be suggested that by emphasizing the narrative properties of *American Psycho* and excising its visual aesthetics, Mary Harron focuses on the more detached critical properties of cinematic language and simultaneously subverts or undermines the spectacular ideology of visual pleasure associated with traditional narrative cinema. In some extended way, Harron is reflecting Ellis's subversive tactics by reversing the dynamics of transgression. Whereas Ellis chooses to include pornographic violence in a genre of cultural production (i.e., "serious" literature) where it is both condemned and unbecoming, informed by the sulfurous reputation and scandalous reception of the novel, Harron is being similarly atypical by purging the graphic violence in a film genre[60] where it is expected and celebrated. From the perspective that Harron's work is a critique of the traditional voyeuristic conventions that have dominated the film medium, it appears that the director responds to Mulvey's political call to destroy the mechanics of scopophilic satisfaction.[61]

Holden's comment regarding the ways in which Harron's film "salvages" the novel adequately echoes the ways in which criticism may affect a novel's perception and reputation and how critical responses can "defend" a work. Yet, Abel considers that by making certain judgments or critical responses, films such as Harron's actually "attack" a work by emphasizing certain aspects while undermining others.[62] Hence, one could contend that by focusing on its representational qualities and dismissing the visceral poetics of the text, Harron's decision to emphasize the satirical aspect neuters the text by separating it from its potential to violate the complacency of the society it addresses. While the novel specifically aims to assault the senses of the readers through a series of visceral shocks in order to trigger an ontological *remise en question* of the system in which they participate, the film positions spectators at a detached distance from the materiality of sexual violence. The "I" of the novel's narrative is a symptom of capitalism's collective violence, whereas the critical detachment produced by the "eye" of the camera allows the spectator to view Bateman as a "consoling fantasy," a product of the material conditions of a historicized epoch. In arguing for a reconsideration of the relation between genre, gender, fantasy, and structures of perversion, Williams reminds us that although horror and pornography may seem to superficially reenact traditional patterns of violence directed toward women, "[t]o dismiss them as bad excess . . . is not to address their function as cultural problem-solving."[63] By excising the scenes of sexual violence from *American Psycho*, Harron seemingly overlooks the discursive function of pornographic horror, and so one could wonder where Harron's satire positions itself with regard to the political economies of the culture industry it supposedly subverts.[64]

## The American Nightmare

Bateman personifies the excesses of consumer capitalism and commodity fetishism, where self-worth is defined by the accumulation of material wealth and interpersonal relationships are commoditized transactions.

Bateman is not the only one preoccupied by these obsessions, and consequently his compulsive behavior cannot be simply dismissed as an individuated neurotic disorder. His consumerist desires make him an integral part of an American culture defined by appearances and possessions. The perceptions that form his *being*, or lack thereof, are entirely shaped by the signs and images of the popular media as a configuration of the collective imaginary. This suggests that the objectification of human existence and the endless pursuit of wealth and status that Bateman embodies also conform to the ideals that have shaped US national consciousness.

Even if the critique of consumer capitalism transcends the precise contextual setting of *American Psycho*, it merits attention. In the 1980s, the US was coming out of a global energy crisis, a bitter recession, and the social and political breakdown caused by the Vietnam War and Richard Nixon's resignation. The political and economic recovery that seemingly occurred when Ronald Reagan took office greatly influenced how America presented itself as a world superpower at the height of the Cold War. From the outset, the text resonates with the free market and consumerist ideologies that have fomented the American financial empire, making Wall Street the capital of the Western hemisphere. In *American Psycho*, the delusional, supercharged, testosterone-filled narrative makes the sublime aura of this exclusive location shine with a sordid magnificence.

Competition is a defining characteristic of the free market ideologies that defined the Reagan era. Bateman and his associates are in competition with each other, an idea best exemplified in the scene where they compare their business cards (44–45) (which was executed with compelling flair in Harron's movie adaptation). *American Psycho* shows how the self-consuming ethos of narcissistic individualism and the Reaganomics of corporate greed, market deregulation, and political irresponsibility have distorted the "American Dream." When consumer capitalism becomes a form of social Darwinism, the dream turns into a nightmare, not only for Bateman's victims, the social others who do not fit into the conformist fantasy of an image-driven society, but for the executioner as well. The society of the spectacle is all encompassing, and the egotistical thrust of self-promotion has paradoxically exacerbated individualism to the point of destroying individuality.

Bateman's surface beauty is the outward projection of a picture-perfect society, which, under the cover of flawless appearances, struggles to hide the vices and vicissitudes of a deeply fragmented and deranged psyche. From a purely materialistic point of view, Bateman has everything he could ever desire, and all with such ease. But he has no sense of human value, only monetary or transactional value. To him everything is an object with a price tag. For example, Bateman dates and has sex with women not because he is intelligent, witty, or charming (he is not), but because he pays them.

Similarly, women are also obsessed by material wealth, for according to Price, "When I tell [girls] what my annual income is, believe me, my behavior couldn't matter less" (53). Moreover, as Reeves exclaims, "Girls dig Bateman" because "He's GQ" (90), but he is also "the boy next door," the archetypical all-American male, and thus interchangeable and undistinguishable from the rest of his crew. Mark Storey points out that Bateman's clichéd masculinity takes the representational elements of dominant masculinity to their logical extreme.[65] Consequently, the hypersexual logos of the male faction also signals a fissure in the construction of this hegemonic type of masculinity. The episode with Luis Carruthers, Bateman's taste in transsexual pornography—evidenced in the multiple references to a pornographic video titled *She-Male Reformatory* (69, 111)—as well as his obsession with his body-image and the implied categorization of "the boy next door" as a gay archetype, all point to the possibility that Bateman is a closet or repressed homosexual who is overcompensating by enacting or projecting misogynistic fantasies as a means to conform to a hypersexual ideal of heterosexual masculinity. Like the male gaze theorized by Mulvey, this misogynistic violence purports to neutralize the paradoxical threat posed to phallocentrism by women and Bateman's own (unconscious) femininity, in part characterized by his obsessive grooming routine. And consequently, the erratic, schizophrenic voice of the narrative effectively marks a crisis in the dominant, hegemonic masculinity Bateman embodies.

Bateman may personify the postindustrial American Dream of financial wealth and class affluence; he also represents the inherent horror of a culture predicated on the logic of competition and accumulation. Bateman's existence is characterized by luxury and excess, but it is also a life plagued by boredom and ennui, where feelings and emotions are null and void. The pointless and endless accumulation of material goods has created an emotional vacuum that translates into vacuous feelings. To escape from the numbness of a life defined by the surface materiality of things, Bateman fantasizes heavily about violence as a means to reawaken his senses. He needs to *feel*, and he can do so only by feeding off the adrenaline rush procured by sensationalized violence. As desire gives way to need in the form of addiction, a vicious circle of increasing sensationalism and subsequent desensitization gradually imposes itself.

If consumer capitalism marks the latest stage of development of Western civilization, then *American Psycho* suggests that as Bataille's epigraph points out, civilized man is indeed no stranger to horror. In her essay on Ellis's hyperrealist aesthetics Frances Fortier asks the reader *"Où est l'insupportable? Dans la violence même ou dans le récit qui le banalise?"* [Wherein lies the unacceptable? Within the violence itself or within the narrative that banalizes it? (translation mine)].[66] Given the recent trends in film as well as social media, wherein ultra-violence, misogyny, hypersexuality, and blatant disregard for civility are the norm, the public at large has grown largely desensitized; the thresholds of tolerance for depictions of obscenity and gore have consistently been pushed further. Ellis claims in an interview for the *New York Times* that he was attempting to convey "how desensitized our culture has become toward violence."[67] Interestingly, this was also the argument made by Michael Haneke in producing *Funny Games U.S.* (2007), his faithful, shot-by-shot remake of his 1997 European film *Funny Games*. But in contrast to Ellis, Haneke decided to excise all display of on-screen violence, a strategy similar to Mary Harron's, which may further support my point that strategies work differently across the two mediums. As I've demonstrated, the critical paradox lies in the fact that through the operation of subjective transfiguration (i.e., through the twofold process of affective projection and response), the text's gratuitous violence works as a critique of gratuitous violence.

Part of the critique rests on the idea that the promulgation of various consumer products of a visual nature has promoted a scopophilic type of voyeurism; turning subjects into objects and undermining the ethical implications of consuming representations of violence and human suffering by classifying them as entertainment. As a celebrated observer of modern life[68] and no stranger to writing scandalous content, Charles Baudelaire addressed the preface of *Les Fleurs du Mal* to a *hypocrite lecteur*, a hypocritical reader, someone who would not want to accept the self-image the poems depict. For Ellis, we are all hypocrites, we all indulge in a dubious lifestyle of voyeuristic consumption. As a satire, *American Psycho* almost perfectly abides by the limitations of its genre. Bakhtin explains that the role of the Menippean satire is to be symptomatic, to reveal the defects of the subject it addresses without attempting to correct them,[69] a point that Jameson similarly emphasizes when he compares postmodern pastiche to the oppositional art of modernism.[70] "THIS IS NOT AN EXIT," the novel concludes, because, quite simply, there is no way out. The ideology of consumerism is so deeply engrained in everyday life that it seems impossible for the public at large to renounce it. At the dawn of the twenty-first century, consumer capitalism represents such a totalizing ideology that the *American Psycho* will carry on.

Bateman is narcissistic, greedy, cruel, proud, and envious. And yet, other than the fact that he *may* be a brutal murderer, he is in many ways not so different from the average US consumer and citizen. The magnitude of American consumerism is rivaled by no other nation in the world and the omnipotence of the media and the spectacle has grown exponentially.[71] Modern-day Americans are obsessed by reality shows, action movies, designer clothing, physical beauty, dieting, money, social networking, and material possessions. The exponential multiplication of social media platforms and online personas has accelerated our "depersonalization," as Bateman would say (282). Capitalist ideology thrives by imposing a system of false needs, and through the omnipotence of media advertising, we are constantly being sold on the belief that consuming certain products will bring us happiness, and that our self-worth is determined by the size of our houses, cars, and egos. Reading *American Psycho* thirty years after it was originally published is a striking reminder that the social Darwinist ethos of 1980s consumerism remains deeply engrained in the American psyche.[72]

In his 2010 *Esquire* column, Stephen Marche asks, "Why in hell are we back in the '80s?" as he traces the current decade's "eighties retrocraze" and tries to understand the nostalgia for what he calls "the shittiest of decades."[73] For many critics and viewers, Oliver Stone's *Wall Street* (1987) remains a cultural reference for its accurate portrayal of the 1980s' neoliberal ideologies of greed and excess. In perhaps one of the most memorable speeches of the film, Gordon Gekko (Michael Douglas), a corporate raider, tells an audience of shareholders:

> The point is, ladies and gentleman, that greed, for lack of a better word, is good. Greed is right, greed works. Greed clarifies, cuts through, and captures the essence of the evolutionary spirit. Greed, in all of its forms; greed for life, for money, for love, knowledge has marked the upward surge of mankind. And greed, you mark my words, will not only save Teldar Paper, but that other malfunctioning corporation called the USA.[74]

Greed was indeed rampant in the decade that spawned a million Gordon Gekkos and Patrick Batemans, but the cultural recycling of 1980s popular culture (including the 2010 sequel to *Wall Street*, *Wall Street Money Never Sleeps*, and Martin Scorsese's own glorification of greed and excess in his 2013 film *The Wolf of Wall Street*) may be a sign that we are indeed back in the 1980s. In fact, the rampant unaccountability of those in positions of political and economic power with regard to the financial scandals and crises of the last two decades suggests that its *spirit* has never left us. The 2016 election of Donald Trump, a celebrated 1980s real estate mogul and Reality TV figurehead widely decried as a sociopathic narcissist and bigoted misogynist, whom Bateman idolizes in the text, is not only a sign that the emperor has no clothes, but that he is alive and well.

# 4

# The Self, the Other, Its Doubles, and Its Shadows

*The Dialectics of Desire in Alain Mabanckou's* African Psycho

> I ask that I be taken into consideration on the basis of my desire. I am
> not only here—now, locked in thinghood. I desire somewhere else
> and something else.
> —Frantz Fanon, *Black Skin, White Masks*

The American debut of Alain Mabanckou, a francophone author from
Congo-Brazzaville whose previous novels have reaped a number of awards
in France,[1] *African Psycho* is set in an undisclosed nation-state in sub-Saharan
Africa. The paratextual reference to Bret Easton Ellis's *American Psycho* is striking and unavoidable. The title and its cover evoke and invoke the Other and
Otherness. Not only does the title call in Ellis's infamous novel, but for a book
originally published in French, it also presents itself as an Anglicism. *African
Psycho* is a francophone text with an English title, and its translation is directed
at an American audience who will inevitably recall the experience of reading
Ellis's book and the infamous history of its reception. But *African Psycho* is not
only a response to *American Psycho*: it is also its shadow and its double.

In *Global Shadows: Africa in the Neoliberal World Order*, James Ferguson
addresses the seemingly paradoxical idea that "Africa" is as much a real cultural and historical locale as it is a construct of Western thought.[2] Decrying
the fact that Africa has consistently been configured as the "dark other" or
"an absent object,"[3] Ferguson claims the continent has almost exclusively
been described in negation (as what it is *not*).[4] Following Achille Mbembe's
observation that "speaking rationally about Africa is not something that has

113

ever come naturally," Ferguson takes into account the role of the imaginary in producing Africa both as a historical and social construct as well as a "real place-in-the-world"—that is, a place that is both real and socially meaningful, and where fantasies about a fictional and constructed Africa collude and collide with actual political and economic processes.[5]

Ferguson notes that the promises of neoliberalism, namely, the idea that free markets will create the conditions for economic opportunities through global interconnectedness, have failed and have had dire consequences on African states as social and political insecurities have only deepened.[6] Echoing the early Western construction of Africa as the "dark continent," these effects have driven political and economic analysts to address Africa in terms of both "shadow economies" and "shadow states," as economic transactions and political power have been negotiated covertly through unofficial means.[7] For Ferguson the idea of a "shadow" also brings in the idea of a *doubling*,[8] wherein Africa's relationship to the West not only points to a negative *other*, a "bad image" of failed modernization for example, but also implies a bond and a relationship:

> A shadow, after all, is not a copy but an attached twin—a shadow is what sticks with you. Likeness here implies not only resemblance but also a connection, a proximity, an equivalence, even an identity. A shadow, in this sense, is not simply a negative space, a space of absence; it is a likeness, an inseparable other-who-is-also-oneself to whom one is bound.[9]

In *African Psycho*, the paratextual reference to *American Psycho* not only confirms the figurative parameters of a relationship between "America" and "Africa," but also emphasizes the model—that is, the "psycho"—on which the relationship is bound. The novel brings into focus the ways in which Ferguson's notions of a doubling and a shadowing can be applied to the discursive formation of African cultural identity and subjectivity, which, I would add, is entangled in a dialectic relationship predicated on configurations of cultural or individual psychosis. Frantz Fanon has already detailed the psychopathology of colonization in depth,[10] and so, one way of approaching *African Psycho* is to inquire what the text can tell us about the psychopathology of the postcolonial subject.

Although the title might temporarily annul the cultural differences between the "American" and the "African" by positioning them in para-textual proximity, the opposition is quickly reinforced in the text itself. Accordingly, Yves Chemla indicates that the world drawn by Grégoire, the protagonist of Mabanckou's novel, stands in opposition to the logic of excess and spectacular consumption that characterizes Bateman's world.[11] Admitting he thoroughly enjoyed Ellis's novel, Mabanckou explains the connection in the following terms:

> My book, *African Psycho*, is deeply rooted in Africa, and I needed to focus on an awkward character who is unable to commit a real murder—Grégoire Nakobomayo. *American Psycho*'s Patrick Bateman is a product of America; he is rich—the image of the successful Manhattan executive. Grégoire is the opposite. He is an orphan. He is poor. He lives on the street. He was adopted by a rich family, but it is not his world. He wants to resemble Angoualima, a mythical serial killer from the other Congo [the Democratic Republic of the Congo, formerly known as Zaïre]. Patrick Bateman is the perfect serial killer. Grégoire is just eternally awkward.[12]

The dyadic relationships the text draws are not limited to the protagonists. Just as Grégoire is related to Bateman as a shadow or a double, the "Africa" depicted in the novel is also related to "America" and, to some extent, the West, even as the precise locale remains undetermined. While there are definite references to the region of the Congo, such as the *Bembé* language (66), the distinct setting of the novel is never named, thereby eluding precise geographical location. The series of playful toponomastic twists, such as "He-Who-Drinks-Water-Is-An-Idiot," the name of the protagonist's neighborhood, further removes the setting from any real or existing locale, even as they more accurately describe the place. In a sense, whereas the context of *American Psycho* was precisely situated both historically and geographically in the epicenter of American culture and civilization, the setting of *African Psycho* is *relative*: in accordance with Ferguson's observations, it is defined as a *double*, a *negation*, or both. The river that cuts the city in two is dubbed the "Seine" (71) as a mirror image of the infamous river that cuts Paris in half, and the numerous references to "the country over there" (possibly pointing to the Democratic Republic of the Congo) aim to emphasize the differences between the two African nation-states. Furthermore, this apparent dissymmetry—such as approximating the Western capital while maintaining the African neighbor at a distance—calls in Ferguson's idea regarding the ways in which Africans aspire to copy Western forms as a means to attain Western norms,[13] even if it means undermining notions of cultural difference and specificity.[14]

The tension between the novel's approximate localization and its clear continental context emphasizes the notion that Africa is not defined in itself but rather through the bonds and relationships it holds with other locales and nation states. Consequently, the novel addresses Ferguson's idea that "Africa" is as much a product of the imagination as it is a real place in the world. Dialogically, the title emphasizes the construction of the "African" as a shadow and a double of the "American." But it also heightens the expectations of the audience: as readers of Ellis's novel, we expect to meet an African version of Bateman, a symptomatic figure revealing the psychosis of the culture he represents. As a result, the following questions arise: How does the novel actualize the audience's expectations and perceptions of African culture? What or who is an African Psycho? What are his or her vices and vicissitudes? How does the protagonist correspond to a Western audience's perceptions of the African and of Africa? If these perceptions are informed and reinforced by media images and representations, how do they address the historical construction of Africa as the "dark continent," which finds its roots in Hegel and is further echoed in Joseph Conrad's novella *Heart of Darkness*? Or is this "African Psycho" a more contemporary figure, the figure of a monster, such as the brutal, ruthless Idi Amin[15] or the narcissistic, delusional dictator "The Ruler" of Ngũgĩ wa Thiong'o's *Wizard of the Crow*? In this chapter and with these questions in tow, I will examine how *African Psycho* critically addresses the reader's beliefs and perceptions about Africa and the African as markers of cultural identity and products of the collective imaginary. In so doing, I will argue that by deconstructing the dialectical model of self-consciousness that arises within and across literary texts and contexts, *African Psycho* addresses the psychopathology of postcolonial subjectivity.

Following Ferguson, we are prompted to consider that by calling in *American Psycho*, Mabanckou's novel is both its double and its shadow. But I would similarly claim that it also *mirrors* Ellis's text. Consequently, we can ask what the African Psycho tells us about the American Psycho and the notion of cultural difference embedded in the play of mirrors. Furthermore, if we are that *hypocrite lecteur* whose self-image is reflected in Bateman as a figure embodying American national consciousness, what does its double and its shadow tell us about the other and, eventually, about ourselves? But before we can try to examine these relationships more in depth, we need to first meet the psycho referred to in the title: who is the African Psycho?

The novel's narrator and protagonist, Grégoire Nakobomayo, is a would-be murderer who lives in the curiously yet appropriately named *He-Who-Drinks-Water-Is-An-Idiot* neighborhood of an unnamed city in sub-Saharan Africa. Grégoire is a "picked-up" child, *un enfant ramassé*, an orphan who spent his childhood in different foster homes. Although he lives in the relative comfort of his own home and is self-employed as a metal-sheet worker, he is consumed by anger and self-loathing. He systematically rants about the dejected state of his neighborhood, the arrogance of the prostitutes from the "country over there," the travesty of the judicial system and the vanity of its public prosecutors, and the gaudy sensationalism of the irrelevant media outlets. Determined to compensate for his apparent ugliness (his head is shaped like a rectangular brick, which lands him the nickname "rectangular head") and overcome his inconsequential life as a manual laborer and petty criminal, he aspires to follow in the footsteps of his deceased idol, the "Great Master Angoualima," the country's most infamous and accomplished serial killer. A figure of mythical proportions, Angoualima becomes Grégoire's imaginary mentor, a "spiritual father" whom Grégoire wants to please by enacting his own murderous deeds. Despite a series of botched criminal attempts, Grégoire believes that murdering Germaine, his live-in girlfriend and a professional streetwalker, will grant him the validation and recognition—from Angoualima, the media, and ultimately, the reader—he so desperately seeks. However, Grégoire not only fails to kill Germaine as he failed to kill his other targets, such as Master Fernandes-Quinoa or the "Girl in White," but also fails as a character and fully realized subject.

### Rants, Raves, and Lies: The Pathological Language of Nonbeing

The narrative unravels in a series of rants and digressions; the thoughts, observations, and events that serve as the context and rationale to the speech act that constitutes the opening sentence and premise to the text: "I have decided to kill Germaine on December 29" (1). Signaling subjectivity, sovereignty, and premeditation, the commissive underlines the agency of the subject in committing the act, but *in-itself* (or *for-itself*) it lacks in factuality,[16] and eventually, curtails its realization. Grégoire's decision allegedly foreshadows the act as the cathartic resolution of the narrative. However, the next sentence highlights the deferral rather than the commitment as the *thinking* shadows the *doing*: "I have been thinking about this for weeks— whatever one may say about it, killing someone requires both psychological and logistical preparedness" (1). The impact of the initial proposition's apparent decisiveness is immediately overturned by the disclosure of excessive premeditation. In *African Psycho*, premeditation equals procrastination. While the commitment allegedly foreshadows the act, it actually foreshadows Grégoire's *failure* in committing the act.

From the start, the narrative is imbued by the absence of assertiveness, and in this sense, the novel reveals the performative paradox inherent to the commissive. Like all speech acts, the commissive is performative, but it also defers the performance of the act to which one is committed. The contradiction actualized in *the performative deferment of the performance* highlights the distance and remoteness of the commissive to the factual. From this perspective, it is the *deferment* and not the act that is put forth. In fact, entire sections of the narrative are devoted to preparing and imagining how the scene will unfold (93–98, 110–12, 125). The opening sentence characterizes to a great extent the narrative progression of the novel, wherein the crime is perpetually deferred as Grégoire errs and wanders in a series of rants, digressions, and projections, repeating his mantra about "preparedness" (77) without ever progressing to the act. He is either ill-prepared or never achieves the desired and necessary level of "psychological and logistical preparedness" for his criminal endeavors even though he seems aware of the perils of deferment: "If I had kept on trying one scenario after another . . . I would never have made up my mind and would still be postponing my gesture indefinitely" (110). The lack of decisiveness that marks the deferral is a sign of Grégoire's past and future failures.

Far from actualizing an individuated agency rooted in assertiveness, Grégoire's narrative is mostly constituted by a series of expressive speech acts that position the psychological front and forward. He claims having "reached the necessary state of mind" (1) and the willpower (77) to carry out his murderous deed, whereas in fact Grégoire is not only an inveterate procrastinator but is also incoherent, erratic, and irrational, if not completely neurotic. His voice recalls that of Dostoevsky's protagonist in *Notes from the Underground* and Ralph Ellison's *Invisible Man*, and in many ways Grégoire shares their bitterness, isolation, and anonymity.

Yves Chemla points out, "African Psycho *est un discours par lequel un 'Je' accède à la souveraineté de sa propre parole, mais en même temps cette parole est minée, et se déconstruit au fur et à mesure de sa prolifération*" [*African Psycho* is a discourse through which an "I" attains the sovereignty of its own *parole*, but at the same time, this *parole* is doomed, and it deconstructs itself as it proliferates (translation mine)]. From the onset, the title qualifies the discourse as pathological, which highlights its nonsense and incongruence. Grégoire's speech is a grotesque collage of fantasies, lies, and phantasmatic projections, and his delusions of grandeur and inner contradictions not only mark him as unreliable but also put into doubt his capacity to act as a free self-determining subject. In fact, his failures are foreshadowed in the patterns of his speech; not only is the discourse characterized by an incessant oscillation between past digressions and future projections—a wandering that eludes action in the present—but every thought appears suspended, as indicated by the ellipses that mark the end of every section of the text.

Wavering in and out of the past and the future without actualizing the present, the discourse constantly tries to reassert itself. Through his incessant blabber, Grégoire anxiously seeks our approval at the same time he seeks recognition from Angoualima, providing motive and rationale to justify his actions and desires. Grégoire professes he is predestined to follow in the footsteps of Angoualima due to his sense of shared history: "I did resemble him. Not in a physical sense, but that he also had cultivated a taste for solitude and that he hadn't been recognized by his parents either" (7–8). Moreover, he similarly claims he is on a "cleaning" mission to restore dignity and honor to the neighborhood of He-Who-Drinks-Water-Is-An-Idiot (18, 78), a place which has nurtured him as parents would (32–33, 79–80). Although Grégoire is well aware of the ways in which persuasion can win over an audience, as he recalls the persuasiveness of the public prosecutor in a well-publicized criminal case (31–32), he lacks the necessary skills to win us over. Calling it a "public health campaign" (64), his apparently noble endeavor to preserve the honor of his territory is quickly overshadowed by the fact that his rationale is deeply rooted in structures of misogyny and xenophobia:

> I was going to clean [the neighborhood] real good, give it back some dignity, rid it of its refuse, of its detritus, of its filth, of its germs, of its amoebas, of its bacilli, yes of its bitches who came from the country over there. (78)

While this train of thought echoes the pitfalls of African nationalism Fanon had already identified in *The Wretched of the Earth*,[17] Grégoire's distinct pathology accentuates its incongruities as the discourse wanders off ineffectually into a senseless rant (77–85).

Grégoire's psychosis is embedded in the ways in which he is incapable of linking thought to action, and in an extended sense, *African Psycho* investigates the relationship between language and being through the protagonist's ambivalence. Ferdinand de Saussure, Ludwig Wittgenstein, and Jacques Lacan situate language as a fundamental, preexisting reality that precedes existence. Humans are born *in* language insofar as they come into being through language. Language informs and shapes subjectivity, from the first violent act of naming,[18] through interpellation, to our own appropriation of its system of signification. Likewise, language allows us to understand our world, but also gives us access to its symbolic order, to the values and meanings of a given cultural milieu. Accordingly, language plays a significant role in constructing Grégoire's subjectivity and his perceptions of the world. In fact, the protagonist seems acutely cognizant of the implications of language; in one particular instance, he explains: *"To kill—a verb I have worshipped since coming of age. Fundamentally, all the small jobs I carried out were done in the hope of later being able to conjugate this verb* in its most immediate and fully realized form" (35). For Grégoire, however, realization often gets lost in a sea of endless chatter and nonsense. Ranting about his failure to kill the "Girl in White," he exclaims:

> On that night, I was convinced that I was going to kill at last, crush, wipe out, I don't give a fuck about words, that I was going to exist at last, that's it, exist, that I was going to be somebody, that I was going to follow in Angoualima's footsteps, come out of the banality of my life as a poor sheet-iron man, a poor auto-body man with large hands, as a good-for-nothing, as a man who does the rounds of He-Who-Drinks-Water-Is-An-Idiot's watering holes, that I was finally going to hear the national press and the press of the country over there to wonder who this new Angoualima was, who is this murderer. (78)

After first dismissing language, he immediately plunges into irrational blather, fluctuating between pathetic self-pity and exaggerated projections of fame and glory.

Grégoire's failure as a subject is in part rooted in a fraught relation with discourse and language. His endless chatter belongs to what Heidegger categorizes as "idle-talk" in his discussion of discourse and language in *Being and Time*.[19] In contrast to authentic discourse, which intelligibly and genuinely shapes our understanding of the ways in which we relate to others, idle-talk "cut[s] off the primary and primordially genuine relations of being toward the world, toward *Mitda-sein*, toward being-in itself."[20] The incessant noise of Grégoire's pathological discourse is overwhelming and overbearing, and its delusions, lies, and incongruities do not allow for an authentic disclosure of Being. To that effect, Angoualima, in his final phantasmatic appearance toward the end of the narrative, tells Grégoire: "you're just a liar . . . you have no personality, that's your problem, Rectangular Head!" (143–44).

Not only is Grégoire a liar, he is also an impostor whose lack of self-worth further distances him from any genuine sense of self. For example, when he meets Germaine, he introduces himself as Angoualima to impress her (115), and in another more notable episode, he pretends to be Angoualima and threatens by phone the host and guest of *Listeners Speak Out*, a popular radio show (52). While he experiences tremendous joy at having successfully impersonated his idol, what is most striking is that Grégoire's sense of self-assertion is derived vicariously by shadowing Angoualima. Existing in a world made of his own lies, where the "Master" from whom he seeks recognition is not only a murderous psychopath but also an abusive and imaginary father figure, Grégoire is incapable of asserting himself as an independent self-consciousness.

## Black Skins, Black Masks

In addition to the obvious paratextual reference to *American Psycho*, Mabanckou's novel also draws an implied and rather subtle hypertextual reference to *Black Skin, White Masks*, Fanon's canonical text on the psychological effects of colonialism. I am prompted to highlight this connection because there are surprising and insightful correspondences between Fanon's chapter that outlines the relationship between "The Man of Color and the White Woman" and *African Psycho*. My argument is that Fanon's analysis of colonial psychosis is transposed to the postcolonial setting through the skewed transfigurations of Jean Veneuse, the "White Woman," and even Germaine Guex, the psychoanalyst whose work Fanon utilizes, in the characters of Grégoire, the "Girl in White," and Germaine, the girlfriend Grégoire plans to murder. Consequently, *African Psycho* dramatizes and somewhat parodies Guex's theories on the neurosis of abandonment.

Grégoire's psyche is deeply scarred by his personal history as a "picked-up" child, a baby abandoned by his parents whom the state literally "picked up" from the mothers who abandoned them and placed in various foster homes in charge of the state (8). In slight contrast to Veneuse, Grégoire is a "real" orphan.[21] However, in similar ways to the subject of Fanon's case study, Grégoire struggles with the pre-oedipal causes and oedipal effects of abandonment. But in the present case, the subject is not desperately trying to live up to standards of Whiteness, as was the case with Veneuse, but to imagined and fictional standards of Blackness, embodied by the psychotic African archetype of Angoualima.

According to Guex, parental abandonment causes deep psychological effects: "The symptomatology of this form of neurosis is based upon the tripod of the *anxiety* aroused by abandonment, the *aggressivity* to which it gives rise, and the resultant *devaluation* of self."[22] Grégoire's erratic narrative voice is an expression of his apparent anxiety, which in turn shapes his murderous tendencies. Finally, his inability to successfully carry them out to gain the recognition of the media and the approval of Angoualima, his "idol and Great Master," triggers feelings of self-loathing that manifest themselves in his imaginary conversation with his mentor.

Interpreting Veneuse's feeling of abandonment, Fanon explains the ways in which the subject rejects the love of others as a result of having been abandoned; in turn, he will make others suffer in order to express his need for revenge.[23] As a foundling, Grégoire deeply resents his mother and fantasizes about eating her heart out: "I would pull out her heart of stone, cook it in my shop's furnace and eat it" (8). His mother's abandonment might also explain his more general misogyny, as he projects treating the body of his female victim in the same way he would his mother's: "I'm going to cut [Germaine] up, then boil her in a big pot thanks to my furnace, and go eat certain parts of her body" (122). Although these cannibal tendencies might recall some of Bateman's most gruesome acts, from a psychosexual standpoint Grégoire is much closer to Houellebecq's Bruno than he is to Ellis's Bateman.

Grégoire describes his life in foster families and, in a satirical nod, the "civilizing mission" of educated civil servants who sent him to catechism, where he would learn the word of God under the crack of the whip (9–10). Most notably, however, Grégoire relates how he defended himself against his foster brother's attempt to abuse him sexually by requesting they play "Mommy and Daddy" (11–13). This event has had a determining effect in establishing Grégoire's proclivity for violence as he not only considers it his first "dangerous deed" (8), but also indicates that his career as a petty criminal began soon thereafter (13).

In addition to setting the stage for Grégoire's inclination toward interpersonal violence, the episode also contains important psychosexual implications. The multilayered juxtaposition of child homosexuality, incestual rape, and role reversal may explain Grégoire's incompetence as well as his relative impotence. In this reconfiguration of domestic rape, Grégoire is asked to play the role of the mother, whom the father/brother wants to abuse sexually: "Take off your pants. We're going to do like daddies and mommies! You're mommy and I'm daddy" (12). But through a clever subterfuge, he turns things to his advantage. Grégoire tricks his foster brother into turning off the lights, claiming that is the way "daddies and mommies do this" (12). To convince his foe he knows what he is talking about, he lies by telling him that he saw his parents having sex. The brother complies and Grégoire acts rapidly, using the element of surprise to completely reverse the dynamics of the encounter:

> He turned off the light. I could still make out his silhouette in the doorway. As soon as his back was turned, I grabbed the stick he used as a whip by surprise. The other end was pointy. He turned around, felt for the switch in the dark. The light came back on, more intense than before. I had only a few seconds to act.
>
> Thinking of the *Zorro* comics I stole from the bookstore-on-the-pavement outside the duo movie theater, I attacked, holding the stick like a spear. Bull's-eye. Immediately I heard the bad boy scream. "Baldy! Baldy!" He cried for help and groped for a cloth to wipe the abundant gooey liquid that oozed from the eye I had just pierced. (13)

By piercing the "eye" of his brother as the symbolic father, Grégoire not only "castrates" him, but he also subverts the violence inherent to the patriarchal gaze. This "first dangerous deed" is a successful self-determining act, yet it is achieved by playing the role of the "mother," the sexual other he so vehemently despises. The psychosexual impact of this episode has some exponential consequences for Grégoire's existence, potentially explaining his repeated failures to act as a sexualized and embodied self. As his model of heterosexual normativity is predicated on castration and role reversal, he is incapable of exerting the phallic violence of the father, contrary to the hypersexualized Angoualima. On the one hand, Grégoire will suffer the impotence of the castrated father in the instance where he wants to rape the "Girl in White" (74–75). On the other, his failure to kill Germaine is both foreshadowed as well as reinforced in domestic role reversal: in projecting the murder scene, he imagines her sitting down after work waiting for him to bring her a beer (97).

From a different perspective, the piercing of the eye brings into focus notable intertextual and narrative ramifications to concepts related to vision and blindness, and more specifically to what we see and experience as a reader. On a first level, the piercing of the eye resonates with the infamous scene from Bunuel's *Le Chien Andalou* and Bataille's idea that the eye is the privileged locus of violence. In so doing, the text draws attention to the aesthetic quality of violence, as is the case in *American Psycho*. More particularly, the description of the foster brother's wound mirrors quite faithfully the episode in *American Psycho* wherein Bateman blinds a bum: " . . . both sockets [are] hollowed out and filled with gore, what's left of his eyes literally oozing over his screaming lips in thick, webby strands" (132). This mirroring effect between the two works is further reinforced by the fact that these episodes mark the first explicit act of violence. But while both texts pick up on the ubiquity and pervasiveness of real and fictionalized violence, this point of convergence only reinforces the divergence between the personal narratives of the protagonists, even if they share a number of distinguishable characteristic traits. In a broader sense, Bateman is more schizoid than neurotic since he does not display any of the peculiarities of Grégoire's psychosexual pathologies (or Bruno's from *Elementary Particles* for that matter). More specifically with regard to the narrative, in *American Psycho*, the textual violence becomes more explicit as it increases in frequency, whereas in *African Psycho*, it vanishes nearly completely as Grégoire is incapable of murdering anyone. For example, when he imagines killing Germaine "through a simulation," the scene does not go further than the description of his knife cutting into her flesh (98). While it is undeniable that both protagonists entertain a brutal misogynistic tendency toward women in general and prostitutes in particular, the vivid and extended descriptions of murder and mutilation by Bateman contrast greatly with Grégoire's "simulations":

> I thought I would blindfold and gag her. The moment she started suspecting something, and therefore started jerking around to try and free herself, it would be too late: I would already have fastened her arms behind her back with cables taken from a moped. Beforehand, even before she came back from work, I would have made the broad-bladed knife red-hot,

more than a thousand degrees, in my shop's furnace. It would then be easier to slash her from the place that separates her anus from her *thing* up to her abdomen while holding her legs wide open with cords . . . (98)

Even as Bateman's descriptions might be a projection of his unconscious desire, they are actualized, both in the protagonist's mind and in that of the reader's through the lack of distancing, the immediacy of the present tense, and the hypersexualized violence of the male pornographic gaze. In contrast, there is a distinctive dose of restraint in Grégoire's voice—the "thing" is never named and he does not appear to be in control when he has sex with Germaine (97)—which accentuates his insecurity and indeterminacy as the titular character. In addition, as with many of his narrative speech acts, the description remains suspended, a temporal distance and deferral further emphasized linguistically by the signal phrase "I thought" and the conditional tense. Grégoire's psychosis, which is deeply rooted in the psychosexual anxieties of abandonment neurosis, differs significantly from that of a brutal murderer and sexual predator in the vein of Bateman or Angoualima.

Not only are the narrative projections of the protagonists' misogynistic desires considerably dissimilar, it is also apparent from the onset that Bateman and Grégoire's respective self-images contrast greatly. There is a way in which the mirroring processes at work between the texts are literally actualized, which not only operate to further differentiate the character's consciousness, but also to reinforce Grégoire's insecurity and inherent failure as a realized subject. Bateman, the all-American golden boy, is reportedly handsome and takes extreme care of his Adonis-like features; narcissistic to the extreme, he is obsessed with his appearance, constantly checking his reflection whenever he can.[24] On the contrary, Grégoire is markedly unattractive; overtly self-conscious of his ugliness, he violently reviles his own appearance: " . . . I looked at myself in the shower . . . I saw the face of an incompetent, of a clumsy individual, and hit my fist hard against the mirror" (37). Both texts reveal, in a dissymmetrical way, that obsessions related to one's body image are not confined within the cultural specificity of their respective milieus. Although Bateman and Grégoire each exhibit psychological anxiety with regard to their body image, their respective comportments disclose divergent psychopathologies.

Bateman's self-image is in a way akin to Dorian Gray's, where the surface beauty works to dissimulate the ugliness of the *fragmented* schizophrenic psyche as a syndrome of postmodern consumer culture. Grégoire's vehement rejection of his reflection is a symptom of a dysmorphic disorder, a syndrome of a deeply *fractured* psyche. Entangled in a dialectic relationship with an imaginary other, he has not resolved the mirror phase of psychosexual development. For Grégoire, his desired self-image is that of an ego-ideal who remains a distinct other (127). Grégoire's identity as a fully sexualized subject remains in jeopardy because he cannot reconcile the image in the mirror with his own. As an aspiring "psycho," Grégoire desires his criminal exploits to reflect those of his Great Master, but he is so consumed by emulating his imaginary idol that he only succeeds in further alienating himself from his own self-image. This dialectical process of self-alienation and self-devaluation is greatly exacerbated because, on the one hand, Grégoire identifies with an imaginary figure of mythical proportions, and on the other, he also relies on gaining validation from a "Master" who will never recognize him as an equal.

**The Monstrous Other as Ego-Ideal**

In the absence of parental figures with whom he could possibly identify, Grégoire chooses the "Great Master Angoualima," the country's most notorious (and deceased) serial killer, as a model to emulate (19). Grégoire's choice is undoubtedly linked to the pervasive influence of the media, and the role it has played in shaping the myth of Angoualima who "was more famous than [the] President and . . . musicians combined," to the extent that he "stole the headlines from them" (40–41). The irony is that even as Grégoire repeatedly rants and raves about the seemingly worthless media (3, 53, 62), his perception and knowledge of both his *being*, the world he inhabits and his place in it, and his *becoming*, his aspirations and desires, are entirely shaped by it. His actions, whether robbing Master Quiroga's office (26) or defending himself from the attack of his foster brother (13), for example, are influenced by what he has read or seen through various media outlets, such as comic books, TV shows, and movies including *Blek le Roc*, *Les tontons flingueurs*, and the notorious *Scarface*. Most notably, the media exclusively informs his knowledge of murder, the very act that will lead to his consecration. In a first instance, he confides:

> Reading news items in our town's dailies, I find that no gesture is as simple as that of bringing someone's life to an end. All you need to do is procure a weapon, whatever it may be, set a trap for the future victim, and finally, proceed. (1)

Later, he confirms that comic strips permitted him to undertake criminal acts (15). His perceptions are skewed to the point that even though he is well aware that the adventures of his heroes are a "figment of the imagination" (15) and that "committing murder is not like acting in a movie" (101), he still considers what happens in the world of fiction to be the norm: "in a normal situation, there would have been a detective like in the movies or in crime novels" (140). In other words, similar to Bateman, Grégoire's perception and understanding of the world he lives in is by and large influenced by the media. The notable difference, however, is that whereas Bateman's consciousness was a cipher, a simulacra of postmodern consumer culture, Grégoire's subjectivity is deeply entangled in a dialectic movement toward recognition that finds its root in colonial subjugation and still resonates presently in the formation of postcolonial subjectivity.

Grégoire seeks the recognition of the media for his deeds as a form of validation, in the hopes of attaining the same notoriety as Angoualima (2). Consequently, what is most dramatic for Grégoire is that his crime might go unnoticed as a "humiliating possibility" (2) or misrepresented in the media. Surprisingly he does not mind if his misdeeds, even his failed murder attempts, are attributed to Angoualima (27). For example, he complains that his failure to kill the "Girl in White" was not only grossly overlooked by the media (5–6) but was also misinterpreted as the act of a "sex maniac" (63). By the same token, Grégoire would like "to be considered [Angoualima's] spiritual heir" (4) and therefore seeks recognition from his "Idol and Great Master" as well, arguing that killing Germaine would not only lead to his "coronation" (4) but would also be "a more coherent gesture . . . that would delight Angoualima" (35). But Grégoire is forever relegated to the ranks of wannabes: a *being* incapable of *becoming*. He is helpless because the recognition he so desperately seeks is foreclosed by evolving in the shadows of his idol, who is both a chimera of his own imagination and the collective imaginary.[25]

Grégoire notes that Angoualima, born with six fingers on each hand, is no "ordinary human being . . . which we find comforting" (2). Grégoire's observation echoes the discussion of the horror genre regarding the figure of the psycho wherein the "normality" of society is reinforced by confirming the "abnormality" of the monster.[26] But as a product of the collective imaginary propagated and perpetuated by the media, Angoualima was also "every man" (42) and "everywhere" (43) to the extent that every single criminal deed was attributed to him (52). In many ways, Angoualima embodies the "consoling fantasy" Freccero describes in her analysis of American historicity referred to in chapter three, but in this case, the fantasy condenses particular perceptions of African culture and mythology.

Angoualima's magical powers and shapeshifting capability is a satirical nod to Anansi, the Ashanti trickster, who figures in many African (and Caribbean) folktales. From a more critical perspective, however, Angoualima also corresponds to the Western projection of the African as a "primitive" or "savage." Voiced by the likes of Hegel in the nineteenth century, this stereotypical projection was famously denounced by Chinua Achebe in his reading of Conrad's *Heart of Darkness*.[27] Nicknamed the "Judge of Darkness," Angoualima reportedly possesses a penis, a *"thing"* as Grégoire calls it on numerous occasions, of gigantic proportions (40). In *La légende du sexe surdimensionné des Noirs*,[28] Serge Bilé argues that the phantasmagorical construction of the comparatively larger sexual organ of the Black male aims to dehumanize him and present him as a savage.[29] In other words, like Hegel's idea that "The Negro . . . exhibits the natural man in his completely wild and untamed state,"[30] the popular myth related to the Black male's oversized penis serves to perpetuate the stereotype that Africans are only gifted in areas that relate to primary instincts and physical capabilities, thus denying them the intellectual capacity to think or reason. What is particularly perverse, Bilé explains, is that many Blacks have internalized the stereotype through the insidious ways in which the cliché has been reinforced by various forms of popular media and particularly in pornography. Additionally, the widely held perception of the Black male's gigantic sex has led lesser-endowed individuals (Blacks and whites alike) to an inferiority complex characterized by sexual anxieties and feelings of inadequacy.

While *African Psycho* parodies the ways in which the media exaggerates and perpetuates the stereotype by calling it "the fifth limb" (40), the text also feeds off our own expectations by revealing how the stereotype affects our cultural biases and anxieties. According to Wood, the figure of the monster and/or the serial killer represents a surplus or excess of sexual energy that has been repressed by societal norms.[31] At the same time, in embodying a form of sexual difference, it also represents the threat of castration. On a first level, *African Psycho* plays into the sexual anxiety (or fantasy) of witnessing the Black monstrous male raping and murdering the white woman. But on another more important level, the text criticizes the particularly perverse effects of racist stereotypes on the African male. In *Black Skins, White Masks*, Fanon argues that the racist attitudes of colonialism have had some particular pernicious effects on the psyche of colonized people, creating a deep complex of inferiority. On the one hand, Angoualima might elude the complex by embodying the collective fantasy of the African psycho serial killer—he is not "an ordinary being" (43), but a bona fide "monster" (40)—and sexual predator bestowed with supernatural attributes and abilities, such as the capacity "to make himself invisible" (39). Grégoire, on the other hand, is not immune to the anxieties associated with the complex. One telling way this is manifested is in his sexual inadequacy and impotence at the moment he is about to rape and kill the "Girl in White" (74–75). Most notably, he blames his failure on the errancies of desire, on the ways in which his sexual desire made him veer off his plan and err as a consequence: "Instead of going straight to the point, instead of killing her nice and neat, suddenly there was this idiotic desire to ride her frontally, to understand what the Great Master Angoualima felt when he raped his victims with his size XXXL *thing . . .*" (81). In fact, his failure is in many ways connected to his inferiority complex toward the legend of Angoualima. Living in the shadow of the myth, of the man with the "fifth limb," he is incapable of rising to the task because he is inhibited by his feelings of inadequacy to the standard of "Blackness" set forth by Angoualima.

Grégoire's phantom relationship with his fictional mentor presents a complex psychological ramification pertaining to the role(s) of the imaginary other in the construction of subjectivity. Grégoire's account of Angoualima's appearance during his visits to his grave corresponds to the extraordinary qualities attributed to him by the media. Partly because he shares the same history as a "picked-up child" (8), Grégoire believes he is predestined to follow on the same path of greatness:

> I recognized myself in each of his gestures, which the whole country decried. I felt admiration for him. In a certain way he preceded me in the type of existence I dreamed of for myself. To fend off despair, I persuaded myself that I resembled him, that his destiny and mine had the same arc, and that little by little I would eventually climb each step until my head . . . deserved a crown of laurels. (3)

Grégoire not only considers Angoualima his mentor and identifies with him as he represents an ego-ideal, he also relates to Angoualima as a son to his father. But Angoualima is not just an imaginary father for Grégoire, he is God Almighty:

> . . . lo and behold the Great Master appeared before me, Imperial, Divine, Colossal, Powerful, Sublime, equal to himself . . . but I immediately lowered my gaze, this mythical character, this charismatic character is none other than my own God and consequently you don't return God's gaze, you are content with believing Him to be alive, eternal, unchangeable, omniscient. . . . (85)

Angoualima is not a beneficent God and his reign is a negative theocracy; he willfully abuses his subjects, insulting Grégoire for his incompetence (87–90). This interaction between Grégoire and Angoualima speaks eloquently of the self-devaluating dimension of Grégoire's neurosis. Moreover, the conversation also clearly sets the stage for a dialectical encounter between self and other.

From the onset, the text presents the ways in which the subject, the "I," is entangled into various intersubjective relationships predicated on recognition. On the one hand, Grégoire explains that his deepest fear is that his deeds will remain "unnoticed" (2), and on the other, he desperately seeks the validation of his existence in his conversations with Angoualima.

Grégoire is under the impression that he will gain recognition by mimicking the acts of the "Great Master." As Fanon tells us in *Black Skins, White Masks*, the drama of Veneuse is that he desperately seeks the recognition and approval of white society, but he erroneously believes he can do so by becoming "white" and rejecting his own racial identity. Grégoire is also in desperate need of recognition, but the validation he seeks is that of a phantasmagoric projection of "African-ness," thus the errancy of his desire partly lies in the belief he has to live up to the myth of African monstrosity. His desire for recognition is further complicated by the fact that the imaginary other is an abusive father whom he also considers his "Master," even as he admits that it is not in his best interest to constantly seek his approval.

The relationship between Angoualima and Grégoire seems to perpetuate the dialectical structure of colonial subjectivity by implying that the postcolonial subject must similarly compare himself to an "Other" in order to attain self-realization. In the chapter entitled "Black Man and Recognition," Fanon argues that the Black man's self-assertion is dependent upon being recognized by the "Other."[32] Adapting Hegel's concept of self-consciousness, Fanon further explains:

> Man is human only to the extent to which he tries to impose himself on another man in order to be recognized by him. As long as he has not been effectively recognized by the other, it is this other who remains the focus of his actions. His human worth and reality depend on this other and on his recognition by the other. It is in this other that the meaning of life is condensed.[33]

The problem for the Black man in former French colonies, argues Fanon, is that he did not have to fight for his freedom to affirm his being, and therefore is unsure of whether the white man considers him as equal. For his part, Grégoire exemplifies the consequences of configuring this other as a phantasmagoric projection, an ego-ideal from whom recognition is perpetually delayed for an ego like his, who confines himself within a structure of self-alienation. In Hegel's account of self-consciousness, the slave/bondsman does not come into being by seeking the validation of the master/lord; rather he transcends his condition by deriving satisfaction from his own labor. This is precisely what Grégoire fails to do because in lieu of affirming his own being through his own becoming, he errs into desiring the recognition of others by mimicking them. Even as Angoualima tells him "it is not by aping what I accomplished that you will get people talking about you" (87), he remains under the spell of the powerful image of his imaginary mentor. Grégoire's errancy is even more surprising since he indicates quite early in the narrative the pitfalls of such an approach to self-determination:

> Now only if I could convince myself that it is not in my interest to compare myself to [Angoualima] or desperately seek his approval as a master of crime, I might be able to start working with a free spirit. To each his own manner and personality. (7)

The permanent shadow of Angoualima keeps Grégoire in the dark, blind to the potential of attaining subjectivity through his own free will and self-determination. Consequently, Angoualima's hold over Grégoire speaks of the pervasive influence of media images over individual subjectivity.

Prefacing his analysis of contemporary Cameroonian cartoons, Mbembé points out:

> In spite of its claim to represent presence, immediacy, and facticity, what is special about an image is its "likeness"—that is, its ability to annex and mime what it represents, while, in the very act of representation, masking the power of its own arbitrariness, its own potential for opacity, simulacrum, and distortion.[34]

In *African Psycho*, the media's construction of Angoualima as a figure of mythical proportion not only emphasizes the media's propensity toward exaggeration,[35] but also the ways in which it creates cartoonish, larger-than-life, even hyperreal, public personalities. At the same time, the overwhelming emphasis given to the greatly exaggerated exploits of the real "African Psycho" (i.e., Angoualima) highlights the media's tendency to glorify and sensationalize violence to draw in the public's attention. More specifically, however, the novel allegorizes the ways in which these imaginary models promote structures of alienation, simulacra that individuals simulate at the cost of their own individuality and authenticity, even when these models are psychotic murderers.

## Spectacle and Subjectivity: A Metanarrative Play of Mirrors

*African Psycho* makes a particular point in stressing the spectacular dimension of societal life in contemporary Africa. Although the African context is clearly situated, it is neither the precolonial Africa of Achebe's *Things Fall Apart*,[36] the colonial setting of Conrad's *Heart of Darkness*, nor the neocolonial post-independence nation-state of Sembène's *Xala*.[37] Rather, it is a postcolonial Africa, which not only remains entangled in historical structures of subjugation and alienation, but has also actualized internal processes of self-alienation by incorporating the neoliberal signifying order of spectacle and simulacra. These aspects are continuously emphasized through the multiple references to the popular media and the role it plays in shaping the collective imaginary, the consciousness of individuals, and institutions of the state. The importance of media theatrics and the gaze is considerably emphasized throughout the text. For example, the "What Then? Trust Me!" television interview parodies the bogus, nonsensical content of television shows as well as the ways in which live television plays with camera angles and montage to add a dramatic, if not dizzying, effect (41–48). In another instance, Grégoire describes at length the ways in which the courthouse is a stage for public prosecutors to practice their oratory skills to the greatest enjoyment of the audience: "I felt like I was going to the movies because we had to stand in line, except that at the courthouse the shows were free and the actors stood a few feet away from us, just like at the theater" (30). Moreover, Mabanckou's novel also stresses the fascination for and popularity of violence in the media by mocking the ways in which it hijacks all aspects of the news from local politics to music and entertainment. In thus representing the society of the spectacle, its structures, and its practices, *African Psycho* maintains close proximity to *American Psycho* and, at a slightly longer distance, *Elementary Particles*.

The titular substitution of "American" by "African" calls our attention to the African, evoking perceived differences between the two locales and their related cultures while at the same time heightening our expectations.

But amid the expected binary construction between American and African, between the first and the developing world, and the paradigmatic consumerist excesses of one culture related to the relative poverty of the other, what stands out is that the ideologies of the culture industry are similarly emphasized and criticized in both texts, marking this critique as a point of convergence between two narratives that diverge considerably. Both Bateman and Grégoire's murderous desires seem to be ignited and fueled by the pervasive and hyperreal quality of images of phallocratic violence as well as a similar cultural obsession for brutal psychopaths. While both struggle to find their own voice amid the constant bombardment of visual noise, each text addresses these issues from opposite angles of the spectrum, retracing the struggle for self-determination and processes of subjectivization from different points of departure.

*African Psycho* undermines the preliminary effect caused in the titular substitution of the African for the American by glossing over potential cultural differences and focusing instead on the anxieties and neuroses of the main character. In *American Psycho*, Bateman's voice is produced by the collective imaginary as a pastiche and conglomerate of media images: a flickering stream of thought that characterizes the schizophrenic hallucinations of the fragmented postmodern psyche. Ellis's narrator is an emotional blank slate, a character that provokes the reader to *project* their affect to fill Bateman's psychological void.

In contrast, Grégoire's consciousness presents a very individuated form of psychosis; a psychosexual disorder rooted in abandonment neurosis, which is further exacerbated as a result of his relationship with Angoualima's ghost. The "I" of Grégoire is an Other that is as alienating as it is self-alienating. In this sense, he is again perhaps much closer to Houellebecq's Bruno. Accordingly, by resisting the narrative process of identification, the reader is prompted to *react* affectively against Grégoire's overbearing psychological discourse, even as they might at first sympathize with his predicament.

As an orphan with no parental guidance or opportunity for identification through a familial process of simultaneous recognition and misrecognition in the mirror phase, Grégoire errs into choosing Angoualima as both a father figure and an ego-ideal. He finds himself in a double bind: his

psychotic neurosis linked to his feeling of abandonment makes him idol-
ize an idealized larger-than-life psychopath. Grégoire's voice is that of the
tortured psychopathological discourse of a character whose fractured self-
image is trapped in the shadows of an idealized Other or ego-ideal. It also
expresses the tragic predicament of the unrealized self who paradoxically
desires to be recognized by a figurative Other; an image which is not only a
figment of his imagination, but also a castrating father, a tyrannical figure
of God-like proportions whose law is as debilitating as it is unavoidable.

Grégoire's desire to emulate and please his idol is emblematic of the
errancy of the desire for recognition in the dialectic encounter between self
and this Other who is "realer than the real." His attempts to mimic and
seek validation from this "Master" only lead to a series of failures, highlighting both his impotency and incapacity as a character. Consequently,
Grégoire's misguided desire leads to his overall failure as an authentic self-
consciousness. In a sense, the novel proposes that Grégoire's failed endeavor
to transcend his condition points to the shortcomings of a dialectical model
of desire and subjectivity, especially when this desire is ignited and fueled
by the simulacra manufactured by the society of the spectacle.

Although both *American Psycho* and *African Psycho* satirize the vicissitudes of media culture, their strategies differ significantly because they
each put into play a very distinct "I/Eye." There is a way in which the
psychopathology of each character, or the apparent lack thereof, can be
mapped on the effects it produces on the reader. Ellis's text implicates the
reader into adopting Bateman's point of view by creating a psychological
vacuum and using cathartic violence as the only release from an otherwise
boring and senseless narrative, even if the descriptions become increasingly
more unbearable. Mabanckou's novel lures the reader in with the *promise*
of violence, both by the paratextual reference to its predecessor and by the
commissive that marks the beginning of the text, but without ever providing it, potentially disappointing the reader at a level similar to Grégoire's
own frustration. Consequently, although the narrative elements of each
text differ considerably, both novels address the reader's desire for textual
violence by involving them affectively. But whereas Ellis's novel suggests
that there is "NO EXIT" to the violent processes of psychological disloca-
tion and objectification at work in contemporary consumer culture, *African*

*Psycho* shows us that there is potentially a way out: it pertains to eluding the self-defeating dialectics of desire.

Simultaneously, there is a broader, metatextual commentary to be found in Grégoire's failures and errancies and in the multiple intertextual references contained in *African Psycho*. Angoualima is a transcendental signifier who is not only cast as an Other, but is also a series of doubles: it is a Master and a God, it is both real and imaginary, and it is both the double and the shadow of Bateman, the American Psycho. Following Fanon, and to some extent Ferguson and Mbembé, we can address Grégoire's predicament as a telling illustration of the "pitfalls of national consciousness" when national or continental identity is constructed according to imaginary constructions of self and other. There is a way in which Grégoire's failure to reconcile his own image with that of his ego-ideal speaks of the disjunction between the postcolonial subject and the discursive construction of the African male as a Monstrous Other. Accordingly, not only does Grégoire fail to live up to the expectations of his mentor, he also fails to live up to the expectations of its (presupposed) Western audience. John Walsh argues that through the 2007 translation of the novel, "Mabanckou now reaches a much wider audience, and one that may soon come to question its own complacency with regard to generally accepted ideas about Africa."[38] However, the novel also points out that the structures of alienation that plague the character, and by extension, the African subject, are also self-imposed; it is undeniable that there is a body of African literature that feeds off the stereotypical projection of this Monstrous Other by transfiguring him as a ruthless dictator.[39]

From a different angle, by making specific references to infamous French literary figures *African Psycho* provides a self-reflexive commentary on the question of literature, not only in terms of its relation to the performativity of language or in issues pertaining to the ethics of representational violence, but also regarding the validity or recognition of a "newer" work or literary tradition in terms of canonical potential. As Walsh points out, "Much like its protagonist, the 'African Psycho,' Mabanckou looks to lure in the reader with apparent pulp only to surprise later with the realization that some greater form of literature is at issue."[40] There is a transfigurative way in which the narrative voice makes a claim for the status of francophone literature vis-à-vis the French Canon in a way parallel to how the postcolonial subject yearns for recognition by an authoritative figure. This idea is clearly implied when Grégoire reacts to the reader's implicit assumption that he is somewhat dim-witted because he only reads comic books:

> But Wait! Don't Get the Wrong Idea, I also threw myself into reading what people call great literature, I did. To each his own. What I was looking for, personally, was action, fear, which I found above all in pulp literature. People said, however, that in order to be an educated man, you had to immerse yourself in the likes of Proust, Genet, Céline, Rousseau and a great many others of that ilk. (15–16)

Evident in Grégoire's intervention is the traditional concept that "great" literature "educates" its readers, an oft-touted yet strongly contested criterion for canonicity. To draw an interesting parallel, it could be argued that Grégoire's anxious discourse and subsequent impotency parodies the sterility of the work operating under Bloom's concept of the "Anxiety of Influence."[41] Consequently, Grégoire's erroneous belief that mimicking his "Father/Master" will bring him widespread recognition similarly marks the failure of an oedipal model for literary greatness.

Situating the novel in the broader context of discursive formations about Africa, Walsh claims, "Mabanckou's approach as a writer is to inscribe violence in his text with the aim of provoking the reader into a dialogue about the causes of violence and about the responsibilities that Africa and the West carry, in order to facilitate a less stereotypical representation of Africa."[42] The paratextual reference to Ellis's novel returns us to some of the political implications alluded to by Ferguson in the introductory section of this chapter. Addressing the complex relationship between Africa and the West, especially as it relates to ideas about modernity and standards of living, Ferguson observes that "Claims of likeness, in this context, constitute not a copying, but a shadowing, even a haunting—a declaration of compatibility, an aspiration to membership and inclusion in the world, and sometimes also an assertion of responsibility."[43] If we consider the triangulation between Grégoire, Angoualima, and Bateman and the titular substitution of the American by the African, Grégoire's desire to be recognized by Angoualima and his failure to mimic him speaks of the African's desire to "exist" according to American or Western norms, which has had negative consequences on the self-determining process of African nation-states in the neoliberal world order. Consequently, what remains at stake are the very definitions of concepts and standards of modernity and globalization that are fundamentally Western and colonial in essence.

# Conclusion

> I'm weeping for myself, unable to find solace in any of this, crying out,
> sobbing, "I just want to be loved," cursing the earth and everything
> I have been taught: principles, distinctions, choices, morals, compro-
> mises, knowledge, unity, prayer—all of it wrong, without any final
> purpose. All it came down to was: die or adapt.
> —Bret Easton Ellis, *American Psycho*

In the introduction, I make a passing reference to a scene from Spike Jonze's *Adaptation* to bring into focus the central prominence of desire in the formation of the subject. But the film also exemplifies how archetypes of masculinity can thrive in a carefully orchestrated balancing act between fact and fiction. As the story unfolds and the central character Charlie eponymously "adapts" to the circumstances dictated by his environment, the film provides a telling example wherein an anxiety-ridden male subject is able to "Man Up" to vanquish his own shortcomings. However, this accomplishment paradoxically requires Charlie's story to conform to prevailing plot conventions that aim at narrative resolution in a gesture that betrays his own desires. Faced with the incongruity between his quest for originality and fidelity and a harsh reality that mocks his pathetic predispositions,

Charlie eventually redirects his efforts into a more comforting, self-affirming fantasy.

Following veteran screenwriter McKee's advice to "wow them in the end" because the "last act makes a film," Charlie discards his original desire to remain faithful to Orlean's whimsical narrative structure devoid of plot. Consequently, the film transitions from a schizophrenic series of fragmentary, digressive, and self-reflexive episodes that chronicle the screenwriter's struggle to adapt the book into a formulaic narrative that reassembles all the different characters' stories into one unified narrative tapestry. The finished product is a film with two easily discernible parts: on the one hand, the film is constructed as an experimental series of supposedly "false starts and wrong approaches," and on the other, a cliché third act that mixes in sex, drugs, and violence and provides narrative resolution as Charlie emerges triumphant by finishing the screenplay and kissing the girl (Amelia, whom he was too timid to kiss previously).

The first part is a Deleuzian "assemblage"[1] of intertextual multiplicities and represents Charlie's errancies of desire: a wandering patchwork of self-reflexive projections and commentaries that revolve around Charlie's repeated mistrials and is interwoven on-screen with his own failures to adapt to the psychopathological realities of his everyday existence. The focalization on Charlie's own insecurities is in fact introduced at the very beginning of the film. As the opening credits roll on a completely dark screen, the audience hears him in voiceover delivering a rambling laundry list of self-disparaging views. Charlie's thoughts provide a telling framework that foreshadows the idea that the film is as much about the process of cinematic adaptation as it is about adaptation per se, with Charlie as a case study for the archetypical "Omega male" close in kind to Bruno from *Elementary Particles*. From an evolutionary perspective, Charlie's struggle to adapt Orlean's book provides an experiential framework that puts into question whether he can adapt to the existential circumstances that seem to exceed him.

Haunted by a debilitating pathos, Charlie is periodically portrayed fantasizing about various women, including Orlean (whom he admires), yet he repeatedly fails to even speak to them, mostly because of an unnerving lack of confidence informed by his self-perceived shortcomings. After he avoids meeting with Orlean as a last-ditch attempt to rescue his script due to his paralyzing shyness, Charlie asks his twin brother Donald to assist him with his screenplay. Donald is a fabrication, an alter ego who, in many ways, acts and thinks as Charlie wishes he could—he is overconfident and extroverted, successfully courts women, and is shamelessly writing a formulaic Hollywood script about a schizophrenic serial killer that employs every cliché in the screenwriter source book. Whereas Charlie routinely mocks Donald through most of the film for his brazen behavior and unashamed credulity, when the style of the film begins to effectively mutate, Charlie's acceptance of Donald is a sign he finally realizes the imperative to adapt to the continuous variations of his environment as a key to survival and success.[2] As a foil to Charlie, Donald reveals how his brother's misdirected passions toward ideals of fidelity, both in screenwriting as in life, are his downfall by affirming, "You are what you love, not what loves you" in an epiphanous moment before he dies in a car crash.

While the second part and climactic third act might bear witness to the overwhelming cultural logic of plot structure and narrative progress, it could also be argued that the film in its entirety, as a combination of multiple point-of-views and fragmentary digressions as well as a more linear and cathartic ending, can be interpreted as an adaptation that has trumped the original in order to palliate its perceived flaws.[3] To that purpose, Lawrence Raw explains insightfully, "through adaptation, we learn to make connections between ourselves and the people around us, analyzing problems and their causes and finding solutions while engaging critically with various texts in different walks of life."[4] The final product is an affirmation that adaptation, in both its creative and cognitive guises, is a process of difference and repetition that betrays the ideal of fidelity. Betrayal is a necessary gesture for Blanchot's Orpheus as it is for the Barthesian lover[5] for it is both a constitutive gesture of the subject as well as testimony to the fluctuations of one's own desires to adapt to new circumstances.

Ultimately, *Adaptation* is as much about the screenwriting practice of adaptation as it is a reflection on the multiple, diverse processes thereof. In a sense, Charlie is the metaphoric embodiment of such processes; his struggle and ultimate triumph, a symbolic journey. By the film's conclusion, Charlie has done away with the phantasmagoric ideal of Orlean (by recasting her as a lonely, washed-out adulteress), fused his alter-ego Donald into an ego-ideal he becomes (by killing him off and absorbing his self-confidence), undermined the dialectics of McKee the Master (by discarding his advice and resorting to a deus ex machina), and eclipsed his self-doubts (as his voiceover narration synchs to the visuals actualizing themselves on screen), thereby absorbing all lines of flight, the schizoid as well as the oedipal, and has *adapted* to the world, free of the anxieties and neuroses that once beset his existence, toward new beginnings.

## To Adapt or Die?

*Adaptation* offers a window into the potentialities of change as progressive and liberating. However, since the film takes an abrupt turn from an assemblage of partially factual episodes to full narrative fiction, one can also infer that the possibilities for one to adapt in such meaningful ways are mostly fictitious, more akin to the myths and mythologies that shape the cultures and identities of men as more cohesive beings than their chaotic becomings. In Joseph Campbell's formulation of the "Monomyth" or the "Hero's Journey," the hero must undergo a symbolic rebirth and resurrection before restoring his world,[6] so it is perhaps no coincidence that Charlie is only able to find himself after the death of his alter-ego Donald.

"The Death of the Subject" or "The Death of Man" is the oft-used phrase used to coin the poststructuralist and/or posthumanist decentralization of the rational subject of enlightenment thought and the diminution of modern ideals of scientific reason and progress with which it was associated. Inspired by Nietzsche's proclamations that "God is dead" and that "Man is something that must be overcome," various strands of poststructuralist thought have led a wide-ranging assault on the concept of the Western European, phallocratic subject as an embodiment of the humanistic ideas of free-will and self-determination, as well as the narratives of human emancipation and progress he stimulated.

In *The Order of Things*, Foucault scrutinizes the historical conditions of knowledge that gave birth to this subject and its subsequent placement at the top of a hierarchy of living beings; that is, "à la place du roi." He argues that "Man" is a product of various structures of institutional and discursive subjugation and oppression, and in the concluding pages, he envisions his disappearance:

> If those arrangements [of knowledge that invented man] were to disappear as they appeared, if some event which we can at the moment do no more than sense the possibility—without knowing either what its form will be or what it promises—were to cause them to crumble, as the ground of Classical thought did, at the end of the eighteenth century, then one can certainly wager that man would be erased, like a face drawn in sand at the edge of the sea.[7]

But, as an eradication of a central locus of knowledge and signification, the "death of man" also implies a rebirth, or a new birth. In *Wretched of the Earth*, Fanon concludes by articulating an edifying critique of European humanism and calls for a "new history of Man" that steers away from "the taints, the sickness, and the inhumanity of Europe."[8]

In contrast to such rebirth narratives, the artificial yet necessary organizational pattern of this work into chapters presents itself as a story of *regression*. As in *Adaptation*, this aporia reveals the deconstructive logic of narrative construction and at the same time interrogates the central role that processes of narrativization play in organizing human experiences. More importantly, however, if my objective in writing this book were to progressively work toward presenting a cohesive picture of transnational postmodern subjectivities operating outside or in the margins of structures of oppression and colonization, then I have failed. In other words, if the rebirth or emancipation of the human subject is the sought-after ideal of progress, what I have proposed in the preceding pages is alarmingly retrogressive.

The masculine subjects examined here—Lurie, Bruno and Michel, Bateman, and Grégoire—present paternalistic, oedipal and/or reterritorialized subjectivities, whose errancies of desire work to reinforce existing Western European or North American capitalistic norms. Lurie is a vestige of the imperial mindset of white male privilege, and Bruno and Michel exhibit characteristic traits of unresolved oedipality, wherein heteronormative male desire operates according to the Lacanian "lack." A similar paradigm haunts Grégoire, whose subject position is additionally coerced by the specters of dialectical desire proper to colonial and postcolonial subject relationships. And while Bateman's subjectivity is a psychological void, a schizophrenic pastiche of postmodern American media culture, his desire is reterritorialized according to the pathos of consumer capitalism and cultural imperialism. Accordingly, the narratives highlight processes of phallogocentric subjectivation and the violence contained therein, even as the immanent critique of the texts operate self-reflexively to denounce these mechanisms.

Thus, the portraits of transatlantic masculinities provided in these texts are a far cry from the more undetermined and differentiated subjectivities proposed by Deleuze and Guattari, or the emancipated "nomadic subject" articulated by Rosi Braidotti. The analyses performed here demonstrate how the errancies of desire dislocate hegemonic and nonhegemonic, as well as colonial and imperial configurations of identity inscribed within geopolitical time and space only to reposition them within a global framework of mediated and monstrous masculinities. Conversely, the fragmented and schizophrenic narrative structure of *Adaptation* actualizes visually the vagrancies of the desiring subject as a rhizomatic multiplicity. In contrast to the narrative and ideological determinisms that frame the masculine subjects presented in the texts, *Adaptation* portrays processes of subjectivities that emphasize the fluid and regenerative potential of desire. Even when the differential lines of flight of the first two acts are eventually harnessed back into a singular unity toward the end, the obvious artificiality of constructing a cohesive narrative is revealed as a coerced subterfuge.

Consequently, my failure to provide any seemingly satisfying resolution also marks my intent, for my objective has never been to perform a narrative of progress, a retelling or mimicry of a (dialectical) struggle toward emancipation. The cultural and literary imaginings of masculinity analyzed herein are eventually reterritorialized by the unrelenting forces exerted by the realities of the everyday, naturalistic scientism, as well as the cultural logic of Hegelianism and consumer capitalism, even as processes and formations of subjectivity cross cultural and national boundaries. In other words, rather than producing a narrative of emancipation, the formal progression of this study regresses into investigating conservative and reactionary—and therefore, fraught—images of masculine desire and male subjectivity. The not-so-arbitrary repartition of the chapters according to the settings of their subject texts is effective in this way. The critical work performed here provides a transnational perspective on issues surrounding masculinity that is both enduring and relevant. The novels of Coetzee, Ellis, Houellebecq, and Mabanckou remind us that conventional gender configurations and processes of identity formation that hinge on the expression of sexual violence and oppression are as unbecoming as they are persistent. Accordingly, the absence of a narrative of emancipation points both to the illusionary quality of narratives of progress, and to the treacherous maze that differentiated transnational subjectivities must navigate under virtual, past, and present conditions of globalization. While there may be much to be celebrated in the dissolution of national boundaries and the nation-state in the wake of transnational movements, there remain a number of concerns with what Shu-mei Shih and Françoise Lionnet have identified as "globalization from above."⁹ Characterized by the instability of global markets and the dubious ideologies of the financial (and political) institutions that support them, the homogenizing forces of global media cultures, and the increasingly oppressive apparatuses of state surveillance and control, the material realities that inform the cultural predicament of a nascent transnational citizenry remain in proximity to problematic constructs of hegemonic masculinity and social dominance.

Notes

Bibliography

Index

# Notes

## Introduction

1. "The End of Men" is the title of an article by Hanna Rosin published in the July/August 2010 issue of *Atlantic,* https://www.theatlantic.com/magazine/archive/2010/07/the-end-of-men/308135/. The article was later expanded into a book-long study of the same name with the added subtitle *And the Rise of Women* (New York: Riverhead Books, 2012).

2. See Elizabeth Badinter, *XY, De l'identité masculine* (Paris: Odile Jacob, 1992), wherein she retraces first the crises of masculinity in seventeenth- and eighteenth-century Europe that concerned the bourgeoisie and the aristocracy, and then, from the end of the nineteenth century to the interwar period, the subsequent crises linked to the industrial revolution and democracy, woman suffrage, and the rise of nationalism and fascism (25–41). In the postwar period in the United States, as the feminist movement began questioning traditional gender roles, social studies on masculinity in the seventies likewise reexamined accepted definitions of manhood (15–16). See also Todd W. Reeser, *Masculinity in Theory* (Oxford, UK: Wiley-Blackwell, 2010), 27–28.

3. The phrase "strong, silent type" is a passing homage to James Gandolfini's Tony Soprano TV character who in therapy sessions kept lamenting the loss of the ideal masculine type seemingly embodied by Gary Cooper.

4. See Jack S. Kahn, *An Introduction to Masculinities* (Oxford, UK: Wiley-Blackwell, 2009), 172–81, and Stephen Whitehead and Frank J. Barrett, "The Sociology of Masculinity," in *The Masculinities Reader,* ed. Stephen Whitehead and Frank J. Barrett (Cambridge, UK: Polity, 2001), 7–8.

5. See, for example, Erik Hayden, "Does Masculinity Need to Be 'Reimagined'?" *Atlantic,* September 21, 2010, https://www.theatlantic.com/national/archive/2010/09/does-masculinity-need-to-be-reimagined/344099/, and R. Albert Mohler Jr., "Man Up or Man Down? Newsweek Redefines Masculinity," *Christian Post,* September 24, 2010, https://www.christianpost.com/news/man-up-or-man-down-newsweek-redefines-masculinity.html.

6. See, for example, Tiffany May, "A 'Masculinity Crisis'? China Says the Boys Are Not All Right," *New York Times,* February 5, 2021, https://www.nytimes.com/2021/02/05/world/asia/china-masculinity-schoolboys.html, and Pankaj Mishra, "The Crisis in Modern

Masculinity," *Guardian*, March 17, 2018, https://www.theguardian.com/books/2018/mar
/17/the-crisis-in-modern-masculinity, for a global perspective; for a report on American
men, see Alia Wong, "The Many Possible Meanings of the 'Masculinity Crisis'," *Atlantic*,
June 26, 2018, https://www.theatlantic.com/family/archive/2018/06/why-american-men
-are-in-crisis/563807/.

7. See Jackson Katz, *Man Enough? Donald Trump, Hillary Clinton, and the Politics of Presidential Masculinity* (Northampton, MA: Interlink Books, 2016).

8. See Liza Featherstone, "Josh Hawley and the Republican Obsession with Manliness," *New York Times*, December 4, 2021, https://www.nytimes.com/2021/12/04/opinion
/josh-hawley-republican-manliness.html, and Joel Mathis, "Why the Republican Party
Loves Grumpy Middle-Aged Men," *Week*, April 12, 2022, https://theweek.com/us/1012470
/why-the-republican-party-loves-grumpy-middle-aged-men.

9. See Stephen Marche, "How Toxic Masculinity Poisoned the 2016 Election," *Esquire*, March 9, 2016, https://www.esquire.com/news-politics/news/a42802/toxic-masculine
-discourse/. Even though the term "toxic masculinity" has garnered considerable cultural
traction, I have decided not to use it, as it has been notably misunderstood by pundits who
may assume a universal cause for sexist or violent behavior in male subjects, which is a
mischaracterization of R. W. Connell's groundbreaking sociological research on masculinities, as Michael Salter points out in "The Problem with a Fight against Toxic Masculinity," *Atlantic*, February 27, 2019, https://www.theatlantic.com/health/archive/2019/02
/toxic-masculinity-history/583411/.

10. See, for example, Michael Kimmel, "Trump's Angry White Men," *World Today*,
December 15, 2017, https://www.chathamhouse.org/publications/the-world-today/2017-12
/trumps-angry-white-men; Stephen Rosen, "Donald Trump and the Crisis of Masculinity," *CounterPunch*, February 26, 2016, https://www.counterpunch.org/2016/02/26/donald
-trump-and-the-crisis-of-masculinity/; and Chidanand Rajghatta, "Donald Trump's Vote
Bank: Angry White Males with No College Degrees," *Economic Times*, July 28, 2016, https://
economictimes.indiatimes.com/news/international/world-news/donald-trumps-vote-bank
-angry-white-males-with-no-college-degrees/articleshow/53428529.cms.

11. See, for example, Stephen Marche, "Donald Trump Is a Parody of American Manhood," *LA Times*, March 27, 2016, https://www.latimes.com/opinion/op-ed/la-oe-marche
-trump-masculine-overcompensation-20160527-snap-story.html, and David French, "Trump's
Counterfeit Masculinity," *National Review*, April 18, 2016, https://www.nationalreview.com
/2016/04/donald-trump-counterfeit-masculinity-feminism-dream/.

12. See Paul Krugman, "The Angry White Male Caucus," *New York Times*, October
1, 2018, https://www.nytimes.com/2018/10/01/opinion/kavanaugh-white-male-privilege
.html, and Jackson Katz, "Are We Witnessing a Crisis in White Male Masculinity," *Newsweek*, January 14, 2018, https://www.newsweek.com/are-we-witnessing-crisis-white-male
-masculinity-781048.

13. See Eugene Scott, "Data about the Capitol Rioters Serves Another Blow to the White, Working-Class Trump-Supporter Narrative," *Washington Post*, April 12, 2021, https://www.washingtonpost.com/politics/2021/04/12/data-about-capitol-rioters-serves-another-blow-white-working-class-trump-supporter-narrative/.

14. The phrase was originally coined by Tarana Burke and later popularized by Hollywood actress Alyssa Milano through social media with the MeToo hashtag. See Cristela Guerra, "Where Did 'Me Too' Come from? Activist Tarana Burke, Long before Hashtags," *Boston Globe*, October 17, 2017, https://www.bostonglobe.com/lifestyle/2017/10/17/alyssa-milano-credits-activist-tarana-burke-with-founding-metoo-movement-years-ago/o2Jv29v6ljObkKPTPB9KGP/story.html.

15. See Karla Adam and William Booth, "A year after It Began, Has #MeToo become a Global Movement?" *Washington Post*, October 5, 2018, https://www.washingtonpost.com/world/a-year-after-it-began-has-metoo-become-a-global-movement/2018/10/05/1fc0929e-c71a-11e8-9c0f-2ffaf6d422aa_story.html; see also Pardis Mahdavi, "How #MeToo Became a Global Movement," *Foreign Affairs*, March 6, 2018, https://www.foreignaffairs.com/articles/2018-03-06/how-metoo-became-global-movement.

16. See Rana Ayyub, "In India, Women Are No Longer Ready to Stay Silent," *Guardian*, October 21, 2018, https://www.theguardian.com/commentisfree/2018/oct/21/india-women-silent-metoo-movement-battle.

17. See Noam Schpancer, "Is Masculinity in Crisis? And If So, What Should Be Done?" *Psychology Today*, June 24, 2020, https://www.psychologytoday.com/us/blog/insight-therapy/202006/is-masculinity-in-crisis-if-so-what-should-be-done.

18. Even though most welcomed this expansionary change, it also triggered the infamous "Canon Wars" of the 1980s and 1990s that pitted so-called "Traditionalists" against "Multiculturalists." For anyone not old enough to remember the debate (or interested in revisiting it), see Rachel Donadio, "Revisiting the Canon Wars" and its associated reading list, *New York Times*, September 16, 2007, https://www.nytimes.com/2007/09/16/books/review/Donadio-t.html?action=click&contentCollection=Sunday%20Book%20Review&module=RelatedCoverage&region=EndOfArticle&pgtype=article.

19. Anne-Marie Slaughter, *Unfinished Business: Women Men Work Family*, (New York: Random House, 2015), 126.

20. See American Psychological Association, Boys and Men Guidelines Group, *APA Guidelines for Psychological Practice with Boys and Men*, August 2018, http://www.apa.org/about/policy/psychological-practice-boys-men-guidelines.pdf; Jessica Schladebeck, "'Traditional Masculinity' Officially Labeled 'Harmful' by the American Psychological Association" *Daily News*, January 9, 2019, https://www.nydailynews.com/news/world/ny-news-traditional-masculinity-harmful-psychological-association-20190109-story.html.

21. See Alex McElroy, "This Isn't Your Old Toxic Masculinity. It Has Taken an Insidious New Form," *New York Times*, January 13, 2022, https://www.nytimes.com/2022/01/13

/opinion/toxic-masculinity.html, wherein the author explains, "Even as men's groups committed to positive change gain prominence, our society still broadly enforces traditional masculinity norms and restrictions. And online there are plenty of spaces where extremely toxic behavior is encouraged and applauded."

22. J. M. Coetzee, *Disgrace* (New York: Penguin Books, 1999).

23. Michel Houellebecq, *Les Particules élémentaires* (Paris: Flammarion, 1998) and Michel Houellebecq, *The Elementary Particles*, trans. Frank Wynne (New York: Vintage, 2000).

24. Bret Easton Ellis, *American Psycho* (New York: Vintage, 1991).

25. Alain Mabanckou, *African Psycho*, trans. Christine Schwartz Hartley (New York: Soft Skull Press, 2007).

26. See Guy de Maupassant, "Le Roman," Preface to *Pierre et Jean* (Paris: Gallimard, 1982), 45–60.

27. See Baruch Spinoza, *Ethics: With the Treatise on the Emendation of the Intellect and Selected Letters*, 2nd ed., ed. and introduced by Seymour Feldman, trans. Samuel Shirley (Indianapolis, IN: Hackett Publishing, 1992), 141.

28. It is beyond the scope of this book to retrace the discourses surrounding desire. However, Judith Butler's *Subjects of Desire* (New York: Columbia Univ. Press, 2005) provides a remarkable synthesis.

29. This idea can be mostly attributed to Gilles Deleuze and Felix Guatarri's concept of "desiring production" in *Anti-Oedipus: Capitalism and Schizophrenia*, trans. Robert Hurley (Minneapolis, MN: Univ. of Minnesota Press, 1983).

30. Maurice Blanchot, "Le Regard d'Orphée," in *L'Espace littéraire* (Paris: Gallimard, 1988).

31. For a surprisingly intelligible explanation of Lacan's interpretation via Slavoj Žižek, see Jeanne L. Schroeder, *The Triumph of Venus: The Erotics of the Market* (Berkeley and Los Angeles: Univ. of California Press, 2004), 84–85.

32. See Rosi Braidotti, *Nomadic Subjects* (New York: Columbia Univ. Press, 1994).

33. See Jessica Bennett, "A Master's Degree in . . . Masculinity?" *New York Times*, August 8, 2015, https://www.nytimes.com/2015/08/09/fashion/masculinities-studies-stonybrook-michael-kimmel.html.

34. See Judith Butler, *Bodies That Matter: On the Discursive Limits of Sex* (New York: Routledge, 2011), 1–5.

35. For a critique, see Juanita Elias and Christine Beasley, "Hegemonic Masculinity and Globalization: 'Transnational Business Masculinities' and Beyond," *Globalizations* 6, no. 2 (2009), 281–96.

36. R. W. Connell, *Masculinities*, 2nd ed. (Berkeley: Univ. of California Press, 2005), xxiv.

37. See mensstudies.org/?p=6296.

38. See, for example, *Rethinking Transnational Men*, ed. Jeff Hearn et al. (New York: Routledge, 2013).

39. Sabrina Qiong Yu, *Jet Li: Chinese Masculinity and Transnational Film Stardom* (Scotland: Edinburgh Univ. Press, 2012).

40. Russell Meeuf, *John Wayne's World: Transnational Masculinity in the Fifties* (Austin: Univ. of Texas Press, 2013).

41. Meeuf, *John Wayne's World*, 3.

42. Meeuf, *John Wayne's World*.

43. Qiong Yu, *Jet Li*, 185.

44. Françoise Lionnet and Shu-mei Shih, *Minor Transnationalism* (Durham, NC: Duke Univ. Press, 2005).

45. See Ferdinand de Saussure, *Course in General Linguistics*, trans. Wade Baskin (New York: Columbia Univ. Press, 2011).

46. See Friedrich Nietzsche, *On Truth and Untruth: Selected Writings*, trans. Taylor Carman (Harper Perennial, 2010), 23, 25.

47. See Jean Baudrillard, *Simulacra and Simulation*, trans. Sheila Glaser (Ann Arbor, Michigan: Univ. of Michigan Press, 1994).

48. See Guy Debord, *The Society of the Spectacle*, trans. Ken Knabb (London: Rebel Press, 2005), 7.

49. Thomas de Zengotita, *Mediated: How the Media Shapes Your World and the Way You Live in It* (New York: Bloomsbury, 2005).

50. de Zengotita, *Mediated*, 107.

51. Carla Freccero, "Historical Violence, Censorship, and the Serial Killer: The Case for American Psycho," *Diacritics* 27, no. 2 (1997), 44–58.

## 1. Predatory Desire

1. Pamela Cooper, "Metamorphosis and Sexuality: Reading the Strange Passions of *Disgrace*," *Research in African Literatures* 36, no. 4 (Winter 2005): 25.

2. Andrew van der Vlies synthesizes the reception of *Disgrace* both in South Africa and abroad, noting that whereas various political parties (including the African National Congress) and writers were overwhelmingly critical of the text locally, many international commentators reviewed the novel positively. Andrew van der Vlies, *J. M. Coetzee's Disgrace: A Reader's Guide* (London: Continuum, 2010), 71–79. Ian Glenn likewise reviews the different responses the novel elicited from various groups of South Africans, ultimately condemning Coetzee to eventual exile to Australia as a sign of the author's cynicism regarding the future of post-apartheid South Africa, especially as he had virulently opposed apartheid. Ian Glenn, "Gone for Good—Coetzee's Disgrace," *English in Africa* 36, no. 2 (October 2009): 79–98.

3. Carine M. Mardorossian, "Rape and the Violence of Representation in J. M. Coetzee's *Disgrace*," *Research in African Literatures* 42, no. 4 (Winter 2011), 73.

4. Glenn, "Gone for Good," 80.

5. Glenn defines the term thus: "Liberal Afro-pessimism incriminates white African settlers and history as agents (though not the only ones) of the dysfunctional post-colonial situation rather than simply victims of it. Liberal Afro-pessimism, driven by a range of events from Rwanda to Sierra Leone, and generally a result of disappointment and comparative despair at Africa's failure to advance as Asian countries have, may be related to earlier forms of racism, but is a far more complex response." Glenn, "Gone for Good," 93.

6. In South Africa, the term "coloured" denotes someone of mixed heritage.

7. The use of the Romantic poets in *Disgrace* has been discussed quite extensively in criticism of the novel. Margot Beard briefly reviews the majority of these apparently insufficient interpretations (59–61) in order to "alert readers to the nuanced texture of the Romantic context of the novel" (62); see Margot Beard, "Lessons from the Dead Masters: Wordsworth and Byron in J. M. Coetzee's *Disgrace*," *English in Africa* 34, no. 1 (May 2007), 59–77.

8. See Cooper, "Metamorphosis and Sexuality," 25.

9. Lucy Valerie Graham, "Reading the Unspeakable: Rape in J. M. Coetzee's *Disgrace*," *Journal of South African Studies* 29, no. 2 (June 2003), 443.

10. Reading *Disgrace* within the perspective of an ethical narrative of salvation, DeKoven makes the arguable case that the "co-presence of middle-aged women and non-human animals . . . [are] possible agents or at least figures of positive change" (847); see Marianne DeKoven, "Going to the Dogs in *Disgrace*," *ELH* 76, no. 4 (Winter 2009), 847–75.

11. Sedgwick argues that because of its commitment to uncover and disentangle patterns of systemic oppression, most criticism is dominated by paranoid positions of knowledge, which are informed by the intellectual tradition of the "hermeneutics of suspicion" that Paul Ricoeur identified in Marx, Nietzsche, and Freud. As an alternative to this "paranoid imperative," Sedgwick suggests that reparative practices of reading may yield additional, unsuspected insights to paranoia's negative gaze; see Eve Sedgwick, "Paranoid Reading and Reparative Reading, Or, You're So Paranoid, You Probably Think This Essay Is about You" in *Touching Feeling: Affect, Pedagogy, Performativity* (Durham, NC: Duke Univ. Press, 2003).

12. See DeKoven, "Going to the Dogs in *Disgrace*"; Sue Kossew, "The Politics of Shame and Redemption in J. M. Coetzee's *Disgrace*," *Research in African Literatures* 34, no. 2 (Summer 2003), 155–62; and Charles Sarvan, "*Disgrace*: A Path to Grace?" *World Literature Today* 78, no. 1 (Jan–Apr 2004), 26–29.

13. Cooper, "Metamorphosis and Sexuality," 22.

14. For a discussion on colonization, sexuality, and interracial desire, see Robert J. Young, *Colonial Desire: Hybridity in Theory, Culture and Race* (New York: Routledge, 1995).

15. For a brief overview, see Julia Kuehn, "Exoticism in 19th Century Literature," *British Library*, May 15, 2014, https://www.bl.uk/romantics-and-victorians/articles/exoticism -in-19th-century-literature, which is partly inspired by Victor Segalen's canonical *Essay on Exoticism: An Aesthetics of Diversity* (Durham and London: Duke Univ. Press, 2002). Also of

note is Anne McClintock's study *Imperial Leather: Race, Gender, and Sexuality in the Colonial Contest* (New York: Routledge, 1995).

16. Mardorossian, "Rape and the Violence of Representation," 78.

17. See, infamously, Gayatri Chakravorty Spivak, "Can the Subaltern Speak?" in *Marxism and the Interpretation of Culture*, ed. Cary Nelson and Lawrence Grossberg (Chicago: Univ. of Illinois Press, 1988), 271–313.

18. Graham suggests that *Disgrace* performs a subversion of the "black peril" narrative by "scripting what Sol T. Plaatje referred to as 'the white peril,' the hidden sexual exploitation of black women by white men that has existed for centuries" (437). Because Lurie mostly desires to possess their bodies without providing much in return, he is representative of an archetype of white men in colonial settings who have exploited women of color (437); see Graham, "Reading the Unspeakable," 433–44.

19. Graham, "Reading the Unspeakable," 438.

20. Graham suggests that Bev and Lurie's use of a condom points to the ways in which their affair will not carry any unforeseen or negative consequences (443), whereas Cooper therein situates an allusion to the possible advent of "white sterility in Africa." Graham, "Reading the Unspeakable," 37.

21. See D. J. Levinson, *The Seasons of a Man's Life* (New York: Ballantine Books, 1978).

22. Cooper argues that the attack by three young black men is symbolic of the "displacement of the white phallus," and that consequently "the black phallus [is] replacing the defunct white one as the features of patriarchal authority are reconfigured in South Africa." Cooper, "Metamorphosis and Sexuality," 29. However, Mardorossian claims that this displacement happens much earlier, when Lucy proposes Lurie work for Petrus (77); see Mardorossian, "Rape and the Violence of Representation," 72–83.

23. Glenn points out that both rape victims in the novel remain silent about their rape, but that Coetzee "can only approach the issue of silence and rape through Lucy's silence." Glenn, "Gone for Good," 94. Therefore, women of color are denied any type of agency (as victims of double colonization) whereas amid her silence, Lucy's decision to stay, even as it "seems to condemn women to perpetual status as suffering victims of sexual violence" (94), confers her an ability to act and speak on behalf of victimized women.

24. Theo Tait, "Is the Film of JM Coetzee's Booker-winner *Disgrace* a Success?" *Guardian*, November 27, 2009, https://www.theguardian.com/culture/2009/nov/28/disgrace-coetzee -film-malkovich-review.

25. In *Rethinking the Novel/Film Debate*, Elliott explains that the "trumping" approach to adaptation inverts the dynamic between the two texts, wherein the adaptation purposely rectifies elements of the original to address criticisms of the original. Kamilla Elliott, *Rethinking the Novel/Film Debate* (Cambridge, UK: Cambridge Univ. Press, 2003).

26. Perhaps most famously, the 2010 movie *Invictus* dramatizes how Mandela was able to bridge the racial divide by supporting South Africa's rugby team as they won the world championship in 1995.

27. Despite the repeal of the 1913 Natives Land Act in 1991, whites still own 72 percent of land in South Africa according to the "Land Audit Report" (November 2017) available on the South African Government website, https://www.gov.za/sites/default/files /gcis_document/201802/landauditreport13feb2018.pdf. The issue garnered international attention in the summer of 2018, when Trump tweeted that the "South African Government is now seizing land from white farmers." South African officials rapidly condemned the claim, explaining that while President Cyril Ramaphosa urged the constitution be amended to accelerate the process of land redistribution, there had not been any land seizures. See "Here's the Story behind That Trump Tweet on South Africa—and Why It Sparked Outrage," https://www.npr.org/2018/08/23/641181345/heres-the-story-behind-that -trump-tweet-on-south-africa-and-why-it-sparked-outra.

28. In his contemporary reading of the novel in the historical context of post-apartheid South Africa, from Mandela's ideal of a "Rainbow Nation" to Zuma's triumph over Mbeki over his and his government's scandals, Glenn argues that the novel "gained in traction as a piece of political and cultural analysis as the rate of (particularly violent) crime increased to the point where André Brink talked of a 'tsunami of crime'"; Glenn, "Gone for Good," 91–92.

29. Interestingly, in contradistinction to the novelistic transformation of the university, South African universities are still dominated by Eurocentric thoughts and ideas. See for example, "Why Are South African Universities Sites of Struggle Today?" by Sabelo J. Ndlovu-Gatsheni, *Joburg Post*, October 21, 2016, http://www.joburgpost.com/articles/12068.

30. N'gugi Wa Thiong'o perhaps made this point most pervasively in *Decolonising the Mind: The Politics of Language in African Literature* (Portsmouth, NH: Heinemann, 1986), but Coetzee also addressed, albeit more allegorically, how an empire utilizes the interlinked mechanisms of language, ideology, and violence to subjugate its enemies in *Waiting for the Barbarians*.

31. van der Vlies, *Disgrace: Reader's Guide*, 59–60.

32. See Edward W. Said, *Orientalism* (New York: Vintage Books, 1994).

33. For an overview, see Michael Prior, *The Bible and Colonialism: A Moral Critique* (Sheffield, UK: Sheffield Academic Press, 1997).

34. See Mardorossian, "Rape and the Violence of Representation," 75.

35. Andrew van der Vlies suggests Lurie may be Jewish; see van der Vlies, *Disgrace: Reader's Guide*, 48–50.

36. See Kirsten Holst Petersen and Anna Rutherford, *A Double Colonization: Colonial and Post-Colonial Women's Writing* (Oxford, UK: Dangaroo Press, 1986).

37. Sarvan, "*Disgrace*: A Path to Grace?," 26.

38. Referring to Coetzee's claim that colonialism and apartheid are responsible for the escalation of a culture of sexual violence toward women, Graham argues, "*Disgrace* points to a context where women are regarded as property, and are liable for protection insofar as they belong to men. As a lesbian, Lucy would be regarded as 'unowned' and therefore

'huntable,' and there is even a suggestion that her sexuality may have provoked her attackers." Graham, "Reading the Unspeakable," 439.

39. Focusing on reading *Disgrace* as a salvific narrative of renunciation, DeKoven argues that Lurie's last utterance of the novel not only echoes Lucy's earlier statement, but also that his gesture toward the destitute dogs in general and Driepoot in particular marks Lurie's renunciation of the "power of the sexually, politically and culturally potent, dominant white male." DeKoven, "Going to the Dogs in *Disgrace*," 871.

40. A detailed analysis of the theme of nonhuman animals in *Disgrace* (and Coetzee's other work such as *The Lives of Animals* and *Elizabeth Costello*) lies beyond the scope of this chapter, but has been given more exclusive consideration elsewhere, particularly from the perspective of Levinesian ethics on Alterity. See for example, Derek Attridge, *J. M. Coetzee and the Ethics of Reading: Literature in the Event* (Chicago: Univ. of Chicago Press, 2004); DeKoven, "Going to the Dogs in *Disgrace*," 847–75; Tom Herron, "The Dog Man: Becoming Animal in Coetzee's *Disgrace*," *Twentieth Century Literature* 51, no. 4 (Winter 2005), 467–90; Sarvan, "*Disgrace*: A Path to Grace?"; Chakravorty Spivak, "Ethics and Politics in Tagore, Coetzee, and Certain Scenes of Teaching," *Diacritics* 32, no. 3–4 (2004), 17–31.

41. Cooper argues that Lucy's conventional position of subjugated wife and mother in "the neomasculinist narrative of futurity in democratic South Africa" (31) marks her appearance as a sacrificial, mythical figure (32). Cooper, "Metamorphosis and Sexuality."

42. Glenn, "Gone for Good," 90.

## 2. The Eschatology of Desire in Michel Houellebecq's *The Elementary Particles*

1. Interestingly, *1984* was propelled to the top of the bestseller list shortly after Trump's election in 2017. See, for example, Michiko Kakutani, "Why '1984' Is a 2017 Must-Read," *New York Times*, January 26, 2017, https://www.nytimes.com/2017/01/26/books/why-1984-is-a-2017-must-read.html; Lynn Neary, "Classic Novel '1984' Sales Are Up in the Era of 'Alternative Facts'," *NPR*, January 25, 2017, https://www.npr.org/sections/thetwo-way/2017/01/25/511671118/classic-novel-1984-sales-are-up-in-the-era-of-alternative-facts; Elisabeth Flock, "George Orwell '1984' Is a Best-Seller Again. Here's Why It Resonates Now," *PBS*, January 25, 2017, https://www.pbs.org/newshour/arts/george-orwells-1984-best-seller-heres-resonates-now.

2. See Michel Foucault, *Surveiller et Punir: Naissance de la prison* (Paris: Gallimard, 1975).

3. In *Society Must Be Defended*, Foucault explains that one of biopolitics' domain is "control over relationships between the human race, or human beings insofar as they are a species, insofar as they are living beings, and their environment, the milieu in which they live." Michel Foucault, *Society Must Be Defended: Lectures at the Collège de France, 1975–76*, ed. Mauro Bertani and Alessandro Fontana, trans. David Macey (New York: Picador, 2003), 244–45.

4. For a more detailed discussion of Sade's ideas, see Vartan Messier, "The Natural Right to Absolute Freedom," *Atenea* 31, no. 1 (December 2011), 31–51.

5. This reading was perhaps first propagated by the surrealists in the 1920s and reappropriated by the various cultural movements of the 1960s on both sides of the Atlantic. It would be important to note, however, that recent scholarship has produced more complex and mitigated understandings of the Marquis and his work; for a comprehensive overview, see James Steintrager, "Liberating Sade," *Yale Journal of Criticism* 18, no. 2 (2005), 351–79.

6. Houellebecq's novels tend to become bestsellers and draw considerable attention at the time of their releases. *Elementary Particles* won France's prestigious "Prix Novembre" but not without controversy, as its founder Michel Dennery seriously disliked the novel and resigned as a result. In addition, although it was a popular success, the novel and its author drew considerable criticism; on the one hand, for the explicit nature of some of the text's passages, and on the other hand, for Houellebecq's rather outrageous comportment during his public appearances. Testifying to the novel's enduring popularity, it was adapted for the screen by German director Oskar Röhler (*Elementarteilchen*, 2006) and for the stage by Julien Gosselin, with a limited run in the fall of 2014 and another in 2017 (see https://www.theatreonline.com/Spectacle/Les-Particules-elementaires/47989#infospectacle).

7. Abecassis claims that it is the inclusion of the private discourse on sexuality in the public discourse of global marketing that has propagated the forms of oppressive violence characteristic of the neoliberal economic model (811); see Jack I. Abecassis, "The Eclipse of Desire: L'Affaire Houellebecq," *MLN* 115, no. 4, French Issue (Sep. 2000), 801–26.

8. Interestingly, but perhaps not so surprisingly, Houellebecq's 2005 novel *The Possibility of an Island* similarly explores themes regarding the pitfalls of desire from the perspective of an imaginary post-human future. For a critique of that novel's scientific discourse, see Douglas Murray, "Houellebecq, Genetics and Evolutionary Psychology" in *The Evolution of Literature: Legacies of Darwin in European Cultures*, ed. Nicholas Saul and Simon J. James (Amsterdam: Rodopi, 2011).

9. See Fredric Jameson, *The Political Unconscious: Narrative as a Socially Symbolic Act* (Ithaca, NY: Cornell Univ. Press, 1981).

10. Abecassis calls it a "hagiography"; Abecassis, "Eclipse of Desire," 804.

11. Jerry Andrew Varsava, "Utopian Yearnings, Dystopian Thoughts: Houellebecq's 'The Elementary Particles' and the Problem of Scientific Communitarianism," *College Literature* 3, no. 4 (Fall 2005), 163.

12. Varsava, "Utopian Yearnings, Dystopian Thoughts," 163.

13. For a critical outlook on the new generation's reconsideration of their forebears' legacy, see François Cusset, *French Theory* (Minneapolis: Univ. of Minnesota Press, 2008), especially the last chapter entitled "Meanwhile, Back in France . . ."; Houellebecq's own allegiances are clearly situated along these lines. Delphine Grass points that "[c]ommenting on contemporary philosophy, [Houellebecq] declares: 'Matter, on its side, seemed to be flying away from success to success. Demagogical and simplistic thinking . . . is still imposed

on us today," quoted in Grass 6–7; see Delphine Grass, "Houellebecq and the Novel as Site of Epistemic Rebellion," *Opticon1826* 1 (Autumn 2006), 1–10.

14. Abecassis, "Eclipse of Desire," 822.

15. Varsava, "Utopian Yearnings, Dystopian Thoughts," 162–63.

16. See Emile Zola, *The Experimental Novel and Other Essays* (New York: Haskell House, 1964), 25.

17. Zola, *Experimental Novel*, 25–26.

18. Friedrich Nietzsche, *Beyond Good and Evil* (Mineola, NY: Dover, 1997), 36.

19. Nietzsche, *Beyond Good and Evil*, 68.

20. Nietzsche, *Beyond Good and Evil*, 31.

21. Abecassis, "Eclipse of Desire," 810.

22. Abecassis, "Eclipse of Desire," 811.

23. Michel Foucault, *The History of Sexuality*, Vol. 1, trans. Robert Hurley (New York: Vintage Books, 1990), 23.

24. Foucault, *History of Sexuality*, 47.

25. In "Preface to Transgression," an essay originally published in 1963 for the "Hommage à Georges Bataille" edition of the journal *Critique* and reprinted in *Language, Counter-Memory, Practice*, Foucault is quite explicit in situating modern sexuality from Sade to Freud not in its "natural" manifestation but rather in the "denatured" realm of language and literature: "it is not through sexuality that we communicate with the orderly and pleasingly profane world of animals; rather, sexuality is a fissure" (30). Michel Foucault, *Language, Counter-Memory, Practice*, ed., trans., and introduction Donald F. Bouchard (Ithaca, NY: Cornell Univ. Press, 1977).

26. Foucault, *History of Sexuality*, 49.

27. See Baudrillard, *Simulacra and Simulation*.

28. In many ways, originally published in 1968, Baudrillard's *The System of Objects*, trans. James Benedict (NY: Verso, 2006) serves as a groundwork preface to Baudrillard's *The Consumer Society*, trans. George Ritzer (London: Sage Publications, 1998) published in France two years later.

29. Gilles Deleuze, "Postscript on the Societies of Control," *October* 59 (Winter 1992): 3–4.

30. Debord, *Society of the Spectacle*, 7.

31. Debord, *Society of the Spectacle*, 9.

32. Deleuze, "Postscript," 5.

33. Zola claims, "And this is what constitutes the experimental novel: to possess a knowledge of the mechanism of the phenomena inherent in man, to show the machinery of his intellectual and sensory manifestations, under the influences of heredity and environment . . . and then finally exhibit man living in social conditions produced by himself. . . ." Zola, *Experimental Novel*, 20–21.

34. Roland Barthes, "The Reality Effect," in *The Rustle of Language*, trans. Richard Howard (Los Angeles: Univ. of California Press, 1986), 148.

35. Jacques Lacan reminds us the fundamental difference between animals and humans is that whereas the former experiences biological *need*, the latter experiences psychological *desire*; see Jean-Michel Rabate, *The Cambridge Companion to Lacan* (Cambridge, UK: Cambridge Univ. Press, 2003), 130.

36. Abecassis dismisses the determinacy of the main character's precise psychological portraits as "the weakest part of the novel" (805) without providing an explanation. This unwarranted dismissal is rather surprising in my view, especially as the narrative is itself quite transparent about the deterministic logic that motivates such precise descriptions. Abecassis, "Eclipse of Desire."

37. Although he originally restricted the oedipal complex to male children exclusively, Freud later revisited his theory to include female children, arguing that the love experienced by daughters for their mothers was homosexual in nature. The weakness of this argument is what partly gave root to subsequent critiques of Freud's original paradigm.

38. Perhaps not surprising the intense release of oxytocin allows for the mother and child to bond at birth.

39. Judith Butler, "Desire," *Critical Terms for Literary Study*, ed. Frank Lentricchia and Thomas McLaughlin (Chicago: Univ. of Chicago Press, 1995), 370.

40. On the one hand, as Varsava intuits, Bruno and Michel are "[l]ittle enough a victim of social circumstance, each is the principal author of his own misery . . . Even Spengler had better reasons for announcing the end of Western Civilization"; see Varsava, "Utopian Yearnings, Dystopian Thoughts," 161. On the other hand, all forms of queerness, alternative fetishes, and sexualities are only mentioned briefly in passing.

41. Varsava, "Utopian Yearnings, Dystopian Thoughts," 162. This view of Houellebecq's protagonists is echoed in reviews of his more contemporary work, where various critics point out that his oeuvre chronicles the slow death of the old white male. See Angelique Chrisafis, "'Vanquished White Male': Houellebecq's New Novel Predicts French Discontent," *Guardian*, January 4, 2019, https://www.theguardian.com/books/2019/jan/04/vanquished-white-male-houellebecqs-new-novel-eerily-predicts-french-discontent.

### 3. Extreme Desires in Bret Easton Ellis's *American Psycho*

1. *American Psycho* is fifty-third on the American Library Association's "100 most frequently challenged books: 1990–1999"; see https://www.ala.org/advocacy/bbooks/frequently challengedbooks/decade1999. In Queensland, Australia, it was outright banned, and in the rest of the country it was sealed in plastic and restricted to those 18 and over; see "X-Rated? Outdated," http://www.theage.com.au/articles/2003/09/19/1063625202157.html?oneclick=true.

2. See David Edelstein, "Torture-Porn: The Sadistic Movie Trend," *New York Magazine*, January 28, 2006, http://nymag.com/movies/features/15622/.

3. A number of cultural theorists have made this claim; for example, Fredric Jameson argues that "the visual is essentially pornographic . . . it has its end in rapt, mindless

fascination." See Fredric Jameson, *Signatures of the Visible* (New York: Routledge Classics, 2007), 1.

4. My use of the term "poetics" is partly derived from Tzvetan Todorov's *The Poetics of Prose*, trans. Richard Howard (Ithaca, NY: Cornell Univ. Press, 1971), and alludes to the ways in which texts combine signifying and structural configurations to produce literary meaning through the reader's interaction. The terms "visual poetics" and "visceral poetics" expand on this notion to refer to the ways in which the combination of linguistic and structural elements produces visual representations to which the reader responds affectively.

5. There are a number of excellent articles that investigate the complexities of Ellis's novel, including Frances Fortier, "L'esthétique hyperréaliste de Bret Easton Ellis," *Tangence* 44 (1994), 45–49; Carla Freccero, "Historical Violence, Censorship, and the Serial Killer: The Case of 'American Psycho'," *Diacritics* 27, no. 2 (1997), 44–58; Alan Murphet, *Bret Easton Ellis's* American Psycho: *A Reader's Guide* (New York: Continuum Contemporaries, 2002); and Elizabeth Young, "The Beast in the Jungle, the Figure in the Carpet," in *Shopping Space: Essays on American "Blank Generation Fiction,"* ed. Elizabeth Young and Graham Caveney (New York: Atlantic Monthly Press, 1992), 85–129. My article "Violence, Pornography, and Voyeurism as Transgression in Bret Easton Ellis' *American Psycho*," *Atenea* 23, no. 2 (June 2004), 73–94, provides a more direct context for the present study.

6. Murphet, *Reader's Guide*, 65–69; Young, "Beast in the Jungle," 86.

7. Murphet, *Reader's Guide*, 15.

8. See Tara Baxter and Nikki Craft, "There Are Better Ways of Taking Care of Bret Easton Ellis Than Just Censoring Him . . . ," in *Making Violence Sexy: Feminist Views on Pornography*, ed. Diana E. H. Russell (New York: Teacher's College Press, 1993), 245–53.

9. While popular reception for *American Psycho* was mostly characterized by outrage and indignation, critical and academic circles have been more welcoming, perceiving that the novel contained material that ought to be examined in more depth. Almost two decades after its date of publication, Ellis's novel has been the subject of various scholarly articles and has also figured in various class discussions and curricula.

10. Alberto Manguel, "Browsing in the Rag-and-Bone Shop," in *Into the Looking-Glass Wood* by Alberto Manguel (San Diego, CA: Harcourt, 2000), 101.

11. Manguel, "Browsing in the Rag-and-Bone Shop," 102.

12. Manguel, "Browsing in the Rag-and-Bone Shop," 99.

13. Mikhail Bakhtin, *The Dialogic Imagination*, ed. Michael Holquist, trans. Caryl Emerson and Michael Holquist (Austin, TX: Univ. of Texas Press, 1988), 26.

14. David W. Price, "Bakhtinian Prosaics, Grotesque Realism, and the Question of the Carnivalesque in Brett Easton Ellis' *American Psycho*," *Southern Humanities Review* 32, no. 4 (Fall 1998), 321–46.

15. See Bakhtin's analysis of Rabelais's *Gargantua et Pantagruel*. Mikhail Bakhtin, *Rabelais and His World*, trans. Hélène Iswolsky (Bloomington, IN: Indiana Univ. Press, 1984).

16. See Fredric Jameson, *Postmodernism, or, the Cultural Logic of Late Capitalism* (Durham, NC: Duke Univ. Press, 1991), where the author notes that works of postmodernism display a clear tendency to blur traditional cultural boundaries (3) and in doing so, they privilege pastiche—i.e., "blank parody," or parody without the laughter—over parody, but that like parody they aim to criticize the idiosyncrasies of the era through mimicry (16–18).

17. Baudrillard, *Simulacra and Simulation*.

18. In their "2019 Year in Review," PornHub (easily the world's most popular porn site) details that 32 percent of their worldwide audience is female; https://www.pornhub.com/insights/2019-year-in-review#gender.

19. Murphet, *Reader's Guide*, 31.

20. Murphet, *Reader's Guide*, 39.

21. Price, "Bakhtinian Prosaics," 327.

22. Messier, "Game Over? The (Re)Play of Horror in Michael Haneke's *Funny Games*," *New Cinemas: Journal of Contemporary Film* 12, no. 1–2 (June 2014), 59–77.

23. For a brief overview of Bataille's theories, see Messier, "*Erotisme* as Transgression in the Writings of Georges Bataille: From *Savoir* to *Jouissance*," in *Transgression and Taboo: Critical Essays*, ed. Vartan P. Messier and Nandita Batra (Mayagüez, Puerto Rico: College English Association-Caribbean Chapter Publications, 2005), 125–37. I also invite the reader to explore Bataille's own explanation; Georges Bataille, *Erotism: Death and Sensuality*, trans. Mary Dalwood (San Francisco: City Lights Books, 1991).

24. Manguel, "Browsing in the Rag-and-Bone Shop."

25. See Linda Williams, "Film Bodies: Gender, Genre, and Excess," *Film Quarterly* 44, no. 4 (Summer 1991), 2–13.

26. Whereas Linda Williams investigates the pleasures derived from the viewing experience of horror films, Carol J. Clover makes the most pervasive argument for the processes of gender identification in "Her Body, Himself," in *The Horror Reader*, ed. Ken Gelder (New York: Routledge, 2000), 294–307.

27. See Stephen King, "Why We Crave Horror Movies," *Playboy* (January 1981), 237.

28. Young, "Beast in the Jungle," 3.

29. See Young, "Beast in the Jungle"; Marco Abel, "Judgment Is Not an Exit: Toward an Affective Criticism of Violence with *American Psycho*," *Angelaki* 6, no. 1 (December 2001); Murphet, *Reader's Guide*.

30. Murphet, *Reader's Guide*, 24.

31. Murphet, *Reader's Guide*, 40.

32. Mark Storey, "'And as things fell apart': The Crisis of Postmodern Masculinity in Bret Easton Ellis's *American Psycho* and Dennis Cooper's *Frisk*," *Critique* 47, no. 1 (2005), 59.

33. Debord, *Society of the Spectacle*, 9.

34. Baudrillard, *Simulacra and Simulation*, 2.

35. Baudrillard, *Simulacra and Simulation*, 3.

36. Max Horkheimer and Theodor W. Adorno, "From the Culture Industry: Enlightenment as Mass Deception," *The Norton Anthology of Theory and Criticism* (New York: Norton, 2001), 1230.

37. Storey, "And things fell apart," 57.

38. Fredric Jameson, "Postmodernism and Consumer Society," in *The Anti-Aesthetic: Essays on Postmodern Culture*, ed. Hal Foster (New York: The New Press, 1999), 111–25.

39. Jameson, "Postmodernism and Consumer Society," 118–19.

40. Jameson, "Postmodernism and Consumer Society," 120.

41. Jameson, "Postmodernism and Consumer Society," 118.

42. The film was released in a DVD uncut edition in 2005.

43. Roger Rosenblatt, "Snuff This Book! Will Brett Easton Ellis Get Away with Murder?" Review of *American Psycho* by Brett Easton Ellis. *New York Times Book Review*, December 16, 1990. https://www.nytimes.com/1990/12/16/books/snuff-this-book-will-bret -easton-ellis-get-away-with-murder.html.

44. Stephen Holden, "Murderer! Fiend! (But Well Dressed)." Review of *American Psycho* directed by Mary Harron. *New York Times*, April 14, 2000. https://www.nytimes.com/2000 /04/14/movies/film-review-murderer-fiend-but-well-dressed.html.

45. See the interview on the 2005 uncut edition DVD, where Turner indicates that having a female director would absorb a lot of the feminist backlash that characterized the release of the book, and this perhaps informs Richard Porton's review of the film, where he points out that the movie was partly conceived as a "feminist project" (44); Richard Porton, "American Psycho," *Cineaste* 25, no. 3 (June 2001). Nevertheless, as various academic critics have clearly demonstrated, Ellis's novel lends itself to a variety of critical approaches, and so it would be interesting to investigate what processes are at work in the general public's perception of authorial ideology with regard to their gender and why it was necessary to instill a female/feminist returning gaze for the public at large to consider reading the text from a feminist perspective.

46. Abel, "Judgment," 138.

47. See Bertolt Brecht, "A Little Organum for the Theater," *Accent: A Quarterly of New Literature* 11, no. 1 (Winter 1951), 14–40.

48. Freccero, "Historical Violence," 48.

49. Freccero, "Historical Violence," 49.

50. Freccero, "Historical Violence," 51.

51. Abel, "Judgment," 142.

52. Laura Tanner, *Intimate Violence: Reading Rape and Torture in Twentieth-Century Fiction* (Indiana Univ. Press, 1994), 28.

53. Georges Bataille, *Visions of Excess: Selected Writings, 1927–1939* (Minneapolis: Univ. of Minnesota Press, 1994), 17.

54. Interestingly, in this interview Ellis also mentions that he is dubious about the possibility that his novels would make good movies; he thinks "[t]hey have cinematic scenes,

they have a lot of dialogue, but often they don't have that narrative momentum a movie needs [ . . . ] So I'm always shocked when people want to make movies out of my books." Randy Shulman, "The Attractions of Bret Easton Ellis," *MetroWeekly*, October 10, 2002. https://www.metroweekly.com/2002/10/the-attractions-of-bret-easton/.

55. Abel, "Judgment," 138.

56. Abel, "Judgment," 147.

57. Abel goes so far as calling them "comical"; Abel, "Judgment," 146.

58. Interestingly enough, a special feature of the DVD, as well as various of its inter-viewees, clearly considers *American Psycho* to be a "time-piece" representative of late 1980s Reaganomics, without ever hinting that Ellis's satire is even more relevant today in the digital age of late capitalism.

59. Browne has noted in "The Spectator-in-the-Text: The Rhetoric of *Stagecoach*" there is usually an ambivalence with regard to narrative positioning of the spectator either outside or inside the text—"the literal place and the imaginary place of the filmic stage"—in concor-dance with the structural organization of the narrative and the narrator's own moral disposi-tion toward the story and its characters. The position of the spectator is further complicated by what Browne dubs "the prohibition against the meeting" between the actor and the specta-tor, insofar as "it places [the spectator] irretrievably outside the action" (116). Nick Browne, "The Spectator-in-the-Text: The Rhetoric of *Stagecoach*," in *Narrative, Apparatus, Ideology: A Film Theory Reader*, ed. Philip Rosen (New York: Columbia Univ. Press, 1986), 102–19.

60. Interestingly, the film has been categorized and marketed as a horror film.

61. Mulvey explains, "The first blow against monolithic accumulation of traditional film conventions (already undertaken by radical filmmakers) is to free the look of the cam-era into its materiality in time and space and the look of the audience into dialectics, pas-sionate detachment. There is no doubt that this destroys the satisfaction, pleasure, and privilege of the 'invisible guest,' and highlights how film has depended on voyeuristic active/passive mechanisms" (209). Laura Mulvey, "Visual Pleasure and Narrative Cinema," *Narrative, Apparatus, Ideology: A Film Theory Reader*, ed. Philip Rosen (New York: Columbia Univ. Press, 1986), 199–209.

62. Abel, "Judgment," 139.

63. Williams, "Film Bodies," 12.

64. It is worth mentioning that the special features of the 2005 uncut edition DVD pay considerable tribute to Ellis's original text. Interestingly, the novel's popularity is such that a musical based on the novel was produced and staged in London and on Broadway in 2013 and 2016, respectively.

65. Storey, "And things fell apart," 60–61.

66. Fortier, "L'esthétique hyperréaliste," 98.

67. Roger Cohen, "Bret Easton Ellis Answers Critics of 'American Psycho'," *New York Times*, March 6, 1991, https://www.nytimes.com/1991/03/06/books/bret-easton-ellis-answers-critics-of-american-psycho.html.

68. See Walter Benjamin, *The Painter of Modern Life: Essays on Charles Baudelaire* (Cambridge, MA: Harvard Univ. Press, 2006).

69. Bakhtin, *Dialogic Imagination*, 26.

70. Jameson, "Postmodernism and Consumer Society," 123–24.

71. The uneasy collusion of spectacle and politics in American life is perhaps best exemplified by Donald Trump. However, another recent noteworthy example is Sarah Palin, who, after being nominated for vice president in the 2008 election, now runs a multimillion-dollar media empire, and is celebrated by Ann Coulter as a "real American" in *Time* magazine's annual "World's Most Influential People" of 2008. See *Time* (May 11, 2009), 120.

72. Bateman remains indelible as a cultural icon. As a cypher for material culture, he is only becoming more relevant in the digital age. In "Twenty Years Later, 'American Psycho' Has Only Grown More Timely," Lazic argues, "Our increasingly materialistic lifestyles have made us carry our brands around not simply in the form of a personalized business card or wardrobe, but also in the electronic devices we use, the diets and social media accounts we follow, and the TV shows and blockbusters we publicly praise. Patrick Bateman's search for identity is a story that has inched closer and closer to our modern existence, even if in less overtly violent ways." Manuela Lazic, "Twenty Years Later, 'American Psycho' Has Only Grown More Timely," *The Ringer*, April 14, 2020, https://www.theringer.com/movies/2020/4/14/21219921/american-psycho-anniversary-christian-bale-patrick-bateman.

73. Stephen Marche, "Why In Hell Are We Back in the '80s?" *Esquire*, June 1, 2010, https://classic.esquire.com/article/2010/6/1/why-in-hell-are-we-back-in-the-80s.

74. The speech was reportedly inspired by the 1986 commencement address at Berkeley's School of Business Administration, in which Ivan Boesky (who was later convicted on insider-trading charges) opined: "Greed is all right, by the way. I want you to know that. I think greed is healthy. You can be greedy and still feel good about yourself."

## 4. The Self, the Other, Its Doubles, and Its Shadows

1. Mabanckou was awarded a number of literary prizes; most notably, *Mémoires de porc-épic* was awarded the Prix Renaudot in 2006. He now partly resides in the United States where he is professor of Francophone literature at UCLA.

2. John Ferguson, *Global Shadows: Africa in the Neoliberal World Order* (Durham, NC: Duke Univ. Press, 2006).

3. Ferguson, *Global Shadows*, 2.

4. Ferguson, *Global Shadows*, 10.

5. Ferguson, *Global Shadows*, 5–7.

6. Ferguson, *Global Shadows*, 9–10.

7. Ferguson, *Global Shadows*, 15.

8. Ferguson, *Global Shadows*, 16.

9. Ferguson, *Global Shadows*, 16.

10. Frantz Fanon, *Black Skins, White Masks*, trans. Richard Philcox (New York: Grove Press, 2008).

11. Yves Chemla, "Variations sur African Psycho," January 1, 2009, http://www.ychemla.net/fic_doc/african_psycho.html.

12. Quoted in John Zuarino, "The African Psycho Comes to America," March 2007, http://www.bookslut.com/features/2007_03_010771.php (Bookslut.com archives no longer available online).

13. This tendency has already been observed by Fanon in *The Wretched of the Earth*; see the chapter entitled "The Pitfalls of National Consciousness." Frantz Fanon, *The Wretched of the Earth*, trans. Richard Philcox (New York: Grove Press, 2004).

14. Ferguson, *Global Shadows*, 19.

15. I might add it would not be a far cry to assume that most contemporary Western audiences are most familiar with Idi Amin through Kevin Macdonald's award-winning film adaptation of Giles Folden's *The Last King of Scotland* (2006).

16. According to John Searle's taxonomy of speech acts in *Expression and Meaning: Studies in the Theory of Speech Acts* (Cambridge, UK: Cambridge Univ. Press, 1976), commissives differ from assertives in the sense that they are not based on facts.

17. Fanon, *Wretched of the Earth*.

18. Jacques Derrida, *Of Grammatology*, trans. Gayatri Chakravorty Spivak (Baltimore, MD: John Hopkins Univ. Press, 1997); see "The Violence of the Letter: From Lévi-Strauss to Rousseau," 101–40.

19. Martin Heidegger, *Being and Time*, trans. Joan Stambaugh (Albany: SUNY Press, 1996); see Part One, Chapter V, Section 35, 157–59.

20. Heidegger, *Being and Time*, 159.

21. I am using the term "real" to contrast Grégoire with Jean Veneuse, whom Fanon considers an "orphan," figuratively speaking, because he was "abandoned" by his parents to attend a lycée in France.

22. Germaine Guex, quoted in Fanon, *Black Skins*, 54.

23. Fanon, *Black Skins*, 56.

24. See Ellis, *American Psycho*, 11, 68, and 230.

25. Achille Mbembé explains that the African has always believed in continuity between the reality and the imaginary, "to the extent that there was no representation of the real world without a relation to the word of the invisible," and that even after colonization, "in spite of the transformations and discontinuities, an imaginary world has remained" (146). Achille Mbembé, *On the Postcolony*, trans. A. M. Berrett, Jane Roitman, Murray Last, and Steven Randall (Berkeley: Univ. of California Press, 2001).

26. Robin Wood explains "the relationship between normality and the Monster . . . constitutes the essential subject of the horror film." See "An Introduction to the American Horror Film," in *American Nightmare: Essays on the Horror Film*, ed. Robin Wood and Richard Lippe (Toronto, CA: Festival of Festivals, 1979), 14.

27. See Chinua Achebe, "An Image of Africa: Racism in Conrad's Heart of Darkness," in *Heart of Darkness: 5th Norton Critical Edition*, ed. Paul. B. Armstrong (New York: Norton, 2016), 306–19

28. Serge Bilé, *La légende du sexe surdimensionné des Noirs* (Paris: Éditions du Rocher, 2005).

29. Interestingly, Bilé's book is a topic of discussion on Mabanckou's old blog; see http://www.congopage.com/Quand-Pierre-Assouline-parle-de-La.

30. Bilé, *La légende*, 209.

31. Wood, "An Introduction to the American Horror Film," 7–28.

32. Fanon, *Black Skins*, 187.

33. Fanon, *Black Skins*, 191.

34. Mbembé, *On the Postcolony*, 142.

35. In an interview, Mabanckou explains, "Congolese journalists like to exaggerate. I wanted, in my novel, to joke on this aspect. I also believe that, in this world, information is often amplified." Quoted in Zuarino, "African Psycho Comes to America."

36. Chinua Achebe, *Things Fall Apart* (New York: Penguin, 1994).

37. Ousmane Sembène, *Xala*, trans. Clive Wake (Chicago, IL: Lawrence Hill, 1976).

38. John Walsh, "Psycho Killer, Qu'est-ce que c'est? Reflections on Alain Mabanckou's *African Psycho*," *Transitions* 100 (2009), 152–63.

39. See, for example, Nuruddin Farrah's "Variations on the Theme of an African Dictatorship" series or Ngũgĩ wa Thiong'o, *Wizard of the Crow* (New York: Anchor Books, 2007).

40. Walsh, "Psycho Killer," 152.

41. Harold Bloom, *The Anxiety of Influence: A Theory of Poetry*, 2nd edition (Oxford Univ. Press, 1997).

42. Walsh, "Psycho Killer," 162.

43. Ferguson, *Global Shadows*, 17.

## Conclusion

1. In *A Thousand Plateaus*, Deleuze and Guattari explain that an assemblage "establishes connections between certain multiplicities . . . so that a book has no sequel nor the world as its object nor one or several authors as its subject," 22–23. Gilles Deleuze and Félix Guattari, *A Thousand Plateaus*, trans. Brian Massumi (Minneapolis, MN: Univ. of Minnesota Press, 1987).

2. Lawrence Raw, "Learning Adaptation," in *Adaptation Studies and Learning: New Frontiers*, ed. Lawrence Raw and Anthony Gurr (Plymouth, UK: Scarecrow Press, 2013), 1–12. Drawing from the work of Charles Darwin and Jean Piaget, Raw approaches adaptation from a perspective that considers the ways in which individuals actively engage with the determining environmental and internal factors that affect their daily lives. Darwin's

idea of a "struggle for existence" posits that the organisms that have adapted best to the continuous changes in their respective environment will thrive and survive.

3. As a reminder, Kamilia Elliott explains that the process of "trumping" inverts the common direction of adaptation criticism by considering not what is presumably wrong with the adaptation, but rather what could be wrong with the original, thus requiring the adaptation to "trump" it, literally.

4. Raw, "Learning Adaptation," 1.

5. See Roland Barthes, *Fragments d'un discours amoureux/A Lover's Discourse: Fragments*, in *Oeuvres Complètes V: 1977–1980* (Paris: Éditions du Seuil, 2002), 25–296.

6. See Joseph Campbell, *The Hero with a Thousand Faces* (Novato, CA: New World Library, 2008), 211.

7. Michel Foucault, *The Order of Things: An Archaeology of Human Sciences* (New York: Vintage, 1994), 387.

8. Fanon, *Wretched of the Earth*, 313–15. Foucault and Fanon's revisualizations for posthuman subjectivities are further echoed in Derrida's concept of "difference" in *Margins of Philosophy*, Deleuze and Guatarri's *Anti-Oedipus*, Braidotti's *Nomadic Subjects*, Hayles's *How We Became Posthuman*, and Haraways's "cyborgs," to cite only a few prominent examples. See Jacques Derrida, *Margins of Philosophy*, trans. Alan Bass (Chicago: Chicago Univ. Press, 1982); Deleuze and Guatarri, *Anti-Oedipus*; Braidotti, *Nomadic Subjects*; N. Katherine Hayles, *How We Became Posthuman: Virtual Bodies in Cybernetics, Literature, and Informatics* (Chicago: Univ. of Chicago Press, 1999); and Donna Haraways, *Simians, Cyborgs, and Women* (New York: Routledge, 1990).

9. See Françoise Lionnet and Shu-mei Shih, *Minor Transnationalism* (Durham, NC: Duke Univ. Press, 2005).

# Bibliography

Abecassis, Jack I. "The Eclipse of Desire: L'Affaire Houellebecq." *MLN* 115, no. 4, French Issue (September 2000): 801–26.

Abel, Marco. "Judgment Is Not an Exit: Toward an Affective Criticism of Violence with *American Psycho*." *Angelaki* 6, no. 1 (December 2001): 137–54.

Aboim, Sofia. *Plural Masculinities: The Remaking of the Self in Private Life*. New York: Routledge, 2010.

Achebe, Chinua. "An Image of Africa: Racism in Conrad's *Heart of Darkness*." In *Heart of Darkness: 5th Norton Critical Edition*, edited by Paul B. Armstrong, 306–19. New York: Norton, 2016.

*Adaptation*. Directed by Spike Jonze. Los Angeles: Columbia Pictures, 2002. DVD.

"All Things Considered: Men in America." *NPR*, Summer 2014.

*American Psycho: Uncut Version*. Directed by Marry Harron. Performances by Christian Bale and Willem Dafoe. 2000. Lion Gates Film, 2005.

Attwell, David. "Coetzee and Post-Apartheid South Africa." Review of *Disgrace*, by J. M. Coetzee. *Journal of Southern African Studies* 27, no. 4 (December 2001): 865–67.

Bakhtin, Mikhail. *Rabelais and His World*. Translated by Hélène Iswolsky. Bloomington, IN: Indiana Univ. Press, 1984.

Bakhtin, Mikhail. *The Dialogic Imagination*, edited by Michael Holquist. Translated by Caryl Emerson and Michael Holquist. Austin, TX: Univ. of Texas Press, 1988.

Barthes, Roland. *Critique et Vérité*. Paris: Éditions du Seuil, 1966.

Barthes, Roland. "The Reality Effect." In *The Rustle of Language*, translated by Richard Howard, 141–48. Los Angeles: UC Press, 1986.

Barthes, Roland. *Fragments d'un discours amoureux/A Lover's Discourse: Fragments*. In *Oeuvres Complètes V: 1977–1980*, 25–296. Paris: Éditions du Seuil, 2002.

Bataille, Georges. *Erotism: Death and Sensuality*. Translated by Mary Dalwood. San Francisco: City Lights Books, 1991.

Bataille, Georges. *Visions of Excess: Selected Writings, 1927–1939*. Minneapolis: Univ. of Minnesota Press, 1994.

Baudrillard, Jean. *Simulacra and Simulation*. Translated by Sheila Glaser. Ann Arbor, MI: Univ. of Michigan Press, 1994.

Baudrillard, Jean. *The Consumer Society: Myths and Structures*. Translated by George Ritzer. London: Sage Publications, 1998.

Baudrillard, Jean. *The System of Objects*. Translated by James Benedict. New York: Verso, 2006.

Baxter, Tara, and Nikki Craft. "There Are Better Ways of Taking Care of Bret Easton Ellis Than Just Censoring Him . . ." In *Making Violence Sexy: Feminist Views on Pornography*, edited by Diana E. H. Russell, 245–53. New York: Teacher's College Press, 1993.

Beard, Margot. "Lessons from the Dead Masters: Wordsworth and Byron in J. M. Coetzee's *Disgrace*." *English in Africa* 34, no. 1 (May 2007): 59–77.

Bilé, Serge. *La légende du sexe surdimensionné des Noirs*. Paris: Éditions du Rocher, 2005.

Blanchot, Maurice. "Le Regard d'Orphée." In *L'Espace littéraire*. Paris: Gallimard, 1988.

Blanchot, Maurice. *The Space of Literature*, Lincoln, NE: Univ. of Nebraska Press, 1989.

Braidotti, Rosi. *Nomadic Subjects: Embodiment and Sexual Difference in Contemporary Feminist Theory*. New York: Columbia Univ. Press, 1994.

Brecht, Bertolt. "A Little Organum for the Theater." *Accent: A Quarterly of New Literature* 11, no. 1 (Winter 1951): 14–40.

Browne, Nick. "The Spectator-in-the-Text: The Rhetoric of *Stagecoach*." In *Narrative, Apparatus, Ideology: A Film Theory Reader*, edited by Philip Rosen, 102–19. New York: Columbia Univ. Press, 1986.

Butler, Judith. *Bodies That Matter: On the Discursive Limits of Sex*. New York: Routledge, 2011.

Butler, Judith. "Desire." In *Critical Terms for Literary Study*, edited by Frank Lentricchia and Thomas McLaughlin, 369–86. Chicago: Univ. of Chicago Press, 1995.

Butler, Judith. *Gender Trouble: Feminism and the Subversion of Identity*. New York: Routledge, 2006.

Chemla, Yves. "Variations sur *African Psycho*." January 1, 2009. http://www.ychemla .net/fic_doc/african_psycho.html.

Coetzee, J. M. *Disgrace*. New York: Penguin Books, 1999.

Coetzee, J. M. *Waiting for the Barbarians*. New York: Penguin, 2010.

Connell, R. W. *Masculinities*. 2nd ed. Berkeley: Univ. of California Press, 2005.

Conrad, Joseph. *Heart of Darkness*. New York: W. W. Norton, 2006.

Cooper, Pamela. "Metamorphosis and Sexuality: Reading the Strange Passions of *Disgrace*." *Research in African Literatures* 36, no. 4 (Winter 2005): 22–39.

Cusset, François. *French Theory*. Minneapolis: Univ. of Minnesota Press, 2008.

Debord, Guy. *The Society of the Spectacle*. Translated by Ken Knabb. London: Rebel Press, 2005.

DeKoven, Marianne. "Going to the Dogs in *Disgrace*." *ELH* 76, no. 4 (Winter 2009): 847–75.

Deleuze, Gilles. "Postscript on the Societies of Control." *October* 59 (Winter 1992): 3–7.

Deleuze, Gilles, and Félix Guattari. *Anti-Oedipus: Capitalism and Schizophrenia*. Translated by Robert Hurley. Minneapolis, MN: Univ. of Minnesota Press, 1983.

Deleuze, Gilles, and Félix Guattari. *A Thousand Plateaus*. Translated by Brian Massumi. Minneapolis, MN: Univ. of Minnesota Press, 1987.

Derrida, Jacques. *Of Grammatology*. Translated by Gayatri Chakravorty Spivak. Baltimore, MD: John Hopkins Univ. Press, 1997.

Derrida, Jacques. *Writing and Difference*. Translated by Alan Blass. Chicago: Univ. of Chicago Press, 1967.

*Disgrace*. Directed by Steve Jacobs. Australia: Paladin, 2009.

Elliott, Kamilla. *Rethinking the Novel/Film Debate*. Cambridge, UK: Cambridge Univ. Press, 2003.

Ellis, Bret Easton. *American Psycho*. New York: Vintage, 1991.

Fanon, Frantz. *Black Skins, White Masks*. Translated by Richard Philcox. New York: Grove Press, 2008.

Fanon, Frantz. *The Wretched of the Earth*. Translated by Richard Philcox. New York: Grove Press, 2004.

Ferguson, John. *Global Shadows: Africa in the Neoliberal World Order*. Durham, NC: Duke Univ. Press, 2006.

Fortier, Frances. "L'esthétique hyperréaliste de Bret Easton Ellis." *Tangence* 44 (1994): 45–49.

Foucault, Michel. *Language, Counter-Memory, Practice*. Edited, translated, and introduction by Donald F. Bouchard. Ithaca, NY: Cornell Univ. Press, 1977.

Foucault, Michel. *Society Must Be Defended: Lectures at the Collège de France, 1975–76*. Edited by Mauro Bertani and Alessandro Fontana. Translated by David Macey. New York: Picador, 2003.

Foucault, Michel. *Surveiller et Punir: Naissance de la prison*. Paris: Gallimard, 1975.

Foucault, Michel. *The History of Sexuality*. Vol. 1. Translated by Robert Hurley. New York: Vintage Books, 1990.

Foucault, Michel. *The Order of Things: An Archaeology of Human Sciences*. New York: Vintage, 1994.

Freccero, Carla. "Historical Violence, Censorship, and the Serial Killer: The Case for 'American Psycho'." *Diacritics* 27, no. 2 (1997): 44–58.

Freud, Sigmund. *Three Essays on the Theory of Sexuality*. Translated by James Strachey. New York: Basic Books, 1975.

Gardner, James. "A Review of *American Psycho*." *National Review* 48, no. 11 (June 17, 1996): 54–57.

Glenn, Ian. "Gone for Good—Coetzee's *Disgrace*." *English in Africa* 36, no. 2 (October 2009): 79–98.

Graham, Lucy Valerie. "Reading the Unspeakable: Rape in J. M. Coetzee's *Disgrace*." *Journal of South African Studies* 29, no. 2 (June 2003): 433–44.

Grass, Delphine. "Houellebecq and the Novel as Site of Epistemic Rebellion," *Opticon1826* 1 (Autumn 2006): 1–10.

Haraway, Donna. *Simians, Cyborgs and Women: The Reinvention of Nature*. New York: Routledge, 1991.

Hayles, N. Katherine. *How We Became Posthuman: Virtual Bodies in Cybernetics, Literature, and Informatics*. Chicago: Univ. of Chicago Press, 1999.

Hegel, G. W. F. *The Phenomenology of Spirit*. Translated by A. V. Miller. Oxford, UK: Oxford Univ. Press, 1979.

Heidegger, Martin. *Being and Time*. Translated by Joan Stambaugh. Albany: SUNY Press, 1996.

Herron, Tom. "The Dog Man: Becoming Animal in Coetzee's *Disgrace*." *Twentieth Century Literature* 51, no. 4 (Winter 2005): 467–90.

Holden, Stephen. "In South Africa, Harsh Losses of Privilege." Review of *Disgrace* directed by Steve Jacobs. *New York Times*, September 17, 2009.

Holden, Stephen. "Murderer! Fiend! (But Well Dressed)." Review of *American Psycho* directed by Mary Harron. *New York Times*, April 14, 2000. https://www.nytimes.com/2000/04/14/movies/film-review-murderer-fiend-but-well-dressed.html.

Houellebecq, Michel. *Les Particules élémentaires*. Paris: Flammarion, 1998.

Houellebecq, Michel. *The Elementary Particles*. Translated by Frank Wynne. New York: Vintage, 2000.

*Invictus*. Directed by Clint Eastwood. Burbank, CA: Warner Bros, 2009.

Jameson, Fredric. "Postmodernism and Consumer Society." In *The Anti-Aesthetic: Essays on Postmodern Culture*, edited by Hal Foster, 111–25. New York: The New Press, 1999.

Jameson, Fredric. *Postmodernism, or, the Cultural Logic of Late Capitalism*. Durham, NC: Duke Univ. Press, 1991.

Kossew, Sue. "The Politics of Shame and Redemption in J. M. Coetzee's *Disgrace*." *Research in African Literatures* 34, no. 2 (Summer, 2003): 155–62.

Kuehn, Julia. "Exoticism in 19th-Century Literature." *British Library*. May 15, 2014. https://www.bl.uk/romantics-and-victorians/articles/exoticism-in-19th -century-literature.

Lacan, Jacques. "The Agency of the Letter in the Unconscious." In *The Norton Anthology of Theory and Criticism*, edited by Vincent B. Leitch, 1285–310. New York: Norton, 2001.

Lacan, Jacques. "The Mirror Stage as Formative of the Function of the I as Revealed in the Psychoanalytic Experience." In *The Norton Anthology of Theory and Criticism*, edited by Vincent B. Leitch, 1285–310. New York: Norton, 2001.

Lacan, Jacques. "The Signification of the Phallus." In *The Norton Anthology of Theory and Criticism*, edited by Vincent B. Leitch, 1285–1310. New York: Norton, 2001.

Lionnet, Françoise, and Shu-mei Shih. *Minor Transnationalism*. Durham, NC: Duke Univ. Press, 2005.

Mabanckou, Alain. *African Psycho*. Translated by Christine Schwartz Hartley. New York: Soft Skull Press, 2007.

Mabanckou, Alain. "Quand Pierre Assouline parle de 'La légende du sexe surdi-mensionné des Noirs' . . ." Accessed November 15, 2018. http://www.congo page.com/Quand-Pierre-Assouline-parle-de-La.

Manguel, Alberto. "Browsing in the Rag-and-Bone Shop." In *Into the Looking-Glass Wood* by Alberto Manguel. San Diego, CA: Harcourt, 2000.

Mardorossian, Carine M. "Rape and the Violence of Representation in J. M. Coetzee's *Disgrace*." *Research in African Literatures* 42, no. 4 (Winter 2011): 72–83.

Mbembé, Achille. *On the Postcolony*. Translated by A. M. Berrett, Jane Roitman, Murray Last, and Steven Randall. Berkeley: Univ. of California Press, 2001.

McClintock, Anne. *Imperial Leather: Race, Gender and Sexuality in the Colonial Contest*. New York: Routledge, 1995.

Meeuf, Russell. *John Wayne's World: Transnational Masculinity in the Fifties*. Austin: Univ. of Texas Press, 2013.

Messier, Vartan. "*Erotisme* as Transgression in the Writings of Georges Bataille: from *Savoir* to *Jouissance.*" In *Transgression and Taboo: Critical Essays,* edited by Vartan P. Messier and Nandita Batra, 125–37. Mayagüez, Puerto Rico: College English Association–Caribbean Chapter Publications, 2005.

Messier, Vartan. "The Conservative, the Transgressive, and the Reactionary: Ann Radcliffe's *The Italian* as a Response to Matthew Lewis's *The Monk.*" *Atenea* 25, no. 2 (December 2005): 37–48.

Mulvey, Laura. "Visual Pleasure and Narrative Cinema." In *Narrative, Apparatus, Ideology: A Film Theory Reader,* edited by Philip Rosen, 199–209. New York: Columbia Univ. Press, 1986.

Murphet, Julian. *Bret Easton Ellis's* American Psycho: *A Reader's Guide.* New York: Continuum Contemporaries, 2002.

Naremore, James, ed. *Film Adaptation.* New Brunswick, NJ: Rutgers Univ. Press, 2000.

Ndlovu-Gatsheni, Sabelo J. "Why Are South African Universities Sites of Struggle Today?" *Joburg Post,* October 21, 2016, http://www.joburgpost.com/articles /12068.

Ngũgĩ wa Thiong'o. *Decolonising the Mind: The Politics of Language in African Literature.* Portsmouth, NH: Heinemann, 1986.

Ngũgĩ wa Thiong'o. *Wizard of the Crow.* New York: Anchor Books, 2007.

Nietzsche, Friedrich. *Beyond Good and Evil.* Mineola, NY: Dover, 1997.

Olson, Greta. "'Like a Dog': Rituals of Animal Degradation in J. M. Coetzee's *Disgrace* and Abu Ghraib Prison." *JNT: Journal of Narrative Theory* 44, no. 1 (Winter 2014): 116–56.

Orlean, Susan. *The Orchid Thief.* New York: Random House, 1998.

Orwell, Georges. *1984.* New York: Signet Classics, 1992.

Petersen, Kirsten Holst, and Anna Rutherford. *A Double Colonization: Colonial and Post-Colonial Women's Writing.* Oxford, UK: Dangaroo Press, 1986.

Piaget, Jean. *The Origins of Intelligence.* Translated by Margaret Cook. New York: International Universities Press, 1952.

Porton, Richard. "American Psycho." *Cineaste* 25, no. 3 (June 2001): 43–45.

Price, David W. "Bakhtinian Prosaics, Grotesque Realism, and the Question of the Carnivalesque in Brett Easton Ellis' *American Psycho.*" *Southern Humanities Review* 32, no. 4 (Fall 1998): 321–46.

Prior, Michael. *The Bible and Colonialism: A Moral Critique.* Sheffield, UK: Sheffield Academic Press, 1997.

Qiong Yu, Sabrina. *Jet Li: Chinese Masculinity and Transnational Film Stardom.* Scotland: Edinburgh Univ. Press, 2012.

Quayson, Ato. "Realism, Criticism, and the Disguises of Both: A Reading of Chinua Achebe's *Things Fall Apart* with an Evaluation of the Criticism Relating to It." *Research in African Literatures* 25, no. 4 (Winter 1994): 117–36.

Radcliffe, Ann. "On the Supernatural in Poetry." *New Monthly Magazine* 16, no. 1 (1826): 145–52.

Raw, Laurence. "Learning Adaptation." In *Adaptation Studies and Learning: New Frontiers,* edited by Lawrence Raw and Anthony Gurr, 1–12. Plymouth, UK: Scarecrow Press, 2013.

Romano, Andrew. "Why We Need to Reimagine Masculinity." *Newsweek.* September 20, 2010. https://www.newsweek.com/why-we-need-reimagine-masculinity-71993#.

Romano, Andrew, and Tony Dokoupil. "Men's Lib." *Newsweek* 156, no. 13 (September 27, 2010): 42–49.

Rosenblatt, Roger. "Snuff This Book! Will Brett Easton Ellis Get Away with Murder?" Review of *American Psycho,* by Brett Easton Ellis. *New York Times Book Review,* December 16, 1990. https://www.nytimes.com/1990/12/16/books/snuff-this-book-will-bret-easton-ellis-get-away-with-murder.html.

Said, Edward W. *Orientalism.* New York: Vintage Books, 1994.

Sarvan, Charles. "*Disgrace*: A Path to Grace?" *World Literature Today* 78, no. 1 (Jan–Apr 2004): 26–29.

Sedgwick, Eve. *Touching Feeling: Affect, Pedagogy, Performativity.* Durham, NC: Duke Univ. Press, 2003.

Shulman, Randy. "The Attractions of Bret Easton Ellis." *MetroWeekly.* October 10, 2002. https://www.metroweekly.com/2002/10/the-attractions-of-bret-easton/.

Slaughter, Anne-Marie. *Unfinished Business.* New York: Random House, 2015.

Spinoza, Baruch. *Ethics: With the Treatise on the Emendation of the Intellect and Selected Letters.* 2nd Edition. Edited and Introduced by Seymour Feldman. Translated by Samuel Shirley. Indianapolis, IN: Hackett Publishing, 1992.

Stam, Robert. *Literature through Film: Realism, Magic, and the Art of Adaptation.* Malden, MA: Blackwell, 2004.

Stam, Robert, and Allessandra Raengo, eds. *A Companion to Literature and Film.* Malden, MA: Blackwell, 2004.

Stam, Robert, and Allessandra Raengo, eds. *Literature and Film: A Guide to the Theory and Practice of Film Adaptation.* Malden, MA: Blackwell, 2004.

Storey, Mark. "'And as things fell apart: The Crisis of Postmodern Masculinity in Bret Easton Ellis's *American Psycho* and Dennis Cooper's *Frisk.*" *Critique* 47, no. 1 (2005): 57–72.

Todorov, Tzvetan. *The Poetics of Prose.* Translated by Richard Howard. Ithaca, NY: Cornell Univ. Press, 1971.

van der Vlies, Andrew. *J. M. Coetzee's Disgrace: A Reader's Guide.* London: Continuum, 2010.

Varsava, Jerry Andrew. "Utopian Yearnings, Dystopian Thoughts: Houellebecq's 'The Elementary Particles' and the Problem of Scientific Communitarianism." *College Literature* 3, no. 4 (Fall 2005): 146–67.

Venuti, Lawrence. "Adaptation, Translation, Critique." *The Journal of Visual Culture* 6, no. 1 (2007): 25–43.

Walker, Ben. "Extremes and Radicalism in the Postmodern and the Popular: A Study of Transgression in Bret Easton Ellis' *American Psycho.*" *The Bakhtin Centre.* September 9, 1998. http://www.shef.ac.uk/uni/academic/A-C/bakh/walker.html (source no longer available online).

Walsh, John. "Psycho Killer, *Qu'est-ce que c'est?* Reflections on Alain Mabanckou's *African Psycho.*" *Transitions* 100 (2009): 152–63.

Williams, Linda. "Film Bodies: Gender, Genre, and Excess." *Film Quarterly* 44, no. 4 (Summer 1991): 2–13.

Wood, Robin. "An Introduction to the American Horror Film." In *American Nightmare: Essays on the Horror Film,* edited by Robin Wood and Richard Lippe, 7–28. Toronto, CA: Festival of Festivals, 1979.

Wood, Robin. *Hollywood from Vietnam to Reagan.* New York: Columbia Univ. Press, 1986.

Young, Elizabeth. "The Beast in the Jungle, the Figure in the Carpet." In *Shopping Space: Essays on American "Blank Generation Fiction,"* edited by Elizabeth Young and Graham Caveney, 85–129. New York: Atlantic Monthly Press, 1992.

de Zengotita, Thomas. *Mediated: How the Media Shapes Your World and the Way You Live in It.* New York: Bloomsbury, 2005.

Zola, Emile. *The Experimental Novel and Other Essays.* New York: Haskell House, 1964.

Zuarino, John. "The African Psycho Comes to America." March 2007. http://www.bookslut.com/features/2007_03_010771.php (Bookslut.com archives no longer available online).

# Index

Abecassis, Jack I., 60–61, 63–64, 65, 69, 158n7

Abel, Marco: "Judgment Is Not an Exit," 99, 100; on selectivity in film, 107

Achebe, Chinua, 129

*Adaptation* (film): about, 7, 138, 143, 144; Charlie (character), 7, 140–41, 142–43; Donald (character), 142, 143; Orlean (character), 141–43

Adorno, Theodor, 96

Africa, shadow economies/shadow states, 114

African aspiration of Western norms, 116

*African Psycho* (Mabanckou): *American Psycho* compared/contrasted with, 113, 136; "He-Who-Drinks-Water-Is-An-Idiot" neighborhood, 115, 117, 120; postcolonial psychopathology of, 114, 116. *See* Great Master Angoualima; Nakobomayo, Grégoire

*African Psycho* (Mabanckou), overview: about, 5, 14–15, 113–17; Black skins, Black masks, 122–27; monstrous Other as ego-ideal, 127–34; pathological language of nonbeing, 118–22; spectacle and subjectivity, 134–39

Amelia (character), 141

American Men's Studies Association, 10

*American Psycho* (Ellis): "aesthetics of boredom," 88–89; *African Psycho*

compared/contrasted with, 113, 136; as bestseller, 80; "boring" passages of, 88–89; censorship of, 77, 160n1; characters as interchangeable/reproducible, 93–94; as consoling fantasy, 15, 100, 101, 129; 1980s popular culture of, 112; paratextual reference to, 14, 113, 114, 122, 136, 138; quote from, 140; as satire, 111; as schizophrenic, 97–98; as social criticism, 90, 99; status symbols, 82; subjectivity as designer labels and brand names, 92–93; uniformity and conformity in, 93; as voice of serial killer, 100; Western objectification of human existence, 82. *See* consumer capitalism

*American Psycho* (Ellis), characters: Luis Carruthers, 109; Christie, 103–4; Courtney, 93; Evelyn, 83, 92, 93; Helga, 94–95; Jean, 83–84; Price, 109; Reeves, 109; Sabrina, 103–4. *See also* Bateman, Patrick

*American Psycho* (Ellis), critics of: Tara Baxter, 80, 99; Tammy Bruce, 80; James Gardner, 86–87; Stephen Holden, 99, 107; Alberto Manguel, 80–81, 85–86, 89, 99; Richard Porton, 163n45; Roger Rosenblatt, 80, 99; Laura Tanner, 101; Guinevere Turner, 99, 163n45

Vartan P. Messier is an associate professor at Queensborough Community College (CUNY) and specializes in contemporary fiction, film and media studies, popular culture, postcolonial studies, and continental philosophy. His work has appeared in *New Cinemas: Journal of Contemporary Film*, *The Journal of Adaptation in Film and Performance*, *Atenea*, and *Interdisciplinary Literary Studies*.